WHAT LIFE
SHOULD MEAN TO YOU

ALFRED ADLER

WHAT LIFE

SHOULD MEAN TO YOU

EDITED BY ALAN PORTER

CAPRICORN BOOKS
NEW YORK

Published by Capricorn Books,
G. P. Putnam's Sons, New York
1958

Fourth Impression

Library of Congress Catalog
Card Number: 58-59753

MANUFACTURED IN THE UNITED STATES OF AMERICA

This book is dedicated to the human family in the hope that its members may learn from these pages to understand themselves better.

CONTENTS

I	*The Meaning of Life*	3
II	*Mind and Body*	25
III	*Feelings of Inferiority and Superiority*	49
IV	*Early Memories*	71
V	*Dreams*	93
VI	*Family Influences*	120
VII	*School Influences*	156
VIII	*Adolescence*	182
IX	*Crime and Its Prevention*	197
X	*Occupation*	239
XI	*Man and Fellow Man*	252
XII	*Love and Marriage*	263
	Index	287

WHAT LIFE
SHOULD MEAN TO YOU

CHAPTER I

The Meaning of Life

Human beings live in the realm of *meanings*. We do not experience pure circumstances; we always experience circumstances in their significance for men. Even at its source our experience is qualified by our human purposes. " Wood " means " wood in its relation to mankind ", and " stone " means " stone as it can be a factor in human life." If a man should try to escape meanings and devote himself only to circumstances he would be very unfortunate: he would isolate himself from others: his actions would be useless to himself or to any one; in a word, they would be meaningless. But no human being can escape meanings. We experience reality always through the meaning we give it; not in itself, but as something interpreted. It will be natural to suppose, therefore, that this meaning is always more or less unfinished, incomplete; and even that it is never altogether right. The realm of meanings is the realm of mistakes.

If we asked a man, " What is the meaning of life? ", he would perhaps be unable to answer. For the most part people do not bother themselves with the question or try to formulate replies. It is true that the question is as old as human history and that in our own time young people — and older people as well — will often break out with the cry, " But what is life for? What does life mean? " We can say, however, that they ask only when they have suffered a defeat. So long as everything is plain sailing and no difficult tests are set before them the question is never put into words. It is in his actions that every man inevitably puts the question and answers it. If we close our ears to his words and observe his actions, we shall find that he has his own individual " meaning of life " and that all his postures, attitudes, movements, expressions, mannerisms, ambitions, habits and character traits accord with this meaning. He behaves as if he could rely upon a certain interpretation of life. In all his actions there is an implicit reckoning up of the world and of himself; a verdict, " I am like this and the universe is like that "; a meaning given to himself and a meaning given to life.

There are as many meanings given to life as there are human beings, and, as we have suggested, perhaps each meaning involves more or less of a mistake. No one possesses the absolute meaning of life, and we may say that any meaning which is at all serviceable cannot be called absolutely wrong. All meanings are varieties between these two limits. Among these varieties, however, we can distinguish some which answer better and some which answer worse; some where the mistake is small and some where it is large. We can discover what it is that the better meanings share in common, what it is that the worse meanings lack. In this way we can obtain a scientific " meaning of life ", a common measure of true meanings, a meaning which enables us to meet reality in so far as it concerns mankind. Here again we must remember that " true " means true for mankind, true for the purposes and aims of human beings. There is no other truth than this; and if another truth existed, it could never concern us; we could never know it; it would be meaningless.

Every human being has three main ties; and it is of these ties that he must take account. They make up reality for him. All the problems which confront him are in the direction of these ties. He must always answer these problems because they are always questioning him; and the answers will show us his individual conception of the meaning of life. The first of these ties is that we are living on the crust of this poor planet, earth, and nowhere else. We must develop under the restrictions and with the possibilities which our place of habitation sets us. In body and mind alike we must develop so that we can continue our personal lives on earth and help to insure the future continuance of mankind. This is one problem which challenges every man for an answer; which no individual can escape. Whatever we do, our actions are our own answer to the situation of human life: they reveal what we think necessary, and fitting, and possible, and desirable. Every answer must be conditioned by the fact that we belong to mankind and that men are beings who inhabit this earth.

Now if we take account of the weakness of the human body and the insecurity in which we are placed, we can see that for our own lives and for the welfare of mankind we must take pains to consolidate our answers, to make them far-seeing and coherent. It is as if we stood before a problem in mathematics; we must work to find a solution. We cannot work haphazard or by guesswork, but we must work consistently, using all the means at our disposal. We shall not find an absolutely perfect answer, an answer established once for all; but, nevertheless, we must use all our ability to find an approximate answer. We must struggle always to find a better answer, and the answer must always be directly applicable to the fact that we are tied to the crust of this poor planet, earth, with all the advantages and disadvantages which our position brings.

Here we come to the second tie. We are not the only members of the human race. There are others around us, and we are living in association with them. The weakness and the limits of the individual human being make it impossible for him to ensure his own aims in isolation. If he lived alone and tried to meet his problems by himself he would perish. He would not be able to continue his own life; he would not be able to continue the life of mankind. He is always tied to other men; and he is tied because of his own weaknesses and insufficiencies and limits. The greatest step for his own welfare and for the welfare of mankind is association. Every answer, therefore, to the problems of life must take account of this tie: it must be an answer in the light of the fact that we are living in association and that we would perish if we were alone. If we are to survive even our emotions must be harmonious with this greatest of problems and purposes and goals — to continue our personal life and to continue the life of mankind, on this planet which we inhabit, in coöperation with our fellow men.

There is a third tie in which we are bound. Human beings are living in two sexes. The preservation of individual and of common life must take account of this fact. The problem of love and marriage belongs to this third tie. No man or woman can escape giving an answer. Whatever a human being does when confronted by this problem, this is his answer. There are many different ways in which human beings attempt to solve this problem: their actions always show their conception of the only way in which the problem is soluble for themselves. These three ties, therefore, set three problems: how to find an occupation which will enable us to survive under the limitations set by the nature of the earth; how to find a position among our fellows, so that we may coöperate and share the benefits of coöperation; how to accommodate ourselves to the fact that we live in two sexes and that the continuance and furtherance of mankind depends upon our love-life.

Individual Psychology has found no problems in life which cannot be grouped under these three main problems — occupational, social and sexual. It is in his response to these three problems that every individual human being unfailingly reveals his own deep sense of the meaning of life. Suppose, for example, we consider a man whose love-life is incomplete, who makes no efforts in his profession, who has few friends and who finds contact with his fellows painful. From the limits and restrictions of his life we may conclude that he feels *being alive* as a difficult and dangerous thing, offering few opportunities and many defeats. His narrow field of action is to be construed as a judgment, " Life means — to preserve myself against hurt, to stockade myself in, to escape untouched." Suppose, on the other hand, we consider a man whose love-life is an intimate and many-sided coöperation, whose work results in useful achievements, whose friends are many and whose contacts with his fellows are wide and fruitful. Of such a man we may conclude that he feels life as a creative task, offering many opportunities and no irrecoverable defeats. His courage in meeting all the problems of life is to be construed as a judgment, " Life means — to be interested in my fellow men, to be part of the whole, to contribute my share to the welfare of mankind."

It is here that we find the common measure of all mistaken " meanings of life " and the common measure of all true " meanings of life." All failures — neurotics, psychotics, criminals, drunkards, problem children, suicides, perverts and prostitutes — are failures because they are lacking in fellow-feeling and social interest. They approach the problems of occupation, friendship and sex without the confidence that they can be solved by coöperation. The meaning they give to life is a private meaning: no one else is benefited by the achievement of their aims and their interest stops short at their own persons. Their goal of success is a goal of mere fictitious personal superiority and their triumphs have meaning only to themselves. Murderers have confessed to a feeling of power when they held a bottle of poison in their hands, but clearly they were confirming their importance only to themselves; to the rest of us the possession of a bottle of poison cannot seem to give them superior worth. A private meaning is in fact no meaning at all. Meaning is only possible in communication: a word which meant something to one person only would really be meaningless. It is the same with our aims and actions; their only meaning is their meaning for others. Every human being strives for significance; but people always make mistakes if they do not see that their whole significance must consist in their contribution to the lives of others.

An anecdote is told of the leader of a small religious sect. One day she called her followers together and informed them that the end of the world was due on the next Wednesday. Her followers were much impressed, sold their property, abandoned all worldly considerations, and waited in excitement for the promised catastrophe. Wednesday passed without unusual occurrences. On Thursday they called in a body to ask an explanation. "See what difficulties we are in," they said. "We abandoned all our security. We told everybody we met that the end of the world was coming on Wednesday, and when they laughed at us we were not discouraged but repeated that we knew it on infallible authority. Wednesday has gone by and the world is still here around us." "But my Wednesday," said the prophetess, "is not your Wednesday." In this way, by a private meaning, she secured herself against challenge. A private meaning can never be put to the test.

The mark of all true "meanings of life" is that they are common meanings — they are meanings in which others can share, and meanings which others can accept as valid. A good solution of the problems of life will always clear the way for others also; for in it we shall see common problems met in a successful way. Even genius is to be defined as no more than supreme usefulness: it is only when a man's life is recognized by others as having significance for them that we call him a genius. The meaning expressed in such a life will always be, "Life means — to contribute to the whole." We are not speaking here of professed motives. We are closing our ears to professions and looking at achievements. The man who meets the problems of human life successfully acts as if he recognized, fully and spontaneously, that the meaning of life is interest in others and coöperation. Everything he does seems to be guided by the interest of his fellow beings; and where he meets difficulties he tries to surmount them only by means consonant with human welfare.

To many people, perhaps, this is a new point of view, and they may doubt whether the meaning we give to life should really be contribution, interest in others and coöperation. They will ask, perhaps, "But what about the individual? If he is always considering other people and devoting himself to their interests, does not his own individuality suffer? Is it not necessary, for some individuals at least, that if they are to develop properly they should consider themselves. Are there not some of us who should learn, first of all, to guard our own interests or to strengthen our own personalities?" This view, I believe, is a great mistake, and the problem it raises is a false problem. If a human being, in the meaning he gives to life, wishes to make a contribution, and if his emotions are all directed to this goal, he will naturally be bound to bring himself into the best shape for contribution. He will fit himself for his goal; he will train himself in social feeling and he will gain skill from practice. Granted the goal, the training will follow. Then and then only will he begin to equip himself to solve the three problems of life and to develop his abilities. Let us take the example of love and marriage. If we are interested in our partner, if we are working to ease and enrich our partner's life, of course we shall make the best of ourselves that we can. If we think that we must develop personality *in vacuo*, without a goal of contribution, we shall merely make ourselves domineering and unpleasant.

There is another hint from which we can gather that contribution is the true meaning of life. If we look around us to-day at the heritage we have received from our ancestors, what do we see? All that survives of them is the contributions they have made to human life. We see cultivated ground; we see roadways and buildings; we see the communicated results of their experience of life, in traditions, in philosophies, in the sciences and the arts, in the technique of dealing with our human situations. These results have all been left by men who contributed to human welfare. What has happened to others? What has happened to those who never coöperated, who gave life a different meaning, who asked only, " What can I get out of life? " They have left no trace behind them. Not only are they dead; their whole lives were futile. It is as if our earth itself had spoken to them and said, " We don't need you. You are not fitted for life. There is no future for your aims and strivings, for the values you held dear, for your minds and souls. Be off with you! You are not wanted. Die out and disappear! " The last judgment for people who give any other meaning to life than coöperation is always, " You are useless. Nobody wants you. Go! " In our present culture, of course, we can find many imperfections. Where we find that it fails we must change it; but the change must always be one which furthers still more the welfare of mankind.

There have always been men who understood this fact; who knew that the meaning of life is to be interested in the whole of mankind and who tried to develop social interest and love. In all religions we find this concern for the salvation of man. In all the great movements of the world men have been striving to increase social interest, and religion is one of the greatest strivings in this way. Religions, however, have often been misinterpreted; and it is difficult to see how they can do more than they are doing already, unless by a closer application to this common task. Individual Psychology arrives at the same conclusion in a scientific way and proposes a scientific technique. It makes, I believe, a step forward. Perhaps science, by increasing the interest of human beings in their fellow human beings and in the welfare of humankind, will be able to approximate closer to the goal than other movements, political or religious. We approach the problem from a different angle, but the goal is the same — to increase interest in others.

Since the meaning given to life works out as if it were the guardian angel or pursuing demon of our careers, it is very clearly of the highest importance that we should understand how these meanings come to be formed, how they differ from one another, and how they can be corrected if they involve big mistakes. This is the province of psychology, as distinct from physiology or biology — the use for human welfare of an understanding of *meanings* and the way in which they influence human actions and human fortunes. From the first days of childhood we can see dark gropings after this " meaning of life." Even a baby is striving to make an estimate of its own powers and its share in the whole life which surrounds it. By the end of the fifth year of life a child has reached a unified and crystallized pattern of behavior, its own style of approach to problems and tasks. It has already fixed its deepest and most lasting conception of what to expect from the world and from itself. From now on, the world is seen through a stable scheme of apperception: experiences are interpreted before they are accepted, and the interpretation always accords with the original meaning given to life. Even if this meaning is very gravely mistaken, even if the approach to our problems and tasks brings us continually into misfortunes and agonies, it is never easily relinquished. Mistakes in the meaning given to life can be corrected only by reconsidering the situation in which the faulty interpretation was made, recognizing the error and revising the scheme of apperception. In rare circumstances, perhaps, an individual may be forced by the consequences of a mistaken approach to revise the meaning he has given to life and may succeed in accomplishing the change by himself. He will never do it, however, without some social pressure, or without finding that if he proceeds with the old approach he is at the end of his tether: and for the most part the approach can best be revised with the assistance of some one trained in the understanding of these meanings, who can join in discovering the original error and help to suggest a more appropriate meaning.

Let us take a simple illustration of the different ways in which childhood situations may be interpreted. Unhappy experiences in childhood may be given quite opposite meanings. One man with unhappy experiences behind him will not dwell on them except as they show him something which can be remedied for the future. He will feel, " We must work to remove such unfortunate situations and make sure that our children are better placed." Another man will feel, " Life is unfair. Other people always have the best of it. If the world treated me like that, why should I treat the world any better? " It is in this way that some parents say of their children, " I had to suffer just as much when I was a child, and I came through it. Why shouldn't they? " A third man will feel, " Everything should be forgiven me because of my un- happy childhood." In the actions of all three men their interpretations will be evident; and they will never change their actions unless they change their interpretations. It is here that individual psychology breaks through the theory of determinism. No experience is a cause of success or failure. We do not suffer from the shock of our experi- ences — the so-called *trauma* — but we make out of them just what suits our purposes. We are *self-determined* by the meaning we give to our experiences; and there is probably something of a mistake always involved when we take particular experiences as the basis for our future life. Meanings are not determined by situations, but we determine ourselves by the meanings we give to situa- tions.

There are, however, certain situations in childhood from which a gravely mistaken meaning is very fre- quently drawn. It is from children in these situations that the majority of failures come. First we must take chil- dren with imperfect organs, suffering from diseases or infirmities during their infancy. Such children are over- burdened, and it will be difficult for them to feel that the meaning of life is contribution. Unless there is some one near them who can draw their attention away from themselves and interest them in others, they are likely to occupy themselves mainly with their own sensations. Later on, they may become discouraged by comparing themselves with those around them, and it may even happen, in our present civilization, that their feelings of inferiority are stressed by the pity, ridicule or avoidance of their fellows. These are all circumstances in which they may turn in upon themselves, lose hope of playing a useful part in our common life, and consider themselves personally humiliated by the world.

I was the first person, I think, to describe the difficulties that confront a child whose organs are imperfect or whose glandular secretions are abnormal. This branch of science has made extraordinary progress, but hardly along the lines in which I should have liked to see it develop. From the beginning I was seeking a method of overcoming these difficulties, and not a ground for throwing the responsibility for failure upon heredity or physical condition. No imperfection of organs compels a mistaken style of life. We never find two children whose glands have the same effects on them. We can often see children who overcome these difficulties and who, in overcoming them, develop unusual faculties for usefulness. In this way Individual Psychology is not a very good advertisement for schemes of eugenic selection. Many of the most eminent men, men who made great contributions to our culture, began with imperfect organs; often their health was poor and sometimes they died early. It is mainly from those people who struggled hard against difficulties, in body as in outer circumstances, that advances and new contributions have come. The struggle strengthened them and they went further ahead. From the body we cannot judge whether the development of the mind will be bad or good. Hitherto, however, the greatest part of children who started with imperfect organs and imperfect glands have not been trained in the right direction; their difficulties have not been understood and they have mainly become interested in their own persons. It is for this reason that we find such a great number of failures amongst those children whose early years were burdened with imperfect organs.

The second type of situation which often provides the occasion for a mistake in the meaning given to life is the situation of the pampered child. The pampered child is trained to expect that his wishes will be treated as laws. He is granted prominence without working to deserve it and he will generally come to feel this prominence as a birthright. In consequence, when he comes into circumstances where he is not the center of attention and where other people do not make it their chief aim to consider his feelings, he will be very much at a loss: he will feel that his world has failed him. He has been trained to expect and not to give. He has never learned any other way of facing problems. Others have been so subservient to him that he has lost his independence and does not know that he can do things for himself. His interest was devoted to himself and he never learned the use and the necessity of coöperation. When he has difficulties before him, he has only one method of meeting them — to make demands on other people. It seems to him that if he can regain his position of prominence, if he can force others to recognize that he is a special person and should be granted everything he wants, then and then only will his situation improve.

These grown-up pampered children are perhaps the most dangerous class in our community. Some of them may make great protestations of good will; they may even become very " lovable " in order to secure an opportunity to tyrannize; but they are on strike against coöperating, as ordinary human beings, in our ordinary human tasks. There are others who are in more open revolt:

when they no longer find the easy warmth and subordination to which they were accustomed, they feel betrayed; they consider society as hostile to themselves and try to revenge themselves upon all their fellows. And if society shows hostility to their way of living (as it almost undoubtedly will) they take this hostility as a new proof that they are *personally* ill-treated. This is the reason why punishments are always ineffective; they can do nothing but confirm the opinion, " Others are against me." But whether the spoiled child goes on strike or openly revolts, whether he tries to dominate by weakness or to revenge himself by violence, he is in fact making much the same mistake. We find people, indeed, who try both methods at different times. Their goal remains unaltered. They feel, " Life means — to be the first, to be recognized as the most important, to get everything I want," and so long as they continue to give this meaning to life, every method they adopt will be mistaken.

The third situation in which a mistake can easily be made is the situation of a neglected child. Such a child has never known what love and coöperation can be: he makes up an interpretation of life which does not include these friendly forces. It will be understood that when he faces the problems of life he will overrate their difficulty and underrate his own capacity to meet them with the aid and good will of others. He has found society cold to him and he will expect it always to be cold. Especially he will not see that he can *win* affection and esteem by actions which are useful to others. He will thus be suspicious of others and unable to trust himself. There is really no experience which can take the place of disinterested affection. The first task of a mother is to give her child the experience of a trustworthy other person: later she must widen and enlarge this feeling of trust until it includes the rest of the child's environment. If she has failed in the first task — to gain the child's interest, affection and coöperation — it will be very difficult for the child to develop social interest and comradely feeling towards his fellows. Everybody has the capacity to be interested in others; but this capacity must be trained and exercised or its development will be frustrated.

If there were a pure type of neglected or hated or unwanted child we should probably find that he was just blind to the existence of coöperation; that he was isolated, unable to communicate with others and completely ignorant of everything that would help him to live in association with human beings. But, as we have already seen, an individual in these circumstances would perish. The fact that a child lives through the period of infancy is proof that he has been given some care and attention. We are therefore never dealing with pure types of neglected children: we are dealing with those who had less than usual consideration, or who were neglected in some respects, though not in others. In short, we need only say that the neglected child is one who never quite found a trustworthy other person. It is a very sad comment on our civilization that so many failures in life come from those children who were orphans or illegitimate; and that we must group such children, on the whole, amongst the neglected children.

These three situations — imperfect organs, pampering, and neglect — are a great challenge to give a mistaken meaning to life; and children from these situations will almost always need help in revising their approach to problems. They must be helped to a better meaning. If we have an eye for such things — which really means, if we have a true interest in them and have trained ourselves in this direction — we shall be able to see their meaning in everything they do. Dreams and associations may prove useful: the personality is the same in dreaming life as in waking life, but in dreams the pressure of social demands is less acute and the personality will be revealed with fewer safeguards and concealments. The greatest of all helps, however, in gaining a quick comprehension of the meaning an individual gives to himself and to life comes through his memories. Every memory, however trivial he may think it, represents to him something *memorable*. It is memorable because of its bearing on life as he pictures it; it says to him, " This is what you must expect ", or "This is what you must avoid ", or " Such is life! " Again we must stress that the experience itself is not so important as the fact that just this experience persists in memory and is used to crystallize the meaning given to life. Every memory is a memento.

The memories of early childhood are especially useful in showing how long standing is the individual's own peculiar approach to life, and in giving the circumstances in which he first crystallized his life-attitude. For two reasons the earliest memory of all has a very notable place. First, the fundamental estimate of the individual and his situation is contained in it; it is his first totalling-up of appearances, his first more or less complete symbol of himself and the demands made of him. Secondly, it is his subjective starting point, the beginning of the autobiography he has made up for himself. We can often find in it, therefore, the contrast between a position of weakness and inadequacy in which he felt himself and the goal of strength and security which he regards as his ideal. It is indifferent for the purposes of psychology whether the memory which an individual considers as first is really the first event which he can remember — or even whether it is a memory of a real event. Memories are important only for what they are " taken as "; for their interpretation and for their bearing on present and future life.

Here we may take a few instances of first memories and see the " meaning of life " which they solidify. " The coffeepot fell off the table and scalded me." Such is life! We should not be surprised to find that the girl whose autobiography began in this way was pursued by a feeling of helplessness and overestimated the dangers and difficulties of life. We should not be surprised either, if, in her heart, she reproached other people for not taking sufficient care of her. Somebody had been very careless to leave so small a child exposed to such risks! A similar picture of the world is presented in another first memory: " I remember falling out of a baby carriage when I was three years old." With this first memory went a recurrent dream, " The world is coming to an end and I wake up in the middle of the night to find the sky bright red with fire. The stars all fall and we collide into another planet. But just before the crash I wake up." This student, when asked if he was afraid of anything, answered, " I am afraid that I won't make a success of life ", and it is clear that his first memory and his recurrent dream act as discouragements and confirm him in fearing failure and catastrophe.

A boy of twelve who was brought to the clinic because of enuresis and continual conflicts with his mother gave as his first memory, " Mother thought I was lost and ran into the street shouting for me and very frightened. All the time I was hidden in a cupboard in the house." In this memory we can read an estimate: " Life means — to gain attention by giving trouble. The way to gain security is through deceitfulness. I am overlooked, but I can fool others." His enuresis, also, was a means well adapted to keeping himself the center of worry and attention, and his mother confirmed him in his interpretation of life by her anxiety and nervousness over him. As in the previous examples, this boy had early gained the impression that life in the outside world was full of dangers and he had concluded that he was only safe if others were apprehensive on his behalf. Only in this way could he reassure himself that they were there to protect him if he needed it.

The first memory of a woman of thirty-five was as follows: " When I was three years old I went down into the cellar. While I was on the stairs in the dark, a boy cousin, a little older than myself, opened the door and came down after me. I was very frightened of him." It seemed probable from this memory that she had not been accustomed to playing with other children and that she was especially ill at ease with the other sex. A guess that she was an only child proved correct; and she was still, at the age of thirty-five, unmarried.

A higher development of social feeling is shown in the following: " I remember my mother letting me wheel my baby sister in the perambulator." In this instance, however, we might look also for signs of being at ease only with weaker people; and perhaps of dependence upon the mother. It is always best when a new child is born to gain the coöperation of the older children in taking care of it;

to interest them in the newcomer and allow them to share the responsibility for its welfare. If their coöperation is gained they will not be tempted to feel the attention given to the baby as a diminution of their own importance.

The desire to be in company is not always a proof of a real interest in others. One girl, when asked for her first memory, replied, " I was playing with my elder sister and two girl friends." Here we can certainly see a child training to be sociable; but we obtain a new insight into her striving when she mentions as her greatest fear, " I am afraid of being left alone." We shall look, therefore, for signs of a lack of independence.

If once the meaning given to life is found and understood, we have the key to the whole personality. It is sometimes stated that human character is unchangeable, but this position can be held only by those who have never found the right key to the situation. As we have already seen, however, no argument or treatment can be successful if it falls short of discovering the original error; and the only possibility of improvement lies in the training for a more coöperative and courageous approach to life. Coöperation is also the only safeguard we have against the development of neurotic tendencies. It is therefore of supreme importance that children should be trained and encouraged in coöperation; should be allowed to find their own way amongst children of their own age, in common tasks and common games. Any block in coöperation will have the most serious results. The spoiled child, for example, who has learned to be interested only in himself, will carry this lack of interest in others to school with him. His lessons will interest him only so far as he thinks he can gain his teacher's favor; he will listen only to what he conceives to be advantageous to himself. As he comes near to adult age, his failure in social feeling will become more and more evidently calamitous. When his error first occurred, he ceased training himself for responsibility and independence; and by now he is painfully ill-equipped for any of life's tests.

We cannot blame him now for his defects: we can only help him to remedy them when he begins to feel the consequences. We do not expect a child who has never been taught geography to answer an examination paper on the subject with success; and we cannot expect a child who has never been trained in coöperation to answer correctly when tasks which demand training in coöperation are set before him. But every problem of life demands an ability to coöperate for its solution; every task must be mastered within the framework of our human society and in a way which furthers our human welfare. Only the individual who understands that life means contribution will be able to meet his difficulties with courage and with a good chance of success.

If teachers and parents and psychologists understand the mistakes that can be made in giving a meaning to life, and if they do not make the same mistakes themselves, we can be confident that children who have been lacking in social interest will come to have a better feeling for their own capacities and for the opportunities of life. When they meet problems, they will not stop their efforts, look for an easy way out, try to escape or throw the burden on the shoulders of others, make claims for tender treatment and especial sympathy, feel humiliated and seek to revenge themselves, or ask, " What is the use of life? What do I get from it? " They will say, " We must make our own lives. It is our own task and we are capable of meeting it. We are masters of our own actions. If something new must be done or something old replaced, no one need do it but ourselves." If life is approached in this way, as a coöperation of independent human beings, we can see no limits to the progress of our human association.

CHAPTER II

Mind and Body

Men have always debated whether the mind governs the body or the body governs the mind. Philosophers have joined in the controversy and taken one position or the other; they have called themselves idealists or materialists; they have brought up arguments by the thousand; and the question still seems as vexed and unsettled as ever. Perhaps Individual Psychology may give some help towards a solution; for in Individual Psychology we are really confronted with the living interactions of mind and body. Some one — mind and body — is here to be treated; and if our treatment is wrongly based we shall fail to help him. Our theory must definitely grow from experience; it must definitely stand the test of application. We are living amongst these interactions, and we have the strongest challenge to find the right point of view.

The findings of Individual Psychology remove much of the tension from this problem. It no longer remains a plain "either . . . or." We see that both mind and body are expressions of life: they are parts of the whole of life. And we begin to understand their reciprocal relations in that whole. The life of man is the life of a moving being, and it would not be sufficient for him to develop body alone. A plant is rooted: it stays in one place and cannot move. It would be very surprising, therefore, to discover that a plant had a mind; or at least a mind in any sense which we could comprehend. If a plant could foresee or project consequences, the faculty would be useless to it. What advantage would it be for the plant to think: " Here is some one coming. In a minute he will tread on me, and I shall be dead underfoot."? The plant would still be unable to move out of the way.

All moving beings, however, can foresee and reckon up the direction in which to move; and this fact makes it necessary to postulate that they have minds or souls.

> " Sense, sure, you have,
> Else you could not have motion." [1]

This foreseeing the direction of movement is the central principle of the mind. As soon as we have recognized it we are in a position to understand how the mind governs the body — it sets the goal for movements. Merely to initiate a random movement from moment to moment would never be enough: there must be a goal for the strivings. Since it is the mind's function to decide a point towards which movement is to be made, it occupies the governing position in life. At the same time, the body influences the mind; it is the body which must be moved. The mind can move the body only in accordance with the possibilities which the body possesses and those which it can be trained to develop. If, for example, the mind proposes to move the body to the moon, it will fail unless it discovers a technique suited to the body's limitations.

Men are more engaged in movement than any other beings. They do not only move in more ways — as we can see in the complicated movements of their hands — but they are also more capable, by means of their movements, of moving the environment around them. We should ex-

[1] " Hamlet ", Act III, Scene 4.

pect, therefore, that the ability to foresee would be most highly developed in the human mind, and that men would give the clearest evidence of a purposive striving to improve their whole position with respect to their whole situation.

In every human being, moreover, we can discover behind all partial movements towards partial goals one single inclusive movement. All our strivings are directed towards a position in which a feeling of security has been achieved, a feeling that all the difficulties of life have been overcome and that we have emerged finally, in relation to the whole situation around us, safe and victorious. With this purpose in view, all movements and expressions must be coördinated and brought into a unity: the mind is compelled to develop as if to achieve a final ideal goal. It is no different with the body; the body also strives to be a unity. It, too, develops towards an ideal goal preëxistent in the germ. If, for example, the skin is broken all the body is busy in making itself whole again. The body, however, is not merely left alone to unfold its potentialities: the mind can help it in its development. The value of exercise and training, and of hygiene in general, have all been proved; and these are all aids for the body supplied by the mind in its striving towards the final goal.

From the first days of life, uninterruptedly till the end, this partnership of growth and development continues. Body and mind are coöperating as indivisible parts of one whole. The mind is like a motor, dragging with it all the potentialities which it can discover in the body, helping to bring the body into a position of safety and superiority to all difficulties. In every movement of the body, in every expression and symptom, we can see the impress of the mind's purpose. A man moves. There is meaning in his movement. He moves his eyes, his tongue, the muscles of his face. His face has an expression, a meaning. It is mind that puts meaning there. Now we can begin to see what psychology, or the science of mind, really deals with. The province of psychology is to explore the meaning involved in all the expressions of an individual, to find the key to his goal, and to compare it with the goals of others.

In striving for the final goal of security, the mind is always faced with the necessity of making the goal concrete; of calculating "security lies in this particular point; it is reached by going in this particular direction." Here, of course, the chance of a mistake occurs; but without a quite definite goal and direction-setting there could be no movement at all. If I lift my hand, there must be a goal for the movement already in my mind. The direction which the mind chooses may be, in reality, disastrous; but it is chosen because the mind conceives it mistakenly as the most advantageous. All psychological mistakes are thus mistakes in choosing the direction of movement. The goal of security is common to all human beings; but some of them mistake the direction in which security lies and their concrete movements lead them astray.

If we see an expression or symptom and fail to recognize the meaning behind it, the best way to understand it is, first of all, to reduce it in outline to a bare movement. Let us take, for example, the expression of stealing. To steal is to remove property from another person to oneself. Let us now examine the goal of the movement: the goal is to enrich oneself, and to feel more secure by possessing more. The point at which the movement sets out is therefore a feeling of being poor and deprived. The next step is to find out in what circumstances the individual is placed and in what conditions he feels deprived. Finally we can see whether he is taking the right way to change these circumstances and overcome his feeling of being deprived; whether the movement is in the right direction, or whether he has mistaken the method of securing what he desires. We need not criticize his final goal; but we may be able to point out that he has chosen a mistaken way in making it concrete.

The changes which the human race has made in its environment we call our culture; and our culture is the result of all the movements which the minds of men have initiated for their bodies. Our work is inspired by our minds. The development of our bodies is directed and aided by our minds. In the end we shall not be able to find a single human expression which is not filled with the purposiveness of the mind. It is by no means desirable, however, that the mind should overstress its own part. If we are to overcome difficulties, bodily fitness is necessary. The mind is engaged, therefore, in governing the environment in such a way that the body can be defended — so that it can be protected from sickness, disease and death, from damage, accidents and failures of function. This is the purpose served by our ability to feel pleasure and pain, to create phantasies and to identify ourselves with good and bad situations. The feelings put the body in shape to meet a situation with a definite type of response. Phantasies and identifications are methods of foreseeing; but they are also more: they stir up the feelings in accordance with which the body will act. In this way the feelings of an individual bear the impress of the meaning he gives to life and of the goal he has set for his strivings. To a great extent, though they rule his body, they do not depend on his body: they will always depend primarily on his goal and his consequent style of life.

Clearly enough, it is not the style of life alone that governs an individual. His attitudes do not create his symptoms without further help. For action they must be reinforced by feelings. What is new in the outlook of Individual Psychology is our observation that the feelings are never in contradiction to the style of life. Where there is a goal, the feelings always adapt themselves to its attainment. We are no longer, therefore, in the realm of physiology or biology; the rise of feelings cannot be explained by chemical theory and cannot be predicted by chemical examination. In Individual Psychology we must presuppose the physiological processes, but we are more interested in the psychological goal. It is not so much our concern that anxiety influences the sympathetic and parasympathetic nerves. We look, rather, for the purpose and end of anxiety.

With this approach anxiety cannot be taken as rising from the suppression of sexuality, or as being left behind as the result of disastrous birth-experiences. Such explanations are beside the mark. We know that a child who is accustomed to be accompanied, helped and supported by its mother may find anxiety — whatever its source — a very efficient weapon for controlling its mother. We are not satisfied with a physical description of anger; our experience has shown us that anger is a device to dominate a person or a situation. We can take it for granted that every bodily and mental expression must be based on inherited material; but our attention is directed to the use which is made of this material in striving to achieve a definite goal.

This, it seems, is the only real psychological approach. In every individual we see that feelings have grown and developed in the direction and to the degree which were essential to the attainment of his goal. His anxiety or courage, cheerfulness or sadness, have always agreed with his style of life: their proportionate strength and dominance has been exactly what we could expect. A man who accomplishes his goal of superiority by sadness cannot be gay and satisfied with his accomplishments. He can only be happy when he is miserable. We can notice also that feelings appear and disappear at need. A patient suffering from agoraphobia loses the feeling of anxiety when he is at home or when he is dominating another person. All neurotic patients exclude every part of life in which they do not feel strong enough to be the conqueror.

The emotional tone is as fixed as the style of life. The coward, for example, is always a coward, even though he is arrogant with weaker people or seems courageous when he is shielded by others. He may fix three locks on his door, protect himself with police dogs and mantraps and insist that he is full of courage. Nobody will be able to prove his feeling of anxiety; but the cowardice of his character is shown sufficiently by the trouble he has taken to protect himself.

The realm of sexuality and love gives a similar testimony. The feelings belonging to sex always appear when an individual desires to approach his sexual goal. By concentration, he tends to exclude conflicting tasks and incompatible interests; and thus he evokes the appropriate feelings and functions. The lack of these feelings and functions — as in impotence, premature ejaculation, perversion and frigidity — is established by refusing to exclude inappropriate tasks and interests. Such abnormalities are always induced by a mistaken goal of superiority and a mistaken style of life. We always find in such cases a tendency to expect consideration rather than to give it, a lack of social feeling, and a failure in courage and optimistic activity.

A patient of mine, a second child, suffered very profoundly from inescapable feelings of guilt. Both his father and his elder brother laid great emphasis on honesty. When the boy was seven years old he told his teacher in school that he had done a piece of homework by himself, although, as a matter of fact, his brother had done it for him. The boy concealed his guilty feelings for three years. At last he went to see the teacher and confessed his awful lie. The teacher merely laughed at him. Next he went to his father in tears and confessed a second time. This time he was more successful. The father was proud of his boy's love of truth; he praised and consoled him. In spite of the fact that his father had absolved him, the boy continued to be depressed. We can hardly avoid the conclusion that this boy was occupied in proving his great integrity and scrupulousness by accusing himself so bitterly for such a trifle. The high moral atmosphere of his home gave him the impulse to excel in integrity. He felt inferior to his elder brother in school work and social attractiveness; and he tried to achieve superiority by a sideline of his own.

Later in life he suffered from other self-reproaches. He masturbated and was never completely free from cheating in his studies. His feelings of guilt always increased before he took an examination. As he went on he collected difficulties of this sort. By means of his sensitive conscience he was much more burdened than his brother;

and thus he had an excuse prepared for all failures to equal him. When he left the university, he planned to do technical work; but his compulsory feelings of guilt grew so poignant that he prayed through the whole day that God would forgive him. He was thus left without time for working.

By now his condition was so bad that he was sent to an asylum, and there he was considered as incurable. After a time, however, he improved and left the asylum, but asked permission to be readmitted if he should suffer a relapse. He changed his occupation and studied the history of art. The time came around for his examinations. He went to church on a public holiday. He threw himself down before the great crowd and cried out, " I am the greatest sinner of all men." In this way again he succeeded in drawing attention to his sensitive conscience.

After another period in the asylum he returned home. One day he came down to lunch naked. He was a well-built man and on this point he could compete well with his brother and with other people.

His feelings of guilt were means to make him appear more honest than others and in this way he was struggling to achieve superiority. His struggles, however, were directed towards the useless side of life. His escape from examinations and occupational work gives a sign of cowardice and a heightened feeling of inadequacy; and his whole neurosis was a purposive exclusion of every activity in which he feared a defeat. The same striving for superiority by shabby means is evident in his prostration in church and his sensational entrance into the dining room. His style of life demanded them and the feelings he induced were entirely appropriate.

It is, as we have already seen, in the first four or five years of life that the individual is establishing the unity of his mind and constructing the relations between mind and body. He is taking his hereditary material and the impressions he receives from the environment and is adapting them to his pursuit of superiority. By the end of the fifth year his personality has crystallized. The meaning he gives to life, the goal he pursues, his style of approach, and his emotional disposition are all fixed. They can be changed later; but they can be changed only if he becomes free from the mistake involved in his childhood crystallization. Just as all his previous expressions were coherent with his interpretation of life, so now, if he is able to correct the mistake, his new expressions will be coherent with his new interpretation.

It is by means of his organs that an individual comes into touch with his environment and receives impressions from it. We can see, therefore, from the way he is training his body, the kind of impression he is prepared to receive from his environment and the use he is trying to make of his experience. If we notice the way he looks and listens and what it is that attracts his attention, we have learned much about him. This is the reason why postures have such an importance; they show us the training of the organs and the use which is being made of them to select impressions. Postures are always conditioned by meanings.

Now we can add to our definition of psychology. Psychology is the understanding of an individual's attitude towards the impressions of his body. We can also begin to see how the great differences between human minds come to arise. A body which is ill-suited to the environment and has difficulty in fulfilling the demands of the environment will usually be felt by the mind as a burden. For this reason children who have suffered from imperfect organs meet with greater hindrances than usual for their mental development. It is harder for their minds to influence, move and govern their bodies towards a position of superiority. A greater effort of mind is needed, and mental concentration must be higher than with others if they are to secure the same object. So the mind becomes overburdened and they become self-centered and egoistic. When a child is always occupied with the imperfection of its organs and the difficulties of movement, it has no attention to spare for what is outside itself. It finds neither the time nor the freedom to interest itself in others, and in consequence grows up with a lesser degree of social feeling and ability to coöperate.

Imperfect organs offer many handicaps but these handicaps are by no means an inescapable fate. If the mind is active on its own part and trains hard to overcome the difficulties, the individual may very well succeed in being as successful as those who were originally less burdened. Indeed, children with imperfect organs very often accomplish, in spite of their obstacles, more than children who start with more normal instruments. The handicap was a stimulus to go further ahead. A boy, for example, may suffer unusual stress through the imperfection of his eyes. He is more occupied in trying to see; he gives more attention to the visible world; he is more interested in distinguishing colors and forms. In the end, he comes to have a much greater experience of the visible world than children who never needed to struggle or to pay attention to small distinctions. Thus an imperfect organ can turn out to be the source of great advantages; but only if the mind has found the right technique for overcoming difficulties. Among painters and poets a great proportion are known to have suffered from imperfections of sight. These imperfections have been governed by well-trained minds; and finally their possessors could use their eyes to more purpose than others who were more nearly normal. The same kind of compensation can be seen, perhaps more easily, among left-handed children who have not been recognized as left-handed. At home, or in the beginning of their school-days, they were trained to use their imperfect right hands. Thus they were really not so well equipped for writing, drawing or handicraft. We might expect, if the mind can be used to overcome such difficulties, that often this imperfect right hand would develop a high degree of artistry. This is precisely what happens. In many instances left-handed children learn to have better handwriting than others, more talent for drawing and painting, or more skill in craftsmanship. By finding the right technique, by interest, training and exercise, they have turned disadvantage into advantage.

Only a child who desires to contribute to the whole, whose interest is not centered in himself, can train successfully to compensate for defects. If children desire only to rid themselves of difficulties, they will continue backward. They can keep up their courage only if they have a purpose in view for their efforts and if the achievement of this purpose is more important to them than the obstacles which stand in the way. It is a question of where their interest and attention is directed. If they are striving towards an object external to themselves, they will quite naturally train and equip themselves to achieve it. Difficulties will represent no more than positions which are to be conquered on their way to success. If, on the other hand, their interest lies in stressing their own drawbacks or in fighting these drawbacks with no purpose except to be free from them, they will be able to make no real progress. A clumsy right hand cannot be trained into a skillful right hand by taking thought, by wishing that it were less clumsy, or even by avoiding clumsiness. It can become skillful only by exercise in practical achievements; and the incentive to the achievement must be more deeply felt than the discouragement at the hitherto existent clumsiness. If a child is to draw together his powers and overcome his difficulties, there must be a goal for his movements outside of himself; a goal based on interest in reality, interest in others, and interest in coöperation.

A good example of hereditary capital and the use to which it may be turned was given me by my investigations into families which suffered from inferiority of the kidney tract. Very often children in these families suffered from enuresis. The organ inferiority is real; it can be shown in the kidney or the bladder or in the existence of a *spina bifida;* and often a corresponding imperfection of the lumbar segment can be suspected from a nævus or birthmole on the skin in that area. The organ inferiority, however, by no means accounts sufficiently for the enuresis. The child is not under the compulsion of his organs; and he uses them in his own way. Some children, for example, will wet the bed at night and never wet themselves during the day. Sometimes the habit will disappear suddenly, upon a change in the environment or in the attitude of the parents. Enuresis can be overcome, except among feeble-minded children, if the child ceases to use the imperfection of his organs for a mistaken purpose.

Mainly, however, children who suffer from enuresis are being stimulated not to overcome it but to continue it. A skillful mother can give the right training; but if the mother is not skillful an unnecessary weakness persists. Often in families which suffer from kidney troubles or bladder troubles everything to do with urinating is overstressed. Mothers will then mistakenly try very hard to stop the enuresis. If the child notices how much value is placed on this point, he will very probably resist. It will give him a very good opportunity to assert his opposition to this kind of education. If a child resists the treatment which his parents give him, he will always find his way to attack them at their point of greatest weakness. A very well-known sociologist in Germany has discovered that a surprising proportion of criminals spring from families which are occupied in the suppression of crime; from the families of judges, policemen, or prison warders. Often the children of teachers are obstinately backward. In my own experience I have often found this true; and I have found also a surprising number of neurotic children among the children of doctors and of delinquent children among the children of ministers of religion. In a similar way, the children whose parents overstress urination have a very clear way open for them to show that they have wills of their own.

Enuresis can also provide us with a good example of how dreams are used to stir up emotions appropriate to the actions we intend. Often children who wet the bed dream that they have got out of bed and gone to the toilet. In this way they have excused themselves; now they are perfectly right to wet the bed. The purpose which enuresis serves is generally to attract notice, to subordinate others, to occupy their attention in the nighttime as well as the day. Sometimes it is to antagonize them; the habit is a declaration of enmity. From every angle, we can see that enuresis is really a creative expression; the child is speaking with his bladder instead of his mouth. The organic imperfection does no more than offer him the means for the expression of his opinion.

Children who express themselves in this way are always suffering from a tension. Generally they belong to the class of spoiled children who have lost their position of being the unique center of attention. Another child has been born, perhaps, and they find it more difficult to secure the undivided attention of their mothers. Enuresis thus represents a movement to come in closer contact with the mother, even by unpleasant means. It says, in effect, " I am not so far advanced as you think: I must still be watched." In different circumstances, or with a different organ imperfection, they would have chosen other means. They might have used sound, for example, to establish the connection, in which case they would have been restless and cried during the night. Some children walk in their sleep, have nightmares, fall out of bed, or become thirsty and call for water. The psychological background for these expressions is similar. The choice of symptom depends in part on the organic situation and in part on the attitude of the environment.

Such cases show very well the influence which the mind exerts over the body. In all probability the mind does not only affect the choice of a particular bodily symptom; it is governing and influencing the whole building-up of the body. We have no direct proof of this hypothesis; and it is difficult to see how a proof could ever be established.

The evidence, however, seems clear enough. If a boy is timid, his timidity is reflected in his whole development. He will not care for physical achievements; or, rather, he will not think of them as possible for himself. In consequence, it will not occur to him to train his muscles in an efficient way, and he will exclude all the impressions from outside that would ordinarily be a stimulus to muscular development. Other children, who allow themselves to be influenced and interested in the training of their muscles, will go farther ahead in physical fitness; he, because his interest is blocked, will remain behind.

From such consideration we can fairly conclude that the whole form and development of the body is affected by the mind and reflects the errors or deficiencies of the mind. We can often observe bodily expressions which are plainly the end results of mental failings, where the right way to compensate for a difficulty has not been discovered. We may be sure, for example, that the endocrine glands themselves can be influenced in the first four or five years of life. Imperfect glands never have a compulsive influence on conduct; on the other hand, they are being continuously affected by the whole environment, by the direction in which the child seeks to receive impressions, and by the creative activity of its mind in this interesting situation.

Another piece of evidence would perhaps be more readily understood and accepted, since it is more familiar and leads towards a temporary expression, not towards a fixed disposition of the body. To a certain degree every emotion finds some bodily expression. The individual will show his emotion in some visible form; perhaps in his posture and attitude, perhaps in his face, perhaps in the trembling of his legs and knees. Similar changes could be found in the organs themselves. If he flushes or turns pale, for example, the circulation of the blood is affected. In anger, anxiety, sorrow or any other emotion, the body always speaks; and each individual's body speaks in a language of its own. When one man is in a situation in which he is afraid, he trembles; the hair of another will start on end; a third will have palpitations of the heart. Still others will sweat or choke, speak in a hoarse voice, or shrink physically and cower away. Sometimes the tonus of the body is affected, the appetite lost, or vomiting induced. With some it is the bladder which is mainly irritated by such emotions, with others the sexual organs. Many children feel stimulated in the sexual organs when taking examinations; and it is well known that criminals will frequently go to a house of prostitution, or to their sweethearts, after they have committed a crime. In the realm of science we find psychologists who claim that sex and anxiety go together and psychologists who claim that they have not the remotest connection. Their point of view depends on their personal experience; with some there is a connection, with others not.

All of these responses belong to different types of individuals. They could probably be discovered to be to some extent hereditary, and physical expressions of this kind will often give us hints of the weaknesses and peculiarities of the family tree. Other members of the family may make a very similar bodily response. What is most interesting here, however, is to see how, by means of the emotions, the mind is able to activate the physical conditions. The emotions and their physical expressions tell us how the mind is acting and reacting in a situation which it interprets as favorable or unfavorable. In an outburst of temper, for example, the individual has wished to overcome his imperfections as quickly as possible. The best way has seemed to be to hit, accuse or attack another individual. The anger, in its turn, influences the organs: mobilizes them for action or lays an additional stress on them. Some people when they are angry have stomach trouble at the same time, or grow red in the face. Their circulation is altered to such a degree that a headache ensues. We shall generally find unadmitted rage or humiliation behind attacks of migraine, or habitual headaches; and with some people anger results in trigeminal neuralgia or fits of an epileptic nature.

The means by which the body is influenced have never been completely explored, and we shall probably never have a full account of them. A mental tension affects both the voluntary system and the vegetative nerve system. Where there is tension, there is action in the voluntary system. The individual drums on the table, plucks at his lip or tears up pieces of paper. If he is tense, he has to move in some way. Chewing a pencil or a cigar gives him an outlet for his tension. These movements show us that he feels himself too much confronted by some situation. It is the same whether he blushes when he is among strangers, begins to tremble or exhibits a tic; they are all results of tension. By means of the vegetative system, the tension is communicated to the whole body; and so, with every emotion, the whole body is itself in a tension. The manifestations of this tension, however, are not as clear at every point; and we speak of symptoms only in those points where the results are discoverable. If we examine more closely we shall find that every part of the body is involved in an emotional expression; and that these physical expressions are the consequences of the action of the mind and the body. It is always necessary to look for these reciprocal actions of the mind on the body, and of the body on the mind, since both of them are parts of the whole with which we are concerned.

We may reasonably conclude from such evidence that a style of life and a corresponding emotional disposition exert a continuous influence on the development of the body. If it is true that a child crystallizes its style of life very early, we should be able to discover, if we are experienced enough, the resulting physical expressions in later life. A courageous individual will show the effects of his attitude in his physique. His body will be differently built up; the tonus of his muscles will be stronger, the carriage of his body will be firmer. Posture probably influences very considerably the development of the body and perhaps accounts in part for the better tonus of the muscles. The expression of the face is different in the courageous individual, and, in the end, the whole cast of features. Even the conformation of the skull may be affected.

To-day it would be difficult to deny that the mind can influence the brain. Pathology has shown cases where an individual has lost the ability to read or write through a lesion in the left hemisphere, but has been able to recover this ability by training other parts of the brain. It often happens that an individual has an apoplectic stroke and there is no possibility of repairing the damaged part of the brain; and yet other parts of the brain compensate, restore the functions of the organs and so complete once more the brain's faculties. This fact is especially important in help-

ing us to show the possibilities of the educational application of Individual Psychology. If the mind can exercise
such an influence over the brain; if the brain is no more
than the tool of the mind — its most important tool, but
still only its tool — then we can find ways to develop and
improve this tool. No one born with a certain standard of
brain need remain inescapably bound by it all his life:
methods may be found to make the brain better fitted for
life.

A mind which has fixed its goal in a mistaken direction — which, for example, is not developing the ability
to coöperate — will fail to exercise a helpful influence on
the growth of the brain. For this reason we find that many
children who lack the ability to coöperate show, in later
life, that they have not developed their intelligence, their
ability to understand. Since the whole bearing of an adult
reveals the influence of the style of life which he built up
in the first four or five years, since we can see visibly
before us the results of his scheme of apperception and the
meaning which he has given to life, we can discover the
blocks in coöperation from which he is suffering, and help
to correct his failures. Already in Individual Psychology
we have the first steps towards this science.

Many authors have pointed out a constant relationship
between the expressions of the mind and those of the
body. None of them, it seems, has attempted to discover
the bridge between the two. Kretschmer, for example, has
described how, in the build of the body, we can discover
a correspondence with a certain type of mind. He is
thus able to distinguish types into which he fits a great
proportion of mankind. There are, for instance, the
pyknoids, round-faced individuals with short noses and

a tendency to corpulence; the men of whom Julius Cæsar speaks:

> " Let me have men about me that are fat;
> Sleek-headed men and such as sleep o' nights." [1]

With such a physique Kretschmer correlates specific mental characteristics; but his work does not make clear the reasons for this correlation. In our own conditions, individuals of this physique do not appear as suffering from organ imperfection; their bodies are well suited to our culture. Physically they feel equal to others. They have confidence in their own strength. They are not tense and, if they wished to fight, they would feel capable of fighting. They have no need, however, to look on others as their enemies or to struggle with life as if it were hostile. One school of psychology would call them extraverts, but would offer no explanation. We should expect them to be extraverts, because they suffer no trouble from their bodies.

A contrasting type which Kretschmer distinguishes is the schizoid, either infantile or unusually tall, long-nosed, with an egg-shaped head. These he believes to be reserved and introspective; and if they suffer from mental disturbances, they become schizophrenic. They are of the other type of which Cæsar speaks:

> " Yond Cassius has a lean and hungry look;
> He thinks too much; such men are dangerous." [2]

Perhaps these individuals suffered from imperfect organs and grew up more self-interested, more pessimistic and

[1] " Julius Cæsar ", Act I, Scene 2.
[2] " Julius Cæsar ", Act I, Scene 2.

more " introverted." Perhaps they made more claims for help, and when they found that they were not sufficiently considered, became bitter and suspicious. We can find, however, as Kretschmer admits, many mixed types, and even pyknoid types who have developed with the mental characteristics attributed to schizoids. We could understand this if their circumstances had burdened them in another way, and they had become timid and discouraged. We could probably, by systematic discouragement, make any child into a person who behaved like a schizoid.

If we had much experience behind us, we could recognize from all the partial expressions of an individual the degree of his ability to coöperate. Without knowing it, people have always been looking for such signs. The necessity for coöperation is always pressing us; and hints have already been discovered, not scientifically but intuitively, to show us how to orient ourselves better in this chaotic life. In the same way we can see that before all the great adjustments of history the mind of the people had already recognized the necessity for adjustment and was striving to achieve it. So long as the striving is only instinctive, mistakes can easily be made. People have always disliked individuals who had very noticeable physical peculiarities, disfigured persons or hunchbacks. Without knowing it, they were judging them as less fitted for coöperation. This was a great mistake, but their judgment was probably founded on experience. The way had not yet been found to increase the degree of coöperation in individuals who suffered from these peculiarities; their drawbacks were therefore overemphasized, and they became the victims of popular superstition.

Let us now summarize our position. In the first four or

five years of life the child unifies its mental strivings and establishes the root relationships between its mind and its body. A fixed style of life is adopted, with a corresponding emotional and physical *habitus*. Its development includes a larger or smaller degree of coöperation; and it is from this degree of coöperation that we learn to judge and understand the individual. In all failures the highest common measure is a small degree of ability to coöperate. We can now give a still further definition of psychology: it is the understanding of deficiencies in coöperation. Since the mind is a unity and the same style of life runs through all its expressions, all of an individual's emotions and thoughts must be consonant with his style of life. If we see emotions that apparently cause difficulties and run counter to the individual's own welfare, it is completely useless to begin by trying to change these emotions. They are the right expression of the individual's style of life, and they can be uprooted only if he changes his style of life.

Here Individual Psychology gives us a special hint for our educational and therapeutic outlook. We must never treat a symptom or a single expression: we must discover the mistake made in the whole style of life, in the way the mind has interpreted its experiences, in the meaning it has given to life, and in the actions with which it has answered the impressions received from the body and from the environment. This is the real task of psychology. It is not properly to be called psychology if we stick pins into a child and see how far it jumps, or tickle it and see how loud it laughs. These enterprises, so common among modern psychologists, may in fact tell us something of an individual's psychology; but only in so far as they give evidence of a fixed and particular style of life. Styles of life are the proper subject-matter of psychology and the material for investigation; and schools which take any other subject-matter are occupied, in the main part, with physiology or biology. This holds true of those who investigate stimuli and reactions; those who attempt to trace the effect of a *trauma* or shocking experience; and those who examine inherited abilities and look to see how they unfold themselves. In Individual Psychology, however, we are considering the psyche itself, the unified mind; we are examining the meaning which individuals give to the world and to themselves, their goals, the direction of their strivings, and the approaches they make to the problems of life. The best key which we so far possess for understanding psychological differences is given by examining the degree of ability to coöperate.

CHAPTER III

Feelings of Inferiority and Superiority

The "inferiority complex", one of the most important discoveries of Individual Psychology, seems to have become world-famous. Psychologists of many schools have adopted the term and use it in their own practice. I am not at all sure, however, that they understand it or use it with the right meaning. It never helps us, for example, to tell a patient that he is suffering from an inferiority complex; to do so would only stress his feelings of inferiority without showing him how to overcome them. We must recognize the specific discouragement which he shows in his style of life; we must encourage him at the precise point where he falls short in courage. Every neurotic has an inferiority complex. No neurotic is distinguished from other neurotics by the fact that he has an inferiority complex and the others have none. He is distinguished from the others by the kind of situation in which he feels unable to continue on the useful side of life, by the limits he has put to his strivings and activities. It would no more help him to be more courageous if we said to him, " You are suffering from an inferiority complex," than it would help some one with a headache if we said, " I can tell you what is wrong with you. You have a headache! "

Many neurotics, if they were asked whether they felt inferior, would answer, " No." Some would even answer, " Just the opposite. I know quite well that I am superior to the people around me." We do not need to ask: we need only watch the individual's behavior. It is there that we shall notice what tricks he uses to reassure himself of his importance. If we see some one who is arrogant, for example, we can guess that he feels, " Other people are apt to overlook me. I must show that I am somebody." If we see some one who gesticulates strongly when he speaks, we can guess that he feels, " My words would not carry any weight if I did not emphasize them." Behind every one who behaves as if he were superior to others, we can suspect a feeling of inferiority which calls for very special efforts of concealment. It is as if a man feared that he was too small and walked on tiptoe to make himself seem larger. Sometimes we can see this very behavior if two children are comparing their height. The one who is afraid that he is smaller will stretch up and hold himself very tensely; he will try to seem bigger than he is. If we asked such a child, " Do you think you are too small? " we should hardly expect him to acknowledge the fact.

It does not follow, therefore, that an individual with strong feelings of inferiority will appear to be a submissive, quiet, restrained, inoffensive sort of person. Inferiority feelings can express themselves in a thousand ways. Perhaps I can illustrate this by an anecdote of three children who were taken to the zoo for the first time. As they stood before the lion's cage, one of them shrank behind his mother's skirts and said, " I want to go home." The second child stood where he was, very pale and trembling, and said, " I'm not a bit frightened." The third glared at the lion fiercely and asked his mother, " Shall I spit at it? " All three children really felt inferior, but each expressed his feelings in his own way, consonant with his style of life.

Inferiority feelings are in some degree common to all of us, since we all find ourselves in positions which we wish to improve. If we have kept our courage, we shall set about ridding ourselves of these feelings by the only direct, realistic and satisfactory means — by improving the situation. No human being can bear a feeling of inferiority for long; he will be thrown into a tension which necessitates some kind of action. But suppose an individual is discouraged; suppose he cannot conceive that if he makes realistic efforts he will improve the situation. He will still be unable to bear his feelings of inferiority; he will still struggle to get rid of them; but he will try methods which bring him no farther ahead. His goal is still " to be superior to difficulties," but instead of overcoming obstacles he will try to hypnotize himself, or auto-intoxicate himself, into *feeling* superior. Meanwhile his feelings of inferiority will accumulate, because the situation which produces them remains unaltered. The provocation is still there. Every step he takes will lead him farther into self-deception, and all his problems will press in upon him with greater and greater urgency. If we looked at his movements without understanding we should think them aimless. They would not impress us as designed to improve the situation. As soon as we see, however, that he is occupied, like every one else, in struggling for a feeling of adequacy but has given up hope of altering the objective situation, all his movements begin to fall into coherence. If he feels weak, he moves into circumstances where he can feel strong. He does not train to be stronger, to be more adequate; he trains to appear stronger in his own eyes. His efforts to fool himself will meet with only a partial success. If he feels unequal to the problems of occu-

pation, he may attempt to reassure himself of his importance by being a domestic tyrant. In this way he may drug
himself; but the real feelings of inferiority will remain.
They will be the same old feelings of inferiority provoked
by the same old situation. They will be the lasting under-
current of his psychic life. In such a case we may truly
speak of an inferiority complex.

It is time now to give a definition of the inferiority
complex. The inferiority complex appears before a problem for which an individual is not properly adapted or
equipped, and expresses his conviction that he is unable to
solve it. From this definition we can see that anger can be
as much an expression of an inferiority complex as tears
or apologies. As inferiority feelings always produce tension, there will always be a compensatory movement
towards a feeling of superiority; but it will no longer be
directed towards solving the problem. The movement
towards superiority will thus be towards the useless side
of life. The real problem will be shelved or excluded.
The individual will try to restrict his field of action and
will be more occupied in avoiding defeat than in pressing
forward to success. He will give the picture of hesitating,
of being at a standstill, or even of retreating, before his
difficulties.

Such an attitude can be seen very simply in cases
of agoraphobia. This symptom is the expression of conviction, " I must not go too far. I must keep myself to
familiar circumstances. Life is full of dangers and I must
avoid encountering them." Where this attitude is carried
out consistently, the individual will keep himself to one
room, or will retire to bed and stay there. The most thoroughgoing expression of a retreat before difficulties is

suicide. Here the individual gives up before all the problems of life, expresses his conviction that he can do nothing to better his situation. The striving for superiority in suicide can be understood when we realize that suicide is always a reproach or a revenge. With every suicide, we can always find some one at whose door he is laying the responsibility for his death. It is as if the suicide said, " I was the tenderest and most sensitive of all people, and you treated me with the utmost brutality."

To some degree or other, every neurotic restricts his field of action, his contacts with the whole situation. He tries to keep at a distance the three real confronting problems of life and confines himself to circumstances in which he feels able to dominate. In this way he builds for himself a narrow stable, closes the door and spends his life away from the wind, the sunlight and the fresh air. Whether he dominates by bullying or by whining will depend on his training: he will choose the device which he has tested best and found most effective for his purposes. Sometimes, if he is dissatisfied with one method, he will try the other. In either case the goal is the same — to gain a feeling of superiority without working to improve the situation. The discouraged child which finds that it can tyrannize best by tears will be a cry-baby; and a direct line of development leads from the cry-baby to the adult melancholiac. Tears and complaints — the means which I have called " water power "— can be an extremely capable weapon for disturbing coöperation and reducing others to a condition of slavery. With such people, as with those who suffer from shyness, embarrassment and feelings of guilt, we should find the inferiority complex on the surface; they would readily admit their weakness and their inability to look after themselves. What they would hide from view would be their heightened goal of supremacy, their desire to be the first at all costs. A child given to boasting, on the other hand, displays its superiority complex at first view; if we examined its behavior rather than its words, we should soon discover the unadmitted feelings of inferiority.

The so-called Œdipus Complex is in reality nothing more than a special instance of the " narrow stable " of the neurotic. If an individual is afraid to meet the problem of love in the world at large, he will not succeed in ridding himself of this problem. If he confines his field of action to the family circle, it will not surprise us to find that his sexual strivings also are elaborated within these limits. From his feeling of insecurity he has never spread his interest outside the few people with whom he is most familiar. He fears that with others he would not be able to dominate in his accustomed way. The victims of the Œdipus Complex are children who were pampered by their mothers, who were trained to believe that their wishes carried with them a right to fulfillment, and who never saw that they could win affection and love by their independent efforts outside the bounds of the home. In adult life they remain tied to their mothers' apron strings. In love they look, not for an equal partner, but for a servant; and the servant of whose support they are surest is their mother. We could probably induce an Œdipus Complex in any child. All we should need is for its mother to spoil it, and refuse to spread its interest to other people, and for its father to be comparatively indifferent or cold.

This picture of restricted movement is given by all the symptoms of neurosis. In the speech of the stammerer we can see his hesitating attitude. His residue of social feeling drives him to make connection with his fellows, but his low opinion of himself, his fear of coming to the test, conflicts with his social feeling, and he hesitates in his speech. Children who are " backward " at school, men and women who have found no occupation by the age of thirty or more, or have shelved the problem of marriage, compulsion neurotics who must carry out the same action again and again, insomniacs who weary themselves for the tasks of the day—all of them reveal the inferiority complex which forbids them to make progress in solving the problems of life. Masturbation, premature ejaculation, impotence and perversion all show a halting style of life, consequent on a fear of inadequacy in the approach to the other sex. The concomitant goal of supremacy will suggest itself if we ask, " Why so afraid of inadequacy? " The answer can only be, " Because the individual has set for himself so high a goal of success."

We have said that inferiority feelings are not in themselves abnormal. They are the cause of all improvements in the position of mankind. Science itself, for example, can arise only when people feel their ignorance and their need to foresee the future: it is the result of the strivings of human beings to improve their whole situation, to know more of the universe and to be able to control it better. Indeed, it seems to me that all our human culture is based upon feelings of inferiority. If we can imagine a disinterested observer visiting our human planet, he would surely conclude, " These human beings, with all their associations and institutions, with all their efforts for security, with their roofs to keep off the rain, their clothes to warm them, their streets to make travel easier — obviously they feel themselves the weakest of all the inhabitants of earth." And in some ways men are the weakest of all creatures. We have not the strength of the lion or the gorilla, and many animals are better fitted to meet the difficulties of life alone. Some animals compensate for their weakness by association — they join together in herds; but human beings have need of more varied and deeper coöperation than we can find anywhere else in the world. The human child is especially weak; it needs care and protection for many years. Since every human being has at one time been the youngest and weakest of mankind, and since mankind, without coöperation, would be completely at the mercy of its environment, we can understand how inescapably a child which has not trained itself in coöperation will be driven towards pessimism and a fixed inferiority complex. We can understand, too, that life will continue to offer problems even to the most coöperative individual. No individual will find himself in the position of having reached his final goal of superiority, of being complete master of his environment. Life is too short; our bodies are too weak; the three problems of life will always admit of richer and fuller solutions. We can always approach to a solution; we can never rest satisfied with our achievement. Striving will continue in any case; but with the coöperative individual it will be hopeful and contributory striving, directed towards a real improvement of our common situation.

Nobody will worry, I think, over the fact that we cannot finally reach the highest goal of our lives. If we could imagine a single individual, or mankind on the whole, as having reached a position where there were no further difficulties, we should think that life in those circumstances must be very dull. Everything then could be foreseen, everything calculated in advance. To-morrow would bring no unexpected opportunities; there would be nothing to look forward to in the future. Our interest in life comes mainly from our lack of certainty. If we were all sure, if we knew everything, there would no longer be discussions or discoveries. Science would have come to an end; the universe around us would be nothing but a twice-told tale. Art and religion, which cheer us with the imagination of our unattained goals, would no longer have any meaning. It is our good fortune that life is not so easily exhausted. The strivings of men are continuous and we can always find or invent new problems, and make new opportunities for coöperation and contribution. The neurotic is blocked at the beginning; his solutions remain at a low level and his difficulties are correspondingly great. The more normal individual puts behind himself an increasingly full solution for his problems; he can advance to new difficulties and arrive at new solutions. In this way he is enabled to contribute to others: he does not lag behind and become a liability for his fellow men; he does not need or demand special consideration; but he proceeds with courage and independence to solve his problems in accordance with social feeling.

The goal of superiority, with each individual, is personal and unique. It depends upon the meaning he gives to life; and this meaning is not a matter of words. It is built up in his style of life and runs through it like a strange melody of his own creation. In his style of life he does not express his goal so that we can formulate it once for all. He expresses it vaguely, so that we must guess at it from the indications he gives. Understanding a style of life is similar to understanding the work of a poet. A poet must use words; but his meaning is more than the mere words he uses. The greatest part of his meaning must be guessed at; we must read between the lines. So, too, with that profoundest and most intricate creation, an individual style of life. The psychologist must learn to read between the lines; he must learn the art of appreciating life-meanings.

It could not be otherwise. The meaning of life is arrived at in those first four or five years of life; and it is not arrived at by a mathematical process, but by dark gropings, by feelings not wholly understood, by catching at hints and fumbling for explanations. The goal of superiority, in a similar way, is fixed by groping and guesswork; it is a life-striving, a dynamic tendency, not a charted and geographically determined point. Nobody knows his own goal of superiority so that he can describe it in full. Perhaps he knows his professional aims, but these give no more than a small part of his strivings. Even where the goal has been made concrete, there can be a thousand varieties of striving towards this goal. One man, for example, will want to be a physician; but to be a physician may mean many different things. Not only may he wish to be a specialist in internal medicine or a specialist in pathology; he will show in his activities his own peculiar degree of interest in himself and interest in others. We shall see how far he trains himself to be of help to his fellows and how far he limits his helpfulness. He has made this his aim as a compensation for a specific feeling of inferiority; and we must be able to guess, from his expressions in his profession and elsewhere, the specific feeling for which he is compensating.

We very frequently find, for example, that physicians in their childhood made early acquaintance with the fact of death; and death was the aspect of human insecurity which made the greatest impression on them. Perhaps a brother or a parent died; and their later training developed towards finding a way, for themselves and others, to be more secure against death. Another man may make it his concrete goal to be a teacher; but we know very well how different teachers may be. If a teacher has a low degree of social feeling, his goal of superiority in being a teacher may be to rule among his inferiors; he may feel secure only with those who are weaker and less experienced than himself. A teacher with a high degree of social feeling will treat his pupils as his equals; he will really wish to contribute to the welfare of mankind. We need not do more than mention here how different the capacities and interests of teachers may be, and how significant of their goal all these expressions will be found. When a goal is made concrete, the individual's potentialities must be curtailed and limited to fit this goal; but the complete goal, the prototype, will always push and pull at these limits and find a way, under any conditions, to express the meaning given to life and the final ideal striving for superiority.

With every individual, therefore, we must look below the surface. An individual may change the way in which he makes his goal concrete, just as he may change one expression of his concrete goal, his occupation. We must still look for the underlying coherence, for the unity of the personality. This unity is fixed in all its expressions. If we take an irregular triangle and place it in different positions, each position will seem to give us quite a different triangle; but if we look hard we shall discover that the triangle is always the same. So, too, with the prototype: its content is never exhausted by any single expression, but we can recognize it in all its expressions. We can never say to a man, " Your striving for superiority would be satisfied if you did this or that . . ." The striving for superiority remains flexible; and, indeed, the nearer to health and normality an individual is, the more he can find new openings for his strivings when they are blocked in one particular direction. It is only the neurotic who feels, of the concrete expressions of his goal, " I must have this or nothing."

We should not attempt to formulate too easily any particular superiority striving; but we can find in all goals one common factor — a striving to be godlike. Sometimes we find children who express themselves quite openly in this way, and remark, " I should like to be God." Many philosophers have had the same idea; and there are educators who would wish to train and educate children to be like God. In old religious disciplines the same objective is visible; disciples should educate themselves in such a way that they become godlike. This ideal of god-likeness appears in a more modest way in the idea of " superman "; and it is revealing — I shall not say more — that Nietzsche when he became insane signed himself in a letter to Strindberg, " The Crucified." Often insane people express their goal of superiority in an undisguised form: they will assert, " I am Napoleon," or " I am the Emperor of China." They wish to be the center of attention through the whole world, to be looked on from all sides, to be connected with the whole world by wireless and overhear all conversations, to predict the future, to be the bearers of supernatural power. In a more reasonable way, perhaps, the same goal of godlikeness comes out in the desire to know everything, to possess universal wisdom, or in the wish to perpetuate our life. Whether it is our earthly life we desire to perpetuate, or we imagine ourselves as coming to earth again and again through many incarnations, or we foresee an immortality in another world, these prospects are all based upon the desire to be like God. In religious teachings it is God who is the immortal being, who survives through all time and eternity. I am not here discussing whether these ideas are right or wrong: they are interpretations of life, they are *meanings*; and to some degree we are all caught up in this meaning,— God and godlikeness. Even the atheist wishes to conquer God, to be higher than God; and we can see that this is a peculiarly strong goal of superiority.

Once the goal of superiority has been made concrete, there are no mistakes made in the style of life. The habits and symptoms of the individual are precisely right for attaining his concrete goal; they are beyond all criticism. Every problem child, every neurotic, every drunkard, criminal or sexual pervert is making the proper movements to achieve what he takes to be the position of superiority. It is impossible to attack his symptoms by themselves; they are exactly the symptoms he ought to have for such a goal. A boy at one school, the laziest boy in the class, was asked by his teacher, " Why do you get on so badly with your work? " He answered, " If I am the laziest boy here, you will always be occupied with me. You never pay any attention to good boys, who never disturb the class and do all their work properly." So long as it was his aim to attract notice and rule over his teacher, he had found the best way to do it. It would be of no use to try to get rid of his laziness; he needed it for his goal. He was perfectly in the right and if he changed his behavior he would be a fool. Another boy was very obedient at home but he seemed to be stupid; he was backward at school and not at all quick-witted at home. He had a brother two years older than he, and his brother was quite different in his style of life. He was intelligent and active but he was always getting into trouble because of his impudence. The younger brother was one day overheard saying to the older brother, " I'd rather be as stupid as I am than as impudent as you are." His stupidity was really quite intelligent if we grant him the goal of escaping trouble. Because of his stupidity less was demanded of him, and if he committed errors he was not blamed for them. Granted his goal, he would have been a fool not to be stupid.

Till the present day, the usual treatment has been to attack the symptom. To this attitude Individual Psychology is entirely opposed, both in medicine and in education. When a child is backward in arithmetic, or has bad school reports, it is useless to concentrate our attention on these points and try to improve him in these special expressions. Perhaps he wants to bother the teacher; or even to escape school altogether by getting himself expelled. If we check him at one point, he will find a new way to reach his goal. It is just the same with the adult neurotic. Suppose he suffers, for example, from migraine. These headaches of his can be very useful to him and they may occur at the precise moment when he has greatest need of them. Through his headaches he may escape solving the problems of society; they may come on whenever he is confronted with the necessity of meeting new people or of making a new decision. At the same time, they may aid him in tyrannizing over his office staff, or over his wife and family. Why should we expect him to give up such a well-tested device? The pain he gives himself, from his present point of view, is no more than a wise investment; it brings him in all the returns he could wish. No doubt we could frighten him out of this symptom by giving him an explanation which shocked him, just as war neurotics were sometimes frightened out of their symptoms by electric shocks or pretended operations. Perhaps medical treatment would relieve him at this point and make it more difficult for him to continue with the particular symptom he has chosen. But, so long as his goal remains the same, if he gives up one symptom he must find another. " Cured " of his headaches, he will develop insomnia, or some other fresh symptom. So long as his goal remains the same, he must continue to pursue it. Neurotics exist who can drop symptoms with astonishing rapidity and take on new ones without a moment's hesitation. They become virtuosos of neurosis, continually extending their repertory. The reading of a book on psychotherapy will suggest to them only some further nervous troubles which as yet they have not had the opportunity of trying out. What we must always look for is the purpose for which the symptom is adopted and the coherence of this purpose with the general goal of superiority.

Suppose in my classroom I sent for a ladder, climbed up it, and perched on top of the blackboard. Any one seeing me would probably think, " Doctor Adler is quite crazy." They would not know what the ladder was for, why I climbed up it, or why I was sitting in such an awkward position. But if they knew, "He wants to sit on the blackboard because he feels inferior unless he is physically higher than other people; he only feels secure if he can look down on his class", they would not think I was quite so crazy. I would have taken an excellent way to attain my concrete goal. The ladder would then seem a very sensible device and my efforts to climb up it would appear well planned and executed. Only on one point would I be crazy — my interpretation of superiority. If I could be convinced that my concrete goal was badly chosen, then I could change my activity. But if the goal remains, and my ladder is taken away, I shall try again with a chair; and if the chair is taken away, I shall see what I can do by jumping and clambering and pulling myself up by my muscles. It is the same with every neurotic: nothing is wrong with his choice of means — they are beyond criticism. It is only his concrete goal we can improve. With a change of goal, the mental habits and attitudes will also change. He will no longer need the old habits and attitudes, and new ones, fitted to his new goal, will take their place.

Let me give the example of a woman of thirty who came to me suffering from anxiety and inability to make friends. She could make no progress with the problem of occupation and in consequence was still a burden upon her family. She would take small jobs from time to time as a stenographer or secretary, but by a miserable fatality, her employers would always make love to her and scare her so much that she had to leave the office. Once, however, she found a place where her employer was not so much interested in her. She felt so humiliated that she left this job also. She had been psychologically treated for many years — for eight years, I believe — but her treatment had not succeeded in making her sociable or putting her in a position where she could earn her living.

When I saw her I traced back her style of life to the first years of her childhood. No one can understand the grown-up who does not learn to understand the child. She had been the youngest in her family, very pretty, and spoiled beyond belief. Her parents were very well off at the time, and she had only to express a wish for it to be granted. " Why," I said when I heard her, " you were brought up like a princess." " That's odd," she replied. " Everybody used to call me Princess." I asked her for her earliest recollection. " When I was four years old," she said, " I remember going out of the house and finding some children who were playing a game. Every so often they jumped up and called out, ' The witch is coming.' I was very frightened and when I got back home, I asked an old woman who was staying with us whether there were really any witches. She answered, ' Yes, there are witches and burglars and robbers, and they will all come after you.' " From this we can see that she was scared to be left alone in the house: and she expressed her fear in her whole style of life. She did not feel strong enough to leave home and those at home must support her and look after her in every way. Another early recollection was as follows: " I had a piano teacher, a man; and one day he tried to kiss me. I stopped playing and went and told my mother. After that, I didn't wish to play the piano any more." Here, too, we can see that she trained to put a great distance between herself and men; and her sexual development was in accordance with the goal of protecting herself against love. She felt that to be in love was a weakness. Here I must say that many people feel weak if they are in love; and to a certain degree they are right. If we are in love we must be tender, and our interest in another human being leaves us open to disturbance. It is only the individual whose goal of superiority is, " I must never be weak, I must never be exposed ", who will avoid the mutual dependence of love. Such people train away from love and are ill-prepared for it. Often you will find that if they feel in danger of falling in love, they turn the situation to ridicule. They laugh and make jokes and tease the person from whom they feel in danger. In this way they try to get rid of their feeling of weakness.

This girl, too, felt weak when she considered love and marriage; and in consequence she was impressed much more strongly than she needed to be when men made love to her in her jobs. She could see no way out but to run away. While she was still confronted with these problems, her mother and father both died and her court almost came to an end. She managed to find relatives to come and look after her; but her position was not nearly so satisfactory. After a while her relatives would become very much bored with her and would stop paying her all the attention she felt she needed. She scolded them and told them how dangerous it was for her to be left alone; and in this way she staved off the tragedy of being left to her own devices. I am convinced that if her family had given up bothering about her altogether, she would have gone mad. The only way to accomplish her goal of superiority was to force her family to support her and allow her to exclude all the problems of life. She kept in her own mind the image, " I do not belong to this planet, but to another planet, where I am a princess. This poor earth does not understand me and acknowledge my importance." One step further would have led her to insanity; but so long as she had some small resources of her own and could still obtain relatives or family friends to take care of her, there was no call for the final step.

Here is another case where both the inferiority complex and the superiority complex can be clearly recognized. A girl of sixteen was sent to me, who had been stealing since she was six or seven and staying out at night with boys since she was twelve. When she was two years old her parents had divorced after a long and bitter personal struggle. She was taken by her mother to live with her in her grandmother's home; and her grandmother, as so often happens, gave herself over to pampering the child. She had been born when the struggle between her parents was at its height and her mother had not welcomed her arrival. She had never liked her daughter and a tension existed between them. When the girl came to see me I talked with her in a friendly way. She told me, " I don't like taking things or running about with boys; but I've got to show my mother that she can't handle me." " You do it for a revenge? " I asked her. " I suppose so," she answered. She wanted to prove herself stronger than her mother; but she had this goal only because she felt weaker. She felt her mother disliked her and she suffered from an inferiority complex. The only way she could think of to assert her superiority was to cause trouble. When children commit thefts or other delinquencies, it is usually for revenge.

A girl of fifteen disappeared for eight days. When

she was found she was taken to the Children's Court; and there she told a tale of having been kidnapped by a man who had bound her and kept her locked in a room for eight days. No one believed her. The doctor spoke very intimately with her and urged her to confess the truth. She was so angry with him for not accepting her story that she slapped him in the face. When I saw her, I asked her what she wanted to be, and gave the impression that I was interested only in her own fate and in what I could do to help her. When I asked her for a dream, she laughed and told me the following dream, " I was in a speak-easy. When I went out, I met my mother. Soon my father came, and I asked my mother to hide me, so that he should not see me." She was afraid of her father and she was fighting him. He used to punish her; and because she was afraid of punishment she was compelled to lie. If ever we hear of a case of lying, we must look for a severe parent. A lie would have no sense unless the truth were felt as dangerous. On the other hand, we can see that this girl had some coöperation with her mother. She now told me that some one had enticed her to a speak-easy, and she had spent the eight days there. She was frightened of confessing because of her father; but at the same time her procedure had been dictated by the desire to get the better of him. She felt subjugated by him; and she could feel the conqueror only by hurting him.

How may people who have mistaken the way to superiority be helped? It is not so difficult if we recognize that the striving for superiority is common to all men. We can then put ourselves in their position and sympathize with their struggles. The only mistake they make is that their strivings are on the useless side of life. It is the striving for superiority which is behind every human creation and it is the source of all contributions which are made to our culture. The whole of human life proceeds along this great line of action — from below above, from minus to plus, from defeat to victory. The only individuals who can really meet and master the problems of life, however, are those who show in their striving a tendency to enrich all others, who go ahead in such a way that others benefit also. If we approach people in the right way, we shall not find them hard to convince. All human judgments of value and success are founded, in the end, upon coöperation; this is the great shared commonplace of the human race. All that we ask of conduct, of ideals, of goals, of actions and traits of character, is that they should serve towards our human coöperation. We shall never find a man who is completely devoid of social feeling. The neurotic and the criminal also know this open secret; we can see their knowledge in the pains they take to justify their style of life or to throw responsibility elsewhere. They have lost courage, however, to proceed on the useful side of life. An inferiority complex tells them, " Success in coöperation is not for you." They have turned away from the real problems of life and are engaged in shadow-fighting to reassure themselves of their strength.

In our human division of labor there is room for a great variety of concrete goals. Perhaps, as we have seen, every goal may involve some small degree of mistakenness; and we could always find something to criticize. To one child, superiority will seem to lie in mathematical knowledge, to another in art, to a third in physical strength. The child with digestive inferiority may come to think that the problems confronting him are mainly problems of nutrition. His interest may turn towards food, since in this way he conceives that he can better his situation. In consequence he may become an expert cook or a professor of dietetics. In all these special goals we can see, together with a real compensation, some exclusion of possibilities, some training towards self-limitation. We can understand, for example, that a philosopher must really from time to time exile himself from society to think and to write his books. But the mistake involved is never great if a high degree of social feeling is bound up with the goal of superiority. Our coöperation has need of many different excellences.

CHAPTER IV

Early Memories

Since the struggle to reach a position of vantage is the key to the whole personality, we shall meet it at every point of the individual's psychic life. To recognize this fact gives us two great aids in our task of understanding an individual style of life. First, we can begin wherever we choose: every expression will lead us in the same direction — towards the one motive, the one melody, around which the personality is built. Secondly, we are provided with a vast store of material. Every word, thought, feeling or gesture contributes to our understanding. Any mistake we might make in considering one expression too hastily can be checked and corrected by a thousand other expressions. We cannot finally decide the meaning of one expression until we can see its part in the whole; but every expression is saying the same thing, every expression is urging us towards the solution. We are like archæologists who find fragments of earthenware, tools, the ruined walls of buildings, broken monuments, and leaves of papyrus; and from these fragments proceed to infer the life of a whole city which has perished. But we are dealing, not with something which has perished, but with the inter-organized aspects of a human being, a living personality which can set before us continuous new manifestations of its own meaning.

It is not an easy task to understand a human being. Individual Psychology is perhaps the most difficult of all psychologies to learn and to practice. We must listen always for the whole. We must be sceptical until the key becomes self-evident. We must gather hints from a multitude of small signs — from the way a man enters a room, the way he greets us and shakes hands, the way he smiles, the way he walks. On one point we may go astray, but others are always forthcoming to correct or confirm us. Treatment itself is an exercise in coöperation and a test of coöperation. We can succeed only if we are genuinely interested in the other. We must be able to see with his eyes and listen with his ears. He must contribute his part to our common understanding. We must work out his attitudes and his difficulties together. Even if we felt we had understood him, we should have no witness that we were right unless he also understood. A tactless truth can never be the whole truth; it shows that our understanding was not sufficient. It is perhaps from a miscomprehension of this point that other schools have derived the concept of " negative and positive transferences ", factors which are never met with in Individual Psychological treatment. To spoil a patient who is accustomed to be spoiled may be an easy way to gain his affections; but his desire for domination will be apparent underneath. If we slight him and overlook him, we may easily incur his enmity: he may break off the treatment, or he may continue it in the hope of justifying himself and making us repent. We shall not be able to help him either by spoiling him or by slighting him: we must show him the interest of one man towards a fellow man. No interest could be truer or more objective. We must coöperate with him in finding his mistakes, both for his own benefit and for the welfare of others. With this aim in view we shall never run the risk of exciting "transfer-ences", of posing as authorities, or of putting him in a position of dependence and irresponsibility.

Among all psychic expressions, some of the most re-vealing are the individual's memories. His memories are the reminders he carries about with him of his own limits and of the meaning of circumstances. There are no "chance memories": out of the incalculable number of impressions which meet an individual, he chooses to re-member only those which he feels, however darkly, to have a bearing on his situation. Thus his memories repre-sent his "Story of My Life"; a story he repeats to him-self to warn him or comfort him, to keep him concen-trated on his goal, to prepare him, by means of past ex-periences, to meet the future with an already tested style of action. The use of memories to stabilize a mood can be plainly seen in everyday behavior. If a man suffers a defeat and is discouraged by it, he recalls previous in-stances of defeat. If he is melancholy, all his memories are melancholy. When he is cheerful and courageous, he selects quite other memories; the incidents he recalls are pleasant, they confirm his optimism. In the same way, if he feels himself confronted with a problem, he will summon up memories which help to prepare the mood in which he will meet it. Memories thus serve much the same purpose as dreams. Many men, when they have decisions to make, will dream of examinations which they have successfully passed. They see their decision as a test, and try to re-create the mood in which they succeeded before. What holds true of the variations of mood within an individual style of life, holds true also of the structure and balance of his moods in general. A melancholiac could not remain melancholiac if he remembered his good moments and his successes. He must say to himself, " All my life I was unfortunate "; and select only those events which he can interpret as instances of his unhappy fate. Memories can never run counter to the style of life. If an individual's goal of superiority demands that he should feel, " Other people always humiliate me ", he will choose for remembrance incidents which he can interpret as humiliations. In so far as his style of life alters, his memories also will alter; he will remember different incidents, or he will put a different interpretation on the incidents he remembers.

Early recollections have especial significance. To begin with, they show the style of life in its origins and in its simplest expressions. We can judge from them whether the child was pampered or neglected; how far he was training for coöperation with others; with whom he preferred to coöperate; what problems confronted him, and how he struggled against them. In the early recollections of a child who suffered from difficulties in seeing and who trained himself to look more closely, we shall find impressions of a visual nature. His recollections will begin, " I looked around me . . .", or he will describe colors and shapes. A child who had difficulties of movement, who wanted to walk or run or jump, will show these interests in his recollections. Events remembered from childhood must be very near to the main interest of the individual; and if we know his main interest we know his goal and his style of life. It is this fact which makes early recollections of such value in vocational guidance. We can find, moreover, the child's relations towards his mother, his father and the other members of the family.

It is comparatively indifferent whether the memories are accurate or inaccurate; what is of most value about them is that they represent the individual's judgment, " Even in childhood, I was such and such a person ", or, " Even in childhood, I found the world like this."

Most illuminating of all is the way he begins his story, the earliest incident he can recall. The first memory will show the individual's fundamental view of life; his first satisfactory crystallization of his attitude. It offers us an opportunity to see at one glance what he has taken as the starting point for his development. I would never investigate a personality without asking for the first memory. Sometimes people do not answer, or profess that they do not know which event came first; but this itself is revealing. We can gather that they do not wish to discuss their fundamental meaning, and that they are not prepared for coöperation. In the main people are perfectly willing to discuss their first memories. They take them as mere facts, and do not realize the meaning hidden in them. Scarcely any one understands a first memory; and most people are therefore able to confess their purpose in life, their relationship to others and their view of the environment in a perfectly neutral and un-embarrassed manner through their first memories. Another point of interest in first memories is that their compression and simplicity allows us to use them for mass investigations. We can ask a school class to write their earliest recollections; and, if we know how to interpret them, we have an extremely valuable picture of each child.

Let me, for the sake of illustration, give a few first memories and attempt to interpret them. I know nothing else of the individuals than the memories they tell — not even whether they are children or adults. The meaning we find in their first memories would have to be checked by other expressions of their personality; but we can use them as they stand for our training, and for sharpening our ability to guess. We shall know what might be true, and we shall be able to compare one memory with another. In especial we shall be able to see whether the individual is training towards coöperation or against it, whether he is courageous or discouraged, whether he wishes to be supported and watched, or to be self-reliant and independent; whether he is prepared to give or anxious only to receive.

1. "Since my sister . . ." It is important to notice which people in the environment occur in first memories. When a sister occurs, we can be pretty sure that the individual has felt greatly under her influence. The sister has thrown a shadow over the other child's development. Generally we find a rivalry between the two, as if they were competing in a race; and we can understand that such a rivalry offers additional difficulties in development. A child cannot extend his interest to others as well when he is occupied with rivalry as when he can coöperate on terms of friendship. We shall not jump to conclusions, however: perhaps the two children were good friends.

"Since my sister and I were the youngest in the family, I was not permitted to attend until she (the younger) was old enough to go." Now the rivalry becomes evident. My sister has hindered me! She was younger, but I was forced to wait for her. She narrowed my possibilities! If this is really the meaning of the memory, we should expect this girl or boy to feel, "It is the greatest danger in my life

when some one restricts me and prevents my free development." Probably the writer is a girl. It seems less likely
that a boy would be held back till a younger sister is ready
to go to school.

" Accordingly we began on the same day." We should
not call this the best kind of education for a girl in her
position. It might well give her the impression that, because she is the older, she must stay behind. In any case,
we see that this particular girl has interpreted it in this
sense. She feels that she is slighted in favor of her sister.
She will accuse some one of this neglect; and probably it
will be her mother. We should not be surprised if she
leaned more towards her father, and tried to make herself his favorite.

" I recall distinctly that mother told every one how
lonely she was on our first day at school. She said, ' I
ran out to the gate many times that afternoon and looked
for the girls. I just thought they would never come.' "
Here is a description of the mother; and a description
which does not show her behaving very intelligently. It
is the girl's portrait of her mother. " Thought we should
never come "— the mother was obviously affectionate,
and the girls knew of her affection; but at the same time
she was anxious and tense. If we could speak to this girl,
she could tell us more of the mother's preference for the
younger sister. Such a preference would not astonish us,
for the youngest child is almost always pampered. From
the whole of this first memory, I should conclude that
the older of the two sisters felt hindered through the
rivalry of the younger. In later life we should expect to
find marks of jealousy and fear of competition. It would
not surprise us to find her disliking women younger than

herself. Some people feel too old all through their lives, and many jealous women feel inferior towards members of their own sex who are younger than they.

2. " My earliest recollection is of my grandfather's funeral, when I was three years of age." This is a girl writing. She is deeply impressed with the fact of death. What does this mean? She has seen death as the greatest insecurity in life, the greatest danger. She drew out of the events that happened to her in her childhood the moral, " Grandfather can die." We shall probably find that she was a favorite of her grandfather and he spoiled her. Grandparents nearly always spoil their grandchildren. They have less responsibility towards them than parents, and often they wish to attach the children to themselves and show that they can still gain affection. Our culture does not make it any too easy for old people to feel convinced of their worth and sometimes they seek to be convinced through easy means — through querulousness, for example. Here we are inclined to believe that the grandfather spoiled this girl when she was a baby and that it was his pampering that fixed him so deeply in her memory. When he died, she felt it as a great blow. A subject and ally had been taken away.

" I remember so vividly seeing him in his coffin, lying there so still and white." I am not sure that it is a good procedure to let a child of three years see a dead man. At least it would be better to prepare the child beforehand. Children have often told me that they had been deeply impressed by the sight of some one who had died and could never forget it. This girl has not forgotten it. Such children strive to diminish or overcome the danger of death. Often their ambition is to become a doctor. They feel that a doctor is better trained than others to fight against death. If a doctor is asked for his first memory, it will often include some remembrance of death. " Lying in the coffin so white and still "— a memory of something visible. Probably this girl is a visual type, interested in looking at the world.

" Then at the grave, as the casket was lowered, I recall those straps being pulled out from underneath the rough box." Again she tells us what she saw; and we are confirmed in our guess that she is a visual type. " This experience seems to have left me with a trembling fear at the mention of any of my relations, friends or acquaintances who have passed to the other life beyond."

Again we can notice that great impression left on her by death. If I had an opportunity of speaking to her, I should ask, " What would you like to be later in life? " and perhaps she would answer, " A doctor." If she made no answer or avoided the question, then I myself would suggest, " Wouldn't you like to be a doctor or a nurse? " When she mentions " the other life beyond ", we can see one type of compensation for the fear of death. What we have learned from her memory as a whole is that her grandfather was friendly to her, that she is a visual type, and that death plays a great rôle in her mind. The meaning she has drawn from life is, " We must all die." This is undoubtedly true; but we shall not find everybody with the same chief interest. There are other points that can occupy our attention.

3. " When I was three years old, my father . . ." Right at the beginning her father occurs. We can suppose that this girl was more interested in her father than her mother. An interest in the father is always a second phase

of development. At first a child is more interested in the
mother, since in the first year or two the coöperation with
the mother is very close. The child needs the mother and
is attached to her; all the child's psychic strivings are
bound up with the mother. If the child turns to the father,
the mother has lost the game. The child is not satisfied
with its situation. This is generally the result of the birth
of a younger child. If we hear in this recollection that
there is a younger child, our guess will be confirmed.

" My father purchased for us a pair of ponies." There
is more than one child, and we are interested to hear
about the other. " He brought them by the halters to the
house. My sister, who was three years older than I . . ."
We must revise our interpretation. We had expected this
girl to be the older sister, and she proves to be the
younger. Perhaps the older sister was the mother's favorite, and it is for this reason that the girl mentions her
father and the present of the two ponies.

" My sister took one strap and led her pony trium-
phantly down the street." Here is a triumph for the older
sister. " My own pony, hurrying after the other, went too
fast for me "— these are the consequences when her
sister takes the lead!—" and trailed me face downward in
the dirt. It was an ignominious end to an experience which
had been gloriously anticipated." The sister has conquered, she has scored a point. We can be quite sure that
this girl means, " If I am not careful!, my older sister will
always win. I am always being defeated, I am always in
the dirt. The only way to be safe is to be first." We can
understand, also, that the older sister had triumphed with
the mother; and that this was the reason why the younger
sister turned to her father.

"The fact that I later surpassed my sister as a horse-woman has never mellowed this disappointment in the least." All our suppositions are now confirmed. We can see what a race there had been between the two sisters. The younger felt, "I am always at the back, I must try to get ahead. I must surpass the others." This is the type I have described, so common among second children or youngest children, which always has a pacemaker for itself, and is always trying to overtake the pacemaker. This girl's memory reinforces her attitude. It says to her, "If any one is ahead of me I am endangered. I must always be the first."

4. "My earliest recollections are of being taken to parties and other social events by my oldest sister, who was about eighteen when I was born." This girl remembers herself as a part of society; perhaps we shall find in this memory a higher degree of coöperation than in the others. Her sister, eighteen years older, had taken the part of a mother to her. She was the member of the family who spoiled her most; but she seems to have spread the child's interest to others in a very intelligent fashion.

"Since my sister was the only girl in a family of four boys until my arrival, she was naturally pleased to show me off." This sounds by no means so good as we thought. When a child is "shown off", it may become interested in being appreciated, instead of in contributing. "She therefore took me about when I was comparatively young. The only thing I can remember about these parties is that I was continually urged to say something; 'Tell the lady your name', and so on." A mistaken method of educa-tion — we should not be surprised to find that this girl stammered or had speech difficulties. When a child stammers, it is generally because too great an interest was shown in its speech. Instead of communicating with others naturally and without stress, it was taught to be self-conscious and to look for appreciation.

" I can also remember that I would say nothing and was invariably scolded when I reached home, so that I came to hate to go out and meet people." Our interpretation must be altogether revised. We can see now that the meaning behind her first memory is, " I was brought into contact with other people, but I found it unpleasant. Because of these experiences, I have hated such coöperation ever since." We should expect, therefore, that even now she dislikes meeting people. We should expect to find her embarrassed and self-conscious with them, believing that it is necessary for her to shine, and feeling that this demand is too heavy. She has trained away from ease and equality among her fellow beings.

5. " One big event stands out in my early childhood. When I was about four years old my great-grandmother came to visit us." We have seen that a grandmother usually spoils her grandchildren: but how a great-grandmother treats them we have not yet experienced. " While she was visiting us we had a four-generation picture taken." This girl is very much interested in her pedigree. Because she remembers so strongly the visit of her great-grandmother and the picture that was taken, we can probably conclude that she is very much bound up in her family. If we are right, we shall discover that her ability to coöperate does not go beyond the limits of her family circle.

" I clearly remember driving to another town and having my dress changed to a white embroidered one after we arrived at the photographer's." Perhaps this girl too is a visual type. " Before having the four-generation picture taken, my brother and I had ours taken." Again we come across the interest in the family. Her brother is a part of the family and we shall probably hear more of her relations with him. " He was placed on the arm of a chair beside me and was given a bright red ball to hold." Here again she remembers visible things. " I stood by the side of the chair and was given nothing to hold." Now we see the main striving of this girl. She says to herself that her brother is preferred to her. We might guess that she felt it disagreeable when her younger brother came and took away her position of being the youngest and most pampered. " We were told to smile." She means, " They tried to make me smile, but what did I have to smile about? They put my brother on a throne and gave him a bright red ball; but what did they give to me? "

" Then came the four-generation picture. Everybody tried to look their best but me. I would not smile." She is aggressive against her family because her family is not good enough to her. In this first memory she has not forgotten to inform us how her family treated her. " My brother smiled so nicely when asked to smile. He was so cute. To this day I detest having my picture taken." Such remembrances give us a good insight into the way most of us meet life. We take one impression and use it to justify a whole series of actions. We draw consequences from it and act as if the consequences were obvious facts. Clearly enough, she had a disagreeable time when this photograph was taken. She still detests having her picture taken. We shall generally find that any one who dislikes something

as much as this chooses a reason for his dislike, selects
something from his experiences to bear the whole burden
of justifying it. This first memory has given us two main
clues to the personality of the writer. First, she is a visual
type; second, and still more important, she is bound to
her family. The whole action of her first memory is placed
within the family circle. She is probably not well adapted
for social life.

6. " One of my earliest recollections, if not the earliest,
is an incident which happened when I was about three
and a half years old. A girl who worked for my parents
had taken my cousin and me down in the cellar and given
us a taste of cider. We liked it very much." It is an interesting experience to discover that we have cellars with
cider in them. This was a journey of exploration. If we
had to make our conclusions already, we might guess one
of two things. Perhaps this girl likes to meet new circumstances and is courageous in her approach to life. Perhaps,
on the other hand, she means that there are people with
stronger wills who can seduce us and lead us astray. The
rest of the memory will help us to decide. " A little later
we determined that we should like another taste, so we
proceeded to help ourselves." This is a courageous girl.
She wants to be independent. " In due time my legs failed
me in their powers of locomotion, and the cellar was rather
damp as we had allowed all of the cider to run out on the
floor." Here we see the making of a prohibitionist!

" I do not know if this incident has anything to do
with my dislike for cider and other intoxicating beverages." One small incident is again made the reason for
a whole attitude to life. If we consider it with common
sense, we cannot see that the incident was sufficiently

weighty to lead to such a conclusion. This girl, however, has secretly taken it as reason enough to dislike intoxicating beverages. We shall probably find that she was a person who understood how to learn from her mistakes. Probably she is really independent and likes to improve if she is in the wrong. This trait may characterize her whole life. It is as if she said, " I make mistakes, but when I see they are mistakes I correct them." If this is so, she will be a very good type: active, courageous in her striving, improving her situation and looking always for the best way of living.

In all these instances we are doing no more than training ourselves in the art of guessing; and before we could be sure that our conclusions were right we should need to see the many other expressions of the personality. Let us now take some cases from practice, where the coherence of the personality in all of its expressions could be seen.

A man of thirty-five came to me suffering from anxiety neurosis. He felt anxiety only when he was away from home. From time to time he was compelled to secure a job; but as soon as he was put in an office he would moan and cry all day and stop only when he came back at night and sat at home with his mother. When asked for his first memory he said, " I remember at four years of age sitting at home close by the window, looking out on the street and being interested to see the people working there." He wants to see others work; he himself wants only to sit by the window and watch them. If his condition is to be changed, we can do it only by freeing him from the belief that he cannot coöperate in the work of others. So far he has thought that the only way to live was to be supported by others. We must change his whole outlook. We shall accomplish nothing by reproaching him. We cannot convince him by medicines or gland extracts. His first memory, however, makes it easier for us to suggest work which will interest him. His main interest is in looking. We find out that he has suffered from nearsightedness; and, because of this disadvantage, he gave more attention to visible things. When he started to meet the problem of occupation he wanted to go on looking, not to work; but the two are not necessarily contradictions. When he was cured, he found an occupation which lay along the line of this main interest. He opened an art shop and in this way he was able to contribute in his own degree to our division of labor.

A man of thirty-two came for treatment, suffering from hysterical aphasia. He could not speak above a whisper. This condition had lasted for two years. It began when he slipped one day on a banana skin and fell against the window of a taxi. He vomited for two days and had migraine afterwards. No doubt he had concussion of the brain; but since there were no organic changes in the throat, the concussion is not enough to explain why he is unable to speak. For eight weeks he was completely speechless. His accident is now a court matter; but the case is not closed. He attributes the accident entirely to the taxi driver and is suing the company for compensation. We can understand that he is in a much better situation with his lawsuit if he can show some disability. We need not say that he is dishonest; but he has no great stimulus to speak loudly. Perhaps he really found it difficult to speak after the shock of his accident and he has not seen a reason for changing.

The patient had seen a throat specialist but the specialist found nothing wrong. Asked for his first memory, he tells us, " I was hanging in the cradle, lying on my back. I remember seeing the hook pull out. The cradle fell and I was badly hurt." Nobody likes to fall, but this man overemphasizes falling. He concentrates on the dangers of falling. It is his chief interest. " The door opened when I fell and my mother came in and was horrified." He had gained his mother's attention by his fall; but the memory is also a reproach,—" She did not take good enough care of me." In the same way the taxi driver was at fault and the company who owned the taxi. None of them took sufficient care of him. This is the style of life of a pampered child: he tries to make others responsible. His next memory tells the same story. " At the age of five I fell twenty feet with a heavy board on top of me. For five or more minutes I was unable to speak." This man is very skillful in losing his speech. He is trained for it and makes falling a reason for refusing to speak. We can not see it as a reason; but he seems to see it so. He is experienced in this method; and, now, if he falls, it follows automatically that he can't speak. He can be cured if he understands that this is a mistake: that there is no connection between falling and loss of speech: especially if he sees that after an accident he need not go about whispering for two years. In this memory, however, he shows us why it is difficult for him to understand. " My mother came out," he continues, " and looked very much excited." On both occasions his falling horrified his mother and drew her attention to him. He was a child who wanted to be pampered, to be the center of attention. We can understand how he wants to be paid for his misfortunes.

Other pampered children might do the same if the same accidents happened. Probably, however, they would not hit on the device of having a speech defect. This is the trademark of our patient; it is part of the style of life he has built up out of his experiences.

A man of twenty-six came to me complaining that he could not find a satisfactory occupation. Eight years ago he had been put in the brokerage business by his father; but he never liked it and he had recently given it up. He had tried to find other work, but he had not been successful. He complained also of sleeplessness and he had had frequent thoughts of suicide. When he threw up his work in the brokerage business, he ran away from home and found a job in another town; but a letter brought news that his mother was ill and he returned to live with the family.

From this history we could already suspect that he had been pampered by his mother and that his father had tried to exert authority over him. We should probably find that his life was a revolt against the strictness of his father. When he was asked about his position in the family, he replied that he was the youngest child and the only boy. He had two sisters; the older of them always tried to boss him and the younger was not much different. His father continually nagged at him and he felt very deeply that he was dominated by all the family. His mother was his only friend.

He went to school until he was fourteen. Afterwards his father sent him to an agricultural school, so that he should be able to help him on a farm which he was planning to buy. The boy got along fairly well at the school, but decided that he did not wish to be a farmer. It was his father who got him the position in the brokerage firm. It is rather surprising that he stuck the work out for eight years; but he gives as his reason that he wanted to do as much as possible for his mother.

As a child he was untidy and timid, afraid of the dark and of being left alone. When we hear of an untidy child, we must always look for some one who tidies up for him. When we hear of a child who is afraid of the dark and does not like to be left alone, we must always look for some one whose attention he can attract and who will console him. With this youth, it was his mother. He had not found it easy to make friends, but he felt sociable enough among strangers. He had never been in love; he was not interested in love and never wished to get married. He looked on the marriage of his parents as unhappy; and this helps us to understand why he excluded marriage for himself.

His father still brings pressure on him to continue in brokerage. He himself would like to go in for advertising, but he is convinced that his family would not give him the money to prepare for this career. At every point we can see that the purpose of his actions is to antagonize his father. While he was in the brokerage firm, it did not occur to him, although he was self-supporting, to use his money to learn advertising. He thinks of it only now, as a new demand on his father.

His first memory clearly reveals the protest of a pampered child against a strict father. He remembers how he worked in his father's restaurant. He liked cleaning the dishes and changing them from one table to another. The way he meddled with them angered his father, who slapped him before the customers. He uses his early experience as a proof that his father is an enemy and his whole life has been a fight against him. He has still no real wish to work. He would be completely satisfied if he could hurt his father.

His ideas of suicide are easy to explain. Every suicide is a reproach; and by thinking of suicide he is saying, " My father is guilty for everything." His dissatisfaction in his occupation is also directed against his father. Every plan that the father proposes, the son rejects; but he is a pampered child and he cannot be independent in his career. He does not really wish to work; he wishes to play; but he still preserves some coöperation with his mother. But how does his fight with his father help to explain his insomnia?

If he is sleepless, next day he is ill equipped for working. His father is waiting for him to work, but the boy is tired and unable to work. Of course, he could say, " I don't want to work, and I won't be forced." But there is his concern for his mother and the bad financial circumstances of the family. If he just refuses to work, his family will think he is quite hopeless and refuse to support him. He must have an alibi; and this he gains by the apparently uninvited misfortune,— sleeplessness.

At first he says that he never dreams; but later he remembers a dream which often recurs. He dreams that somebody is throwing a ball against the wall and the ball always bounces away. This seems a trivial dream. Can we find a connection between the dream and his style of life? We ask him, " What happened then? What did you feel when the ball bounced away? " He tells us, " Whenever it bounces away I wake up." Now he has revealed the whole structure of his sleeplessness. He uses the dream as an alarm clock to waken him up. He imagines that everybody wishes to push him forward, to drive him and to compel him to do things that he does not wish to do. He dreams that somebody is throwing a ball against the wall. At this point he always wakes up. In consequence he is tired next day; and when he is tired he cannot work. His father is very anxious for him to work; and so, by this roundabout method, he has defeated his father. If we were to look only at his fight with his father, we should think him very intelligent to discover such weapons. His style of life, however, is not very satisfactory, either for him or for others, and we must help him to change it.

When I explain his dream, he stops dreaming; but he tells me he still wakes up sometimes in the night. He has no longer the courage to continue with his dream, because he sees its purpose can be found out; but he still tires himself for the next day. What can we do to help him? The only possible way would be to reconcile him with his father. So long as all his interest goes towards irritating and defeating his father, nothing will come right. I begin, as we must always begin, by admitting that there is justification for the patient's attitude. " Your father seems to be completely wrong ", I say. " It is very unwise of him to try to use his authority and to boss you the whole time. Perhaps he is a sick man and should be treated. But what can you do? You cannot expect to change him. Suppose it rains; what can you do? You can take an umbrella or a taxi; but it is no use to try to fight the rain or overpower it. At present you are spending your time fighting the rain. You believe that this is strength. You believe that you are getting the better of it. But your victories damage yourself more than any one." I show him the coherence of all his expressions — his uncertainty over his career, his thoughts of suicide, his running away from home, his sleeplessness; and I show him how in all of them he is punishing himself to punish his father.

I give him also a piece of advice: " When you go to sleep to-night, imagine that you want to waken yourself up from time to time, so that you can be tired to-morrow. Imagine that to-morrow you are too tired to go to work and your father explodes into a fit of temper." I want him to face the truth. His main interest is to annoy and hurt his father. As long as we fail to stop this fight, treatment will be useless. He is a pampered child. We can all see it; and now he can see it himself.

The situation closely resembles the so-called Œdipus Complex. This youth is occupied in damaging his father; and he is very much attached to his mother. It is not a sexual affair, however. His mother has pampered him and his father has been unsympathetic. He has suffered from a mistaken training and a mistaken interpretation of his position. Heredity plays no part in his trouble. He has not derived it as an instinct from savages who killed and consumed the head man of the tribe. He has created it himself out of his own experiences. Attitudes like this could be provoked anew with every child. We need only give the child a mother to pamper it, as this mother did; and a father who is harsh, as this father was. If the child revolts against its father, and fails to proceed independently in solving the problems before it, we can understand how easy it was to adopt such a style of life.

CHAPTER V

Dreams

Almost every human being dreams, but those who understand their dreams are very few. This state of affairs might well seem astonishing. Here is a general activity of the human mind. Men have always been interested in dreams and have always been puzzled to know what they meant. Many people feel that their dreams have a deep significance: they feel them as queer and momentous. We can find this interest expressed from the earliest ages of mankind. Yet, on the whole, men have still no conception of what they are doing when they dream, or why they dream at all. As far as I know, there are only two theories of dream-interpretation which attempt to be comprehensive and scientific. The two schools which claim to understand and interpret dreams are the Freudian school of psychoanalysis and the school of Individual Psychology. Of these two, perhaps only the Individual Psychologists would claim that their explanation was wholly in agreement with common sense.

Previous attempts to understand dreams were not, of course, scientific, but they deserve consideration. At least they will reveal how men have regarded their dreams, what their attitude towards dreaming has been. Since dreams are a part of the mind's creative activity, if we find out what men have expected from dreams we shall come very close to seeing the purpose of dreams. Right at the beginning of our investigation we meet a striking fact. It seems always to have been taken for granted that dreams had some bearing on the future. People often felt that in dreams some master spirit, some god or ancestor, would take possession of their minds and influence them. They used their dreams to obtain guidance when they were in difficulties. Ancient dream books offered to explain what a dream meant for the future fortunes of the man who dreamed it. Primitive peoples looked for omens and prophecies in their dreams. The Greeks and the Egyptians went to their temples in the hope of obtaining a sacred dream that would influence their future lives. Such dreams were looked on as curative, as removing physical or mental difficulties. The American Indians, by purification, fasting and sweat baths, took great pains to induce dreams, and based their conduct on the interpretation they gave them. In the Old Testament dreams are always interpreted as revealing something of future events. Even to-day there are individuals who insist that they have had dreams which later came true. They believe that in dreams they are clairvoyant, and that the dream, somehow or other, can reach over into the future and prophesy what is going to occur.

From a scientific standpoint, such views seem ridiculous to us. From the time when I first attempted to solve the problem of dreams, it seemed clear to me that a man who is dreaming is in a worse position to foretell the future than a man who is awake and in more complete possession of his faculties. It seemed clear that dreams would be found, not more intelligent and prophetic than everyday thinking, but more confused and confusing. Yet we must take note of this tradition of mankind, that dreams are somehow connected with the future; and perhaps we shall find it, in some sense, not entirely false. If we look on it in true perspective, it may provide us with the very key which has been missing. We can see already that men have regarded dreams as offering a solution to their problems. We may conclude that the individual's purpose in dreaming is to seek guidance for the future, to seek a solution for his problems. This is very far from committing us to a prophetic view of dreams. We have still to consider what sort of a solution he seeks and where he hopes to get it from. It still seems evident that any solution offered by a dream would be worse than a solution arrived at by common-sense thinking, with the whole situation before us. Indeed, it is not too much to say that in dreaming an individual is hoping to solve his problems in his sleep.

In the Freudian view we find a real effort to treat the dream as having a meaning which can be scientifically understood. In several points, however, the Freudian interpretation has taken the dream out of the region of science. It supposes, for example, a gap between the work of the mind during the day and its work during the night. "Conscious" and "unconscious" are placed in contradiction to each other, and the dream is given its own special laws contradictory to the laws of everyday thinking. Wherever we see such contradictions, we must conclude an unscientific attitude of mind. In the thinking of primitive peoples and of ancient philosophers, we always meet this desire to put concepts in strong antithesis, to treat them as contradictions. The antithetic attitude can be illustrated very clearly among neurotics. People often believe that left and right are contradictions, that man and woman, hot and cold, light and heavy, strong and weak are contradictions. From a scientific standpoint, they are not contradictions, but varieties. They are degrees of a scale, arranged in accordance with their approximation to some ideal fiction. In the same way, good and bad, normal and abnormal, are not contradictions but varieties. Any theory which treats sleep and waking, dream thoughts and day thoughts, as contradictions is bound to be unscientific.

Another point of difficulty in the original Freudian view is that dreams were referred to a sexual background. This, too, separated them from the ordinary strivings and activities of men. If it were true, dreams would have a meaning as an expression not of the whole personality, but only of a part of the personality. The Freudians themselves found a sexual interpretation of dreams insufficient, and Freud suggested that we could also see in dreams the expression of an unconscious desire to die. Perhaps we can find a sense in which this is true. Dreams, as we have noticed, are an attempt to reach an easy solution for problems, and they reveal the individual's failure of courage. The Freudian term, however, is highly metaphoric, and it does not bring us any closer to finding how the whole personality is reflected in dreams. Once again, the dream life seems rigorously separated from the daytime life. In the Freudian attempts, we are given many interesting and valuable hints. Especially useful, for example, is the hint that it is not the dream itself which is important, but the underlying thoughts of the dream. In Individual Psychology we arrive at a somewhat similar conclusion. What is missing from psychoanalysis is the very first requisite for a science of psychology — a recognition of the coherence of the per-

sonality and of the unity of the individual in all his expressions.

This lack can be observed in the Freudian answer to
the crucial question of dream interpretation, " What is the
purpose of dreams? What do we dream for at all? " The
psychoanalyst answers, " To satisfy the individual's un-
fulfilled desires." But this view would by no means explain everything. Where is the satisfaction if the dream
is lost, if the individual forgets it or cannot understand
it? All mankind is dreaming and scarcely any one understands his dreams. What pleasure can we get from dreaming? If the dream life is separated from the day life, and
the satisfaction given by a dream takes place in a life of
its own, we can perhaps understand the purpose of dreams
for the dreamer. But now we have lost the coherence of
the personality. Dreams have now no purpose for the
waking man. From a scientific point of view, the dreamer
and the waking man are the same individual, and the purpose of dreams must be applicable to this one coherent
personality. It is true that in one type of human being,
we could connect the striving for wish-fulfillment in
dreams with the whole personality. This type is the pampered child, the individual who always is asking, " How
can I get gratification? What does life offer me? " Such
an individual might look for gratification in his dreams,
just as he does in all his other expressions. And, indeed,
if we look closely we shall find that the Freudian theory
is the consistent psychology of the pampered child, who
feels that his instincts must never be denied, who looks
on it as unfair that other people should exist, who asks
always, " Why should I love my neighbor? Does my
neighbor love me? " Psychoanalysis starts with the prem-

ises of a pampered child, and works out these premises in the most thoroughgoing detail. But the striving for gratification is only one of the million varieties of the striving for superiority; and we cannot take it as the central motive of all expressions of personality. If we really discover the purpose of dreams, moreover, we must also be helped to see what purpose it serves to forget dreams or not to understand them.

This was the most vexing problem before me when I started, some quarter of a century ago, to try to find the meaning of dreams. I could see that the dream is not a contradiction to waking life; it must always be in the same line as other movements and expressions of life. If, during the day, we are occupied with striving towards the goal of superiority, we must be occupied with the same problem at night. Every one must dream as if he had a task to fulfill in dreaming, as if he had to strive towards superiority also in his dreams. The dream must be a product of the style of life, and it must help to build up and enforce the style of life.

One consideration helps immediately to make clear the purpose of dreams. We dream, and in the morning we generally forget our dreams. Nothing is left. But is this true? Is nothing left at all? Something remains — we are left with the feelings our dreams have aroused. None of the pictures persist: no understanding of the dream is left: only the feelings which remain behind. The purpose of dreams must be in the feelings they arouse. The dream is only the means, the instrument, to stir up feelings. The goal of the dream is the feelings it leaves behind.

The feelings an individual creates must always be in conformity with his style of life. The difference between dream thought and day thought is not absolute; there is no rigid division between the two. To put the difference in a few words, in dreaming more relations with reality are excluded. There is no break with reality. When we sleep we are still in contact with reality. If we are disturbed with problems, our sleep is disturbed also. The fact that, during our sleep, we can make the adjustments which prevent us from falling out of bed shows that connections with reality are still present. A mother can sleep through the loudest noises in the street and yet waken at the slightest movement of her child. Even in sleep we remain in touch with the world outside us. In sleep, however, sense perceptions, though not absent, are diminished and our contact with reality is lessened. When we dream we are alone. Demands of society are not so urgently present with us. In our dream thought we are not stimulated to reckon so honestly with the situation around us.

Our sleep can be undisturbed only if we are free from tension and sure of the solution of our problems. One disturbance of calm and tranquil sleep is dreaming. We can conclude that we dream only if we are not sure of the solution of our problems, only if reality is pressing in on us even in our sleep and offering us difficulties. This is the task of the dream: to meet the difficulties with which we are confronted and to provide a solution. Now we can begin to see in what way our minds will attack problems in our sleep. Since we are not dealing with the whole situation, the problems will appear easier, and the solution offered will demand as little as possible adaptation from our own side. The purpose of the dream will be to support and back the style of life, to arouse the feelings suited to it. But why does the style of life need support? What can attack it? It can only be attacked by reality and common sense. The purpose of dreams, therefore, is to support the style of life against the demands of common sense. This gives us an interesting insight. If an individual is confronted by a problem which he does not wish to solve along the lines of common sense, he can confirm his attitude by the feelings which are aroused in his dreams.

At first this may seem a contradiction to our waking life; but there is no contradiction. We may stir up feelings in precisely the same way when we are awake. If some one meets a difficulty and wishes not to face it by using his common sense, but to continue in his old style of life, then he will do everything he can to justify his style of life and make it seem sufficient. His goal, for example, is to get money in an easy way, without struggling and working for it, without making a contribution to others. Gambling occurs to him as a possibility. He knows that many people have lost their money and suffered disaster through gambling; but he wishes to have an easy time, he wishes to enrich himself in an easy way. What will he do? He fills his mind with thoughts of the advantages of money. He pictures himself making money through speculation, buying a car, living in luxury, being known by his fellows as a rich man. By these pictures he is stirring up feelings to push him forward. He turns away from common sense and begins to gamble. The same thing happens in more commonplace circumstances. If we are working and some one tells us of a play he has seen and enjoyed, we begin to feel like stopping our work and going to the theater. If a man is in love he pictures the future for himself; and if he is really attracted he will picture the future as pleasant. Sometimes, if he feels pessimistic, he will have gloomy pictures of the future, but in any case he will be stirring up his feelings, and we can always tell what sort of man he is by noticing the kind of feelings which he arouses.

But if nothing remains behind from a dream but feelings, what has happened to common sense? Dreaming is the adversary of common sense. We shall probably find that people who do not like to be deluded by their feelings, who prefer to proceed in a scientific way, do not dream often or do not dream at all. Others, who are further away from common sense, do not want to solve their problems by normal and useful means. Common sense is an aspect of coöperation; and people who are badly trained for coöperation dislike common sense. Such people have very frequent dreams. They are anxious that their style of life should conquer and be justified; they wish to avoid the challenge of reality. We must arrive at the conclusion that dreams are an attempt to make a bridge between an individual's style of life and his present problems without making any new demands of the style of life. The style of life is the master of dreams. It will always arouse the feelings that the individual needs. We can find nothing in a dream that we shall not find in all the other symptoms and characteristics of the individual. We would approach problems in the same way whether we dreamed or not; but the dream offers a support and justification for the style of life.

If this is true, we come to a new and most important step in understanding dreams. In dreams we are fooling ourselves. Every dream is an auto-intoxication, a self-hypnosis. Its whole purpose is to excite the mood in which we are prepared to meet the situation. We should be able to see in it exactly the same personality that we find in everyday life; but we should see him, as it were, in the workshop of the mind, preparing the feelings which he will utilize during the day. If we are right, we shall be able to see self-deception even in the construction of a dream, in the means which it employs.

What do we find? First of all, we find a certain choice of pictures, incidents, occurrences. We have mentioned these selections before. When an individual is looking back on his past he makes an anthology of pictures and incidents. We have found that his selection is tendencious; that he chooses from memory only those incidents which support his personal goal of superiority. It is his goal that rules his memory. In the same way in the construction of a dream we pick out only such incidents as agree with our style of life and express what the style of life demands when confronted by our present problems. The meaning of the selection can be nothing but the meaning of the style of life in relation to the difficulties in which we find ourselves. In a dream the style of life is demanding its own way. To meet the difficulties realistically would call for common sense, but the style of life refuses to give way.

On what other means does a dream draw? From the earliest times it has been observed, and in our own day Freud has especially emphasized, that dreams are mainly built up out of metaphors and symbols. As one psychologist says, " We are poets in our dreams." Now why does ˹ dream not speak in simple straightforward language instead of in poetry and metaphors? If we speak plainly, without metaphors or symbols, we cannot escape common sense. Metaphors and symbols can be abused. They can combine different meanings; they can say two things at the same time, one of which, perhaps, is quite false. Illogical consequences can be drawn from them. They can be employed to stir up feelings. We find it, again, in everyday life. We wish to correct some one and say, " Don't be a baby! " We ask, " Why do you cry? Are you a woman? " Something irrelevant, something addressed merely to the feelings, always creeps in when we use metaphors. Perhaps a large man is angry with a small man and says, " He is a worm. He ought to be trodden on." By his metaphor he is making it easy to support his anger.

Metaphors are wonderful instruments of speech; but by them we can always deceive ourselves. When Homer describes the army of the Greeks overrunning the fields like lions, he gives us a magnificent image. Do we believe that he really wished to say exactly how these poor, dirty soldiers crept over the fields? No; he wanted us to think of them as lions. We know that they are not really lions; but if the poet had described how the soldiers breathed heavily and sweated, how they stopped to pluck up courage or to avoid danger, how old their armor was and a thousand such details, we should not be so much impressed. Metaphors are used for beauty, for imagination and fantasy. We must insist, however, that the use of metaphors and symbols is always dangerous in the hands of an individual who has a mistaken style of life.

A student is faced with an examination. The problem is straightforward and he should approach it with courage and common sense. But if it is his style of life that he wants to run away, he may dream that he is fighting in a war. He pictures this straightforward problem in a heightened metaphor and now he is far more justified in being afraid. Or he dreams that he is standing before an abyss and that he must run back to avoid falling in. He must create feelings to help him to avoid the examination, to escape from it; and he fools himself by identifying the examination with the abyss. In this we can find another means employed very frequently in dreams. It is to take a problem and to curtail it and boil it down until only a part of the original problem is left. The remainder is then expressed in a metaphor and treated as if it were the same as the original problem. Another student, for example, more courageous and looking more towards the future, wishes to complete his task and go through with his examination. He still wishes for support, however; he still wishes to reassure himself — his style of life demands it. The night before the examination he dreams that he is standing on top of a mountain. The picture of his situation is very much simplified. Only the smallest part of all the circumstances of his life is represented. The problem is a great one to him; but by excluding many aspects of it and concentrating himself on his prospect of success, he stirs up feelings to help him. Next morning he gets up feeling happy, fresh, and more courageous than before. He has succeeded in minimizing the difficulties he must face. In spite of the fact that he has reassured himself, he has really been fooling himself. He has not been occupied in facing the whole problem in a common sense way, but he has been stirring up a mood of confidence.

This stirring up of feelings is nothing unusual. A man who wants to jump over a stream will perhaps count three before he jumps. Is it really so important that he should count three? Is there a necessary connection between jumping and counting three? Not the slightest connection. He

counts three, however, to stir up his feelings and to collect
all his powers. We have all the means ready in our human
minds to elaborate a style of life, to fix it and to reinforce
it, and one of the most important means is the ability to
stir up feelings. We are engaged in this work every night
and every day; but it comes out more clearly, perhaps, in
the night.

Let me illustrate the way in which we fool ourselves
by a dream of my own. During the war I was the head
of a hospital for neurotic soldiers. When I saw soldiers
who were not prepared for war, I tried to relieve them
as much as I could by giving them easier tasks. A great
deal of tension was taken from them and this practice was
often quite successful. One day a soldier came to me who
was one of the best built and strongest men I have ever
seen. He was very depressed and as I examined him I
wondered what could be done with him. I should have
liked, of course, to send home every soldier who came
to me; but all my recommendations had to pass before
a superior officer and my benevolence had to be kept within
bounds. It was not easy to decide in this soldier's case;
but when the time came I said, " You are neurotic, but you
are very strong and healthy. I will give you easier work
to do so that you need not go to the front."

The soldier looked pitiable and answered, " I am a
poor student and I have to support my old father and
mother by giving lessons. If I cannot give lessons they
will starve. They will both die if I can't help them." I
thought that I should have to find him still easier service
— send him back home to work in an office; but I was
afraid that if this was my recommendation my superior
officer would get angry and send him to the front. In the

end I decided to do the utmost I honestly could. I would certify him as fit only for service on guard. When I went home at night and slept I had a terrible dream. I dreamed that I was a murderer and was running round in dark, narrow streets trying to think whom I had murdered. I could not remember who, but I felt, " Because I have committed murder I am done for. My life is over. Everything is finished." And so, in the dream, I stood still and sweated.

My first thought when I awoke was, " Whom have I murdered? " Then it occurred to me, " If I don't give this young soldier service in an office, perhaps he will be sent to the front and killed. Then I should be the murderer." You see how I stirred up feelings to deceive me. I had not been a murderer; and if this disaster really occurred, I should still not be guilty. But my style of life would not permit me to run the risk. I am a doctor; I am to save life, not to endanger it. I thought again that if I gave him an easier job my superior would send him to the front and the position would be no better. It occurred to me that if I wanted to help him the only thing to do was to follow rules of common sense and not bother about my own style of life. I, therefore, certified him as fit for service on guard. Later events confirmed the fact that it is always better to follow common sense. My superior read my recommendation and struck it out. I thought, " Now he is going to send him to the front. I should have given him office service after all." My superior wrote, " Six months' office service." It turned out that this officer had been bribed to let the soldier off easily. The youth had never given a lesson in his life and nothing he said had been true. He had told his story only so that I should give him an easier task and the bribed superior should be able to sign my recommendation. Since that day I have thought it better to give up dreaming.

The fact that dreams are designed to fool us and intoxicate us accounts for the fact that they are so rarely understood. If we understood our dreams they could not deceive us. They could no longer arouse in us feelings and emotions. We should prefer to proceed in common-sense ways, and we should refuse to follow the promptings of our dreams. If dreams were understood, they would lose their purpose. The dream is a bridge between the present real problem and the style of life; but the style of life should need no reinforcement. It should be directly in contact with reality. There are many varieties of dreams and every dream reveals where reinforcement of the style of life is felt to be necessary in view of the particular situation which confronts the individual. The interpretation of dreams is therefore always individual. It is impossible to interpret symbols and metaphors by formula; for the dream is a creation of the style of life, drawn from the individual's own interpretation of his own peculiar circumstances. If I describe briefly some of the more typical forms of dreams, I am not doing it to provide a rule-of-thumb interpretation; but only to help towards understanding dreams and their meaning.

Many people have experienced dreams of flying. The key to these dreams, as to others, is in the feelings they arouse. They leave behind them a mood of buoyancy and courage. They lead from below to above. They picture the overcoming of difficulties and the striving for the goal of superiority as easy; and they allow us to infer, therefore, a courageous individual, forward looking, and ambitious, who can not get rid of his ambition, even when he is asleep. They involve the problem, " Should I go on or not? "; and the answer suggested is, " There are no obstacles in my way." There are very few people who have not experienced dreams of falling. This is very remarkable; it shows that the human mind is more often occupied with self-preservation and the fear of defeat than with a striving to overcome difficulties. This becomes comprehensible when we remember that our tradition of education is to warn children and put them on their guard. Children are always admonished, " Don't get on the chair! Leave the scissors alone! Keep away from the fire! " They are always being surrounded by fictitious dangers. Of course, there are real dangers too; but to make an individual cowardly will never help him in meeting these dangers.

When people dream frequently that they are paralyzed or that they failed to catch a train the meaning is generally, " I should be glad if this problem would pass by without any need for interference on my part. I must make a detour, I must arrive too late, so that I am not confronted. I must let the train go by." Many people dream of examinations. Sometimes they are astonished to find themselves taking an examination so late in life, or having to pass an examination on a subject in which they have already passed long ago. With some individuals the meaning would be, " You are not prepared to face the problem before you." With others it would mean, " You have passed this examination before and you will pass the test before you at present." One individual's symbols are never the same as another's. What we must consider chiefly in the dream is the mood residue and its coherence with the whole style of life.

A neurotic patient, thirty-two years of age, came for treatment. She was a second child and, like most second children, was very ambitious. She always wished to be the first and to solve all her problems in an irreproachable manner. She came with a nervous breakdown. She had had a love relation with a married man who was older than herself, and her lover had failed in his business. It had been her wish to marry him, but he was unable to get a divorce. She dreamed that a man to whom she had rented her apartment while she was in the country married shortly after he moved in but earned no money. He was not an honest or hard-working man. Because he could not pay the rent for his apartment she was compelled to evict him. At the first glance we can see that this dream has some connection with her present problem. She was considering whether she should marry a man who has failed in business. Her lover was poor and unable to support her. What especially strengthened the comparison is that he had taken her out to dinner without having enough money to pay for it. The effect of the dream is to stir up feelings against marriage. She is an ambitious woman, and she does not wish to be connected with a poor man. She uses a metaphor and asks herself, " If he had rented my apartment and could not pay for it, what could I do with such a tenant? " The answer is, " He would have to leave."

This married man, however, is not her tenant and he cannot properly be identified with him. A husband who cannot support a family is not the same as a tenant who cannot pay the rent. To relieve her problem, however, to follow her style of life with more assurance, she gives herself the feeling, " I must not marry him "; and by this means she avoids approaching the whole problem in a common-sense way and selects only a small part of it. At the same time she minimizes the whole problem of love and marriage as if it could be sufficiently expressed by the metaphor, " A man rents my apartment. If he cannot pay he must be thrown out."

As the technique of Individual Psychological treatment is always directed towards increasing the individual's courage in meeting the problems of life, it is easy to understand that dreams will change in the course of treatment and reveal a more confident attitude. The last dream of a melancholiac patient before her cure was as follows: " I was sitting all alone on a bench. Suddenly a heavy snowstorm came on. Fortunately I escaped it, since I hurried indoors to my husband. Then I helped him to look for a suitable position in the advertisement columns of a newspaper." The patient was able to interpret the dream for herself. It shows clearly her feeling of reconciliation with her husband. At first she had hated him and had complained bitterly of his weakness and lack of enterprise in failing to earn a good living. The meaning of the dream is, " It is better to stay by my husband than to expose myself to dangers alone." Though we may agree with the patient in her view of the circumstances, the way in which she reconciles herself to her husband and her marriage still suggests too much the sort of advice which anxious relatives are accustomed to give. The dangers of being alone are overemphasized and she is still not quite ready to coöperate with courage and independence.

A boy of ten years of age was brought to the clinic. His school teacher complained that he was mean and vicious with other children. He stole things at school and put them in the desks of other boys, so that they should get blamed. Such conduct is only possible if a child feels a need to bring others down to his own level. He wants to humiliate them, to prove that *they* are mean and vicious, not he. If this is his approach, we can guess that it must have been trained in the family circle, that there must be some one at home whom he wished to make guilty. When he was ten years old, he threw stones at a pregnant woman in the street and got into trouble for it. If he was ten years old he probably knew what pregnancy is. We can suspect that he does not like pregnancy and we must look to see if there is not a younger brother or sister whose arrival did not please him. On the teacher's report he is called " the pest of the neighborhood "; he bothers his fellow children, calls them names and tells scandals about them. He chases small girls and strikes them. Now we are prepared to believe that it is a younger sister with whom he is in competition.

We learn that he is the elder of two children, with a younger sister four years old. His mother says that he loves his younger sister and is always good to her. This strains our credulity to the limit; it is impossible that such a boy should love his younger sister. We shall see later on that our scepticism is justified. The mother claims also that the relation between herself and her husband is ideal. This is a great pity for the child. Obviously his parents are not responsible for any of his faults; they must come from his own wicked nature, from fate, or perhaps from some remote ancestor! We often hear of these ideal marriages: such excellent parents and such a horrid child! Teachers, psychologists, lawyers and judges all bear witness to these mishaps. And indeed an " ideal " marriage may be a great difficulty for a boy like this: if he sees that his mother is devoted to his father, it may irritate him. He wants to monopolize his mother's attention and he may resent any show of affection to any one else. What are we to do, then, if happy marriages are bad for children and unhappy marriages are worse? We must make the child coöperative from the first; we must really take him into the marriage relationship. We must avoid letting him cling to one parent only. This boy we are considering is a pampered child; he wants to keep his mother's attention and he is training in the direction of causing trouble whenever he feels that he is not given attention enough.

Here again we find confirmation immediately. The mother never punishes the child herself; she waits for the father to come home and punish him. Probably she feels weak; she feels that only a man can order and command; only a man is strong enough to punish. Perhaps she wishes to keep the boy attached to her and is afraid of losing him. In either case she is training the boy away from interest and coöperation with his father; and friction is bound to develop between the two. We hear that the father is devoted to his wife and family, but he hates to come home after the day's work because of the boy. He punishes him very severely and beats him frequently. The boy has no dislike for his father, we are told. This, again, is impossible; the boy is not feeble-minded. He has learned to be very skillful in hiding his feelings.

He loves his sister, but he does not play nicely with

her and he often slaps her or kicks her. He sleeps in the
dining room on a day bed: his sister sleeps on a cot in her
parents' room. Now if we can identify ourselves with this
boy, if we can have sympathy with him, this cot in the
parents' room will bother us. We are trying to think, feel
and see through the boy's mind. He wants to occupy his
mother's attention. At night his sister is in so much closer
proximity to his mother. He must fight to bring her
nearer. The boy's health is very good: his birth was normal
and he was breast fed for seven months. When he was
first placed on the bottle he vomited; and his vomiting
spells continued till he was three years old. In all probability he had an imperfect stomach. He is now well fed
and well nourished, but his interest in the stomach has
persisted. He considers it a weak point. We can understand
a little better now why he threw stones at a pregnant
woman. He is very finicky about his food. If he is dis-
pleased with his meals, his mother gives him money and
he goes out and buys what he likes. Nevertheless he goes
around to the neighbors and complains that his parents
do not give him enough to eat. This is a trick he has
mechanized. It is always the same. His way to recover the
feeling of superiority is to slander somebody.

We are now in a position to understand a dream he
told when he came to the clinic. "I was a cowboy in the
West," he said. "They sent me to Mexico and I had to
fight my way through to the United States. When one
Mexican came against me I kicked him in the stomach."
The feeling of the dream is, "I am surrounded by
enemies. I must struggle and fight." In America cowboys
are looked on as heroes; he thinks that chasing little girls
and kicking people in the stomach is heroic. We saw al-

ready that the stomach plays a great rôle in his life — he takes it as the most vulnerable point. He himself suffered from stomach weakness and his father has a nervous stomach trouble and is always complaining about it. The stomach has been elevated in this family to a position of the highest importance. The boy's aim is to hit people at their weakest point. His dream and his actions show exactly the same style of life. He is living in a dream; and if we are not able to waken him from it, he will go on living in the same way. He will not only fight his father, his sister, little children and girls especially, but he will want to fight the doctor who tries to stop his fighting. His dream impulse will stimulate him to go on, to be a hero, to conquer others; and unless he can see how he is fooling himself there is no treatment that can help him.

His dream is explained to him at the clinic. He feels he is living in a hostile country and everybody who wants to punish him and hold him back is a Mexican; they are all his enemies. Next time he comes to the clinic we ask him, " What has happened since we saw each other last? " " I've been a bad boy," he answers. " What did you do? " " I chased a little girl." Now this is far more than a confession; it is a boast and an attack. This is a clinic where people are trying to improve him and he insists that he has been a bad boy. He is saying, " Don't hope for any improvement. I will kick you in the stomach." What are we to do with him? He is still dreaming; he is still playing the hero. We must diminish the satisfaction he gets from his rôle. " Do you believe," we ask him, " that this hero of yours would really chase a little girl? Isn't that a rather bad imitation of heroism? If you are going to be a hero, you should chase a big, strong girl. Or perhaps you shouldn't chase a girl at all." This is one side of the treatment. We must open his eyes and make him less eager to continue his style of life, " spit in his soup," as the proverb says. After this, he will not like this soup of his any longer. The other side is to give him courage to coöperate, to seek significance on the useful side of life. Nobody takes to the useless side of life unless he fears that he will be defeated if he remains on the useful side.

A girl of twenty-four years old, living alone and doing secretarial work, complains that her boss makes life intolerable for her by his bullying manner. She feels that she is not able to make friends and keep them. Experience would lead us to believe that if an individual cannot keep friends it is because he wishes to dominate others; he is really interested only in himself and his goal is to show his personal superiority. Probably her boss is the same sort of person. They both wish to rule others. When two such people meet, there are bound to be difficulties. The girl is the youngest of seven children, the pet of the family. She was nicknamed " Tom " because she always wanted to be a boy. This increases our suspicion that she has identified her goal of superiority with personal domination; to be masculine, she thinks, is to be the master, to control others and not to be controlled herself. She is pretty, but she thinks that people only like her because of her pleasant face and she is afraid of being disfigured or hurt. Pretty girls find it easier in our time to impress and control others; and this fact she understands quite well. She wants to be a boy, however, and to dominate in a masculine way: in consequence she is not elated by her prettiness.

Her earliest memory is of being frightened by a man; and she confesses that she is still frightened of being attacked by burglars and maniacs. It might appear odd that a girl who wanted to be masculine should be afraid of burglars and maniacs; but it is not really so strange. It is her feeling of weakness which dictates her goal. She wants to be in circumstances where she can rule and subjugate and she would like to exclude all other situations. Burglars and maniacs cannot be controlled and she would like to extinguish them all. She wishes to be masculine in an easy way and to keep extenuating circumstances for herself if she fails. With this very wide-spread dissatisfaction with the feminine rôle, the " Masculine Protest ", as I have called it, there always go feelings of tension — " I am a man fighting against the disadvantage of being a woman."

Let us see whether we can trace the same feelings in her dreams. Frequently she dreams of being left alone. She was a spoiled child: her dream means, " I must be watched. It isn't safe to leave me alone. Others could attack and subjugate me." Another dream she frequently experiences is that she has lost her purse. " Take care," she is saying " you are in danger of losing something." She does not want to lose anything at all; in especial, she does not want to lose power of controlling others; but she chooses one thing in life, the loss of a purse, to stand for the whole. We have another illustration of how dreams reinforce the style of life by creating feelings. She has not lost her purse, but she dreams she has lost it, and the feeling remains behind. A longer dream helps us still more to see her attitude. " I had gone to a swimming pool where there were a lot of people," she says. " Somebody noticed that I was standing on the heads of the people there. I felt that some one screamed to see me and I was in great danger of falling down." If I were a sculptor, I should carve her in just this way, standing on the heads of others, using others as her pedestal. This is her style of life; these are the feelings she likes to arouse. She sees her position, however, as precarious, and she thinks that others should realize her danger too. Others should watch her and be careful, so that she can continue to stand on their heads. Swimming in the water she is not safe. This is the whole story of her life. She has fixed as her goal, "To be a man in spite of being a girl." She is very ambitious, as most youngest children are; but she wants to seem superior, rather than to achieve adequacy to her situation, and she is pursued all the time by the fear of defeat. If we are to help her, we must find the way to reconcile her to her feminine rôle, to take away her fear and over-valuation of the other sex, and to make her feel friendly and equal among her fellow beings.

A girl whose younger brother had been killed in an accident when she was thirteen gave as her earliest recollection: "When my brother was a baby and was learning to walk, he grabbed hold of a chair to pull himself up and the chair fell on him." Here is another accident and we can see that she is deeply impressed by the dangers of the world. "My most frequent dream," she related, "is very queer. I am usually walking along the streets where there is a hole that I do not see. Walking along, I fall into the hole. It is filled with water, and as I touch the water I wake with a jump, with my heart beating terribly fast." We shall not find the dream as strange as she finds it herself; but if she is to continue to alarm herself with it, she must think it mysterious and fail to understand it. The dream says to her, " Be cautious. There are dangers about that you know nothing of." It tells us more than this, however. You cannot fall if you are down. If she is in danger of falling, she must imagine that she is above the others. As in the last example, she is saying, " I am superior, but I must always take care not to fall."

In another case we will see if we can find the same style of life at work in a first memory and a dream. A girl tells us, " I remember being very much interested in seeing an apartment house being built." We can guess that she is coöperative. A small girl cannot be expected to take part in building a house, but she can show her liking to share in the tasks of others by her interest. " I was a little tot, and I was standing by a very tall window, and the panes of glass are as clear to me as if it were yesterday." If she notices that it is tall, she must have a contrast in her mind between tall and small. She means, " The window was big, and I was little." I should not be surprised to hear that she is undersized, and it is this that interests her so much in comparative sizes. Her mentioning that she remembers it so clearly is a sort of boast. Now let us tell her dream. " Several other people were riding with me in a car." She is coöperative, as we thought; she likes to be with others. " We drove until we stopped in front of a wood. Every one got out and ran into the woods. Most of them were larger than I." Again she notices the difference of size. " But I managed to arrive in time to get into the elevator, and it went down into a mine-working about ten feet deep. If we stepped out, the air would poison us, we thought." She pictures a danger now. Most people are afraid of some dangers;

mankind is not very courageous. " We stepped out perfectly safe." You see the optimistic view. If an individual is coöperative, he is always courageous and optimistic. " We stayed there a minute, then came up again and ran quickly to the car." I am convinced that this girl is always coöperative, but she has the impression that she must be larger and taller. We shall find some tension here, as if she was standing on tiptoe; but it will be offset by her liking for others and her interest in common achievements.

CHAPTER VI

Family Influences

From the moment of birth a baby seeks to connect himself with his mother. This is the purpose of his movements. For many months his mother plays overwhelmingly the most important rôle in his life: he is almost completely dependent upon her. It is in this situation that the ability to coöperate first develops. The mother gives her baby the first contact with another human being, the first interest in some one other than himself. She is his first bridge to social life; and a baby who could make no connection at all with his mother, or with some other human being who took her place, would inevitably perish.

This connection is so intimate and farreaching that we are never able, in later years, to point to any characteristic as the effect of heredity. Every tendency which might have been inherited has been adapted, trained, educated and made over again by the mother. Her skill, or lack of skill, has influenced all the child's potentialities. We mean nothing else by a mother's skill than her ability to coöperate with her child and to win the child to coöperate with herself. This ability is not to be taught by rules. New situations arise every day. There are thousands of points in which she must apply her insight and understanding to the child's needs. She can be skillful only if she is interested in her child and occupied in winning his affection and securing his welfare.

In all her activities we can see her attitude. Whenever

she takes the baby up, carries him, speaks to him, bathes him or feeds him, she has opportunities to connect him with herself. If she is not trained in her tasks or not interested in them, she will be clumsy and the baby will resist. If she has never learned how to bathe a child, he will find bathing an unpleasant experience. Instead of making a connection with her, he will try to get rid of her. She must be skillful in the way she puts her baby to bed, in all her movements and in the noises she makes. She must be skillful in watching him or in leaving him alone. She must consider his whole environment — fresh air, the temperature of the room, nutrition, sleeping times, physical habits and cleanliness. On every occasion she is providing an opportunity for the child to like her or dislike her, to coöperate or reject coöperation.

There is no mystical power in the skill of motherhood. All skill is the result of long interest and training. The preparation for motherhood begins very early in life. The first steps can be seen in a girl's attitude to younger children, her interest in babies and in her future tasks. It is never advisable to educate boys and girls as if they had precisely the same tasks ahead of them. If we are to have skillful mothers, girls must be educated for motherhood and educated in such a way that they like the prospect of being a mother, consider it a creative activity, and are not disappointed by their rôle when they face it in later life.

Unfortunately it happens frequently in our culture that the part of a woman in motherhood is regarded as having only a minor value. If boys are preferred to girls, if their rôle is taken to be superior, it is natural for girls to dislike their future tasks. No one can be content with a subordinate position. When such girls marry and face the prospect of having children of their own, in one way or another they show their resistance. They are not willing and prepared to have children; they do not look forward to it; they do not feel it as a creative and interesting activity. This is perhaps the greatest problem of our society and little effort is made to meet it. The whole of human society is bound up with the attitude of women to motherhood. Almost everywhere the woman's part in life is undervalued and treated as secondary. Even in childhood we find boys looking at housekeeping as if it were a job for servants; as if their dignity demanded that they should never lift a hand to help in the housework. Housekeeping and home-making are too often regarded, not as contributions open to women, but as drudgery relegated to them. If a woman can really see housekeeping as an art in which she can be interested and through which she can lighten and enrich the lives of her fellows, she can make it a task equal to any other in the world. If, on the other hand, it is thought of as work too mean for a man, need we wonder when women resist their tasks, revolt against them, and set out to prove — what should be obvious from the first — that women are the equals of men and no less entitled to consideration and to the opportunity to develop their capacities? It is true that capacities can be developed only through social feeling; but social feeling will lead them in the right way, without any extraneous limits and restrictions placed on their development.

Where the woman's part is undervalued, the whole harmony of married life is destroyed. No woman who considers that to be interested in children is an inferior task can train herself for the skill, care, understanding and sympathy that are so necessary if children are to be given a favorable position in the beginning of their lives. A woman who is dissatisfied with her rôle has a goal in life which prevents her from making the best connection with her children. Her goal does not run in the same way as their goals; she is often occupied in proving her personal superiority; and for this purpose the children can be only a bother and distraction. If we trace back the cases of failure in life, we almost always discover that the mother did not fulfill her functions properly: she did not give the child a favorable start. If the mothers fail, if they are dissatisfied with their tasks and lack interest in them, the whole of mankind is endangered.

We cannot regard the mother, however, as guilty for failures. There is no guilt. Perhaps the mother herself was not trained for coöperation. Perhaps she is suppressed and unhappy in her married life. She is confused and worried by her circumstances; and sometimes she grows hopeless and despairing. There are many disturbances to the development of a good family life. If the mother is sick she may wish to coöperate with the children but feel herself too much handicapped. If she goes to work she is perhaps exhausted when she comes home. If economic conditions are bad, food, clothing and temperature may all be wrong for the child. Moreover, it is not the child's experiences which dictate his actions; it is the conclusions which he draws from his experiences. When we enquire into the story of a problem child, we see difficulties in the relation between himself and his mother; but we can see the same difficulties among other children who have answered them in a better way. We come back here to the fundamental view of Individual Psychology. There are no reasons for the development of character; but a child can make use of experiences for his goal and turn them into reasons. We cannot say, for example, that if a child is badly nourished he will become a criminal. We must see what conclusion he has drawn.

It is easy to understand that if a woman is dissatisfied with her rôle as a woman she will incur difficulties and tension. We know the strength of the striving for motherhood. Investigations have made it clear that a mother's tendency to protect her children is stronger than all other tendencies. Among animals, among rats and apes, for instance, the drive for motherhood has been shown to be stronger than the drives of sex or hunger; so that if they must choose between following one drive or another, it is the drive of motherhood which prevails. The foundation of this striving is not sexual; it derives from the goal of coöperation. A mother often feels her child as a part of herself. Through her children she is connected with the whole of life; she feels herself the master of life and death. In every mother we could find, in one degree or another, the feeling that through her children she has accomplished a work of creation. She feels, we might almost say, that she has created as God creates — out of nothing she has brought forth a living being. The striving for motherhood is really one aspect of the human striving for superiority, the human goal of godlikeness. It gives us one of the clearest examples of how this goal can be used for the sake of mankind in the interest of others and with the deepest social feeling.

A mother, of course, may exaggerate a feeling that her child is a part of herself and press him into the service of her goal of personal superiority. She may try to make the child wholly dependent upon herself and control his life so that he shall always remain bound to her. Let me quote the case of a peasant woman of seventy years of age. Her son, at the age of fifty, was still living with her; and both of them contracted pneumonia at the same time. The mother survived, but the son was taken to the hospital and died. When the mother was told of his death, she replied, " I always knew that I should never bring the boy up safely." She felt responsible for the whole life of her child. She had never tried to make him an equal part of our social life. We can begin to understand what a mistake is involved when a mother does not widen the connection she has made with her child and lead him to coöperate equally with the rest of his environment.

The relationships of a mother are not simple and even her connection with her children must not be overstressed. This is true for their sake as well as for hers. Where one problem is overstressed all other problems suffer; and even the single problem with which we are occupied cannot be met as well as if we put less weight upon it. A mother is related with her children, with her husband, and with the whole social life around her. These three ties must be given equal attention: all three must be faced calmly and with common sense. If a mother considers only her tie with her children, she will be unable to avoid pampering and spoiling them. She will make it hard for them to develop independence and the ability to coöperate with others. After she has succeeded in connecting the child with herself, her next task is to spread his interest towards his father; and this task will prove almost impossible if she herself is not interested in the father. She must turn the child's interest also to the social life around him; to the other children of the family, to friends, relatives and fellow human beings in general. Her task is thus twofold. She must give the child his first experience of a trustworthy fellow being; and she must then be prepared to spread this trust and friendship until it includes the whole of our human society.

If the mother is occupied only with interesting the child in herself, later on he will resent all attempts to interest him in others. He will always look for support from his mother and feel hostile to all whom he can regard as competitors for her attention. Any interest she shows in her husband or in the other children of the family will be felt as a deprivation, and the child will develop the view, " My mother belongs to me and to no one else." For the most part modern psychologists have misunderstood the situation. In the Freudian theory of the Œdipus Complex, for example, it is supposed that children have a tendency to fall in love with their mothers and wish to marry them and to hate their fathers and wish to kill them. Such a mistake could never arise if we understood the development of children. The Œdipus Complex could appear only in a child who wished to occupy his mother's whole attention and get rid of every one else. Such a desire is not sexual. It is a desire to subjugate the mother, to have complete control of her and to make her into a servant. It can occur only with children who have been pampered by their mothers and whose feeling of fellowship has never included the rest of the world. In rare cases it has happened that a boy who had always remained connected only with his mother made her the center also of his attempts to meet the problem of love and marriage; but the meaning of such an attitude would be that he could not conceive of coöperation with any one but his mother. No other woman could be trusted to be equally subservient. An Œdipus Complex would thus be always an artificial product of mistaken training. We have no need to suppose inherited incestuous instincts, or, indeed, to imagine that such an aberration, in its origin, has anything to do with sexuality.

When a child whose mother has bound him only to herself is placed in a situation where he is no longer connected with her, trouble always begins. When he goes to school, for example, or plays with children in the park, his goal will always be to remain connected with his mother. Whenever he is separated from her he will resent it. He wishes always to drag his mother along with him, to occupy her thoughts and to make her attentive to him. There are many means which he can use. He may become a mother's darling, always weak and affectionate and craving for sympathy. He may weep or fall sick at any reverse, to show how much he needs to be looked after. On the other hand, he may have outbursts of temper; he may be disobedient or fight with his mother in order to be noticed. Among problem children we find thousands of varieties of spoiled children, struggling for the attention of their mothers and resisting every demand from their environment.

A child quickly becomes experienced in finding out the means by which he can best succeed in occupying attention. Pampered children are often afraid of being left alone and especially of being left alone in the dark. It is not the dark itself of which they are afraid; but they utilize fear in the attempt to bring their mothers closer to them. One such pampered child always cried in the dark. One night, when his mother came in response to his cries, she asked him, " Why are you afraid? " " Because it is so dark," he answered. But his mother had now seen the purpose of his behavior. " And after I have come," she said, " is it less dark? " The darkness itself is unimportant and his fear of darkness meant only that he disliked being separated from his mother. If such a child is separated from his mother, all his emotions, all his strength and all his mental powers are engaged in preparing a situation in which his mother has to approach him and be connected with him again. He will strive to bring her near by screaming, by calling out, by being unable to sleep or by making a nuisance of himself in some other way. One means which has always attracted the attention of educators and psychologists is fear. In Individual Psychology we no longer concern ourselves with finding out causes of fear, but rather with identifying its purpose. All pampered children suffer from fear: it is by means of their fears that they can attract attention and they build up this emotion into their style of life. They make use of it to secure their goal of regaining connection with the mother. A child that is timid is a child that has been pampered and wants to be pampered again.

Sometimes these pampered children have nightmares and cry out in their sleep. This is a well-known symptom; but so long as sleep was thought to be a contradiction of waking it was impossible to understand. This was a mistake, however; sleep and waking are not contradictions but varieties. In his dreams a child behaves in much the same way as during the day. His goal of changing the situation to his advantage influences his whole body and mind; and after some training and experience he finds out the most successful means to approach his goal. Even in his sleep thoughts, pictures and memories come into his mind which are appropriate to his purposes. A pampered child, after a few experiences, discovers that if he is to connect himself again with his mother, thoughts which terrify him will be of great service. Even when they grow up, pampered children often keep their anxiety dreams. To be afraid in dreams was a well-tested device for gaining attention which has now become mechanized into a habit.

This use of anxiety is so obvious that we should be very surprised to hear of a pampered child who never made trouble during the night. The repertory of tricks to attract attention is very large. Some children will find the bed-clothes uncomfortable or call for glasses of water. Others will be afraid of burglars or wild animals. Some are unable to go to sleep unless their parents sit by their bedsides. Some dream; some fall out of bed and some wet the bed. One pampered child whom I treated seemed to give no trouble at all at night. Her mother said that she slept soundly without dreaming or waking up and caused no trouble at all. It was only during the day that she made trouble. This was very surprising. I suggested all the symptoms which could serve to attract the attention of the mother and draw her closer; this girl showed none of them. At last the explanation occurred to me. " Where does she sleep? " I asked her mother. " In my bed," she replied.

Sickness is often a refuge for pampered children; for when they are sick they are pampered more than ever. It often happens that such a child begins to show himself a problem child sometime after an illness and it appears at first that it is the illness that made him a problem child. The fact is, however, that when he is well again he remembers the fuss that was made over him when he was ill. The mother can no longer pamper him as he was pampered then; and he takes his revenge by becoming a problem. Sometimes a child who notices how another child, through being sick, became the center of attention, will wish to fall sick himself and will even kiss the sick child in the hope of catching his disease.

One girl had been in a hospital for four years and had been very much spoiled by the doctors and nurses. At first, when she returned home, she was spoiled by her parents; but after a few weeks their attention decreased. If ever she was denied something she wanted, she would put her finger in her mouth and say, " I have been in hospital." She reminded others she had been sick and she tried to continue the favorable situation in which she had found herself. We can find the same behavior in adults, who often like to speak of their diseases or the operations which they have undergone. On the other hand, it sometimes occurs that a child who has been a problem to his parents recovers after an illness and no longer bothers them. We have already seen that imperfect organs are an additional burden to a child; but we have seen also that they are not sufficient to explain bad traits of character. We can doubt, therefore, whether the removal of the organic difficulty has, in itself, anything to do with the change. One boy, the second boy in the family, gave much trouble by lying, stealing, playing truant, and being cruel and disobedient. His teacher did not know what to do with him and urged that he should be put in a reformatory. At this time the boy fell ill. He suffered from tuberculosis of the hip and for half a year he was lying in plaster of Paris. When he recuperated he became the best boy of the family. We cannot believe that his illness had had such an effect on him; and it soon came out very clearly that the change was due to a recognition of his previous mistakes. He had always thought that his parents preferred his brother and had always felt himself slighted. During his illness he found himself the center of attention, taken care of and helped by everybody; and he was intelligent enough to get rid of the idea that he was always neglected.

It is ridiculous to imagine that the best way to remedy the mistakes that mothers often make would be to take all children from the care of their mothers and hand them over to nurses or to institutions. Whenever we try to find a substitute for a mother, we are looking for some one who will play a mother's part — who will interest the child in herself just as a mother does. It is much easier to train the child's own mother. Children who grow up in orphan asylums often show a lack of interest in others: there was no one who could make the personal bridge between the child and his fellow beings. Sometimes an experiment has been made with children in institutions who were not developing very well. A nurse or a sister has been found to give the child her individual care; or he has been placed with a family where the mother could look after him as well as her own children. The result has always been a great improvement if the foster-mothers were well chosen. The best means of bringing up such children is to find a substitute for a mother and father and for a family life; and all we should be doing if we took children from their parents would be hunting around for other people who could fulfill the tasks of parents. The importance of a mother's affection and interest can be seen also from the fact that so many failures come from among orphans, illegitimate or unwanted children and the children of broken marriages. It is notorious that the part of a stepmother is very difficult, and the children often fight against her. The problem is not insoluble and I have seen it met with good success; but too often the woman does not understand the situation. Perhaps, when the mother died, the children turned towards the father and were pampered by him. Now they feel deprived of his attention and attack their stepmother. She feels that she must fight back and the children have now a real grievance. She has challenged them and they fight more than ever. A fight with a child is always a losing fight: he can never be beaten or won to coöperation by fighting. In these struggles the weakest always carries the day. Something is demanded of him which he refuses to give; something which can never be gained by such means. An incalculable amount of tension and useless effort would be spared in this world if we realized that coöperation and love can never be won by force.

The part of the father in family life is equally important with the mother's part. At first his relationship with the child is less intimate and it is later on that his influence has its effect. We have already described some of the dangers if a mother is unable to spread the child's interest towards his father. The child suffers a serious block in the development of his social feeling. Where the marriage is unhappy, the situation is full of danger for the child. His mother may feel herself unable to include the father in the family life; she may wish to keep the child entirely to herself. Perhaps both parents use the child as a pawn in their personal warfare. Each wishes to attach the child to himself; to be more loved than the partner. If children find dissension between their parents, they are very skillful in playing them off against each other. Thus a competition may arise to see who can govern the child better or spoil him more. It is impossible to train a child in coöperation with such an atmosphere around him. The first coöperation among other people which he experiences is the coöperation of his parents; and if their coöperation is poor, they cannot hope to teach him to be coöperative himself. Moreover, it is from the marriage of their parents that children gain their first idea of marriage and the partnership of the sexes. The children of unhappy marriages, unless their first impression is corrected, will grow up with a pessimistic view of marriage. Even when they are adults they will feel that marriage is bound to turn out badly. They will attempt to avoid the other sex or they will be sure that they will fail in their approach. A child is thus very gravely handicapped if the marriage of his parents is not a coöperative part of social life, a product of social life, and a preparation for social life. The meaning of marriage is that it should be a partnership of two people for their mutual welfare, for the welfare of their children, and for the welfare of society; and if it fails in any of these respects it is not in coherence with the demands of life.

Since marriage is a partnership, no one member should be supreme. This point needs much closer consideration than we are accustomed to give it. In the whole conduct of the family life there is no call for the use of authority; and it is unfortunate if one member is especially prominent or considered more than the others. If the father is high-tempered and tries to dominate the rest of the family, the boys will get a false view of what is expected from a man. The girls will suffer still more. In later life they will picture men as tyrants. Marriage will seem to them a kind of subjugation and slavery. Sometimes they will seek to secure themselves against the other sex by perversion. If the mother is dominating and nags the other members, the position is reversed. The girls will probably imitate her and become sharp and critical themselves. The boys will always be on the defensive, afraid of criticism and keeping watch for attempts to subjugate them. Sometimes it is not only the mother who is tyrannical, but sisters and aunts all join to keep a boy in his place. He grows reserved and never wants to come forward and join in social life. He is afraid that all women will have the same nagging, censorious attitude and he wishes to be rid of the whole sex. Nobody likes to be criticized; but if an individual makes it the main interest of his life to escape criticism, all his relations with society are interfered with. He looks at every event and judges it only in accordance with his scheme of apperception, " Am I the conqueror or the conquered? " No comradeship is possible to those who look at relations with others as opportunities of defeat or victory.

The task of a father can be summed up in a few words. He must prove himself a good fellow man to his wife, to his children and to society. He must meet in a good way the three problems of life — occupation, friendship and love — and he must coöperate on an equal footing with his wife in the care and protection of the family. He should not forget that the woman's part in the creation of family life can never be surpassed. It is not his part to dethrone the mother, but to work with her. Especially with regard to money we should emphasize that if the financial support of the family comes through him it is still a common affair. He should never make it appear that he gives and the others receive. In a good marriage the fact that the money comes through him is only a result of the division of labor in the family. Many fathers use their economic position as a means of ruling the household. There should be no ruler in the family and every occasion for feelings of inequality should be avoided. Every father should be aware of the fact that our culture has overemphasized the privileged position of the man, and that in consequence his wife, when he married her, was probably in some degree afraid of being dominated and put in an inferior position. He should know that his wife is not on a lower level than he merely because she is a woman and does not support the family in the same way as he supports it. Whether or no the wife contributes in money to the support of the family, if the family life is a real coöperation, there will be no question who makes the money and to whom it should belong.

The father's influence on his children is so important that many of them look on him, throughout their lives, either as their ideal or as their greatest enemy. Punishment, especially corporal punishment, is always harmful to children. Any teaching which cannot be given in friendship is wrong teaching. It is unfortunately frequent that the father of the family is given the task of punishing the children. There are many reasons why this is unfortunate. First of all, it reveals a conviction on the mother's part that women are not really able to educate their children;

that they are really weak creatures who need a strong hand to help them. If a mother tells her children, " You wait till father comes home ", she is preparing them to regard men as the final authorities and the real powers in life. Secondly, it disturbs the relation of the children with their father and makes them fear him, instead of feeling him a good friend. Perhaps some women are afraid of losing their hold over their children's affections if they punish them themselves; but the solution is not to delegate the punishment to the father. The children will not reproach their mother any the less because she has summoned an executioner to her aid. Many women still use the threat of " telling father " as a means of compelling their children's obedience. What sort of conclusion will the children draw about the man's part in life?

If the father is meeting the three problems of life in a useful way he will be an integral part of the family, a good husband and a good father. He must be at ease with others and able to make friends. If he makes friends he is already making his family a part of the social life around him. He will not be isolated and bound to traditional ideas. Influences from outside the home are finding their way into it and he is showing his children the way to social feeling and coöperation. There is a real danger, however, if the husband and wife have different friends. They should live in the same society and avoid being separated through their friendships. I do not mean, of course, that they should cling together and never go out by themselves; but there should be no difficulty in the way of their being together. Such a difficulty occurs, for example, if the husband does not want to introduce his wife into the circle of his friends. The center of his social life, in that case, is outside of the family. It is very valuable in the development of children that they should learn that the family is a unit of a larger society and that outside the family there exist also trustworthy human beings and fellow men.

It is a favorable sign of the ability to coöperate if the father is on good terms with his own parents, sisters and brothers. Of course, he must leave his family and become independent; but this does not imply that he should dislike his closest relatives and break with them. Sometimes two people will marry when they are still dependent on their parents and will exaggerate the connection which binds them to their families. When they speak of " home " they will refer to the home of their parents. If they are involved in the idea that their parents are still the center of the family, they will not be able to establish a real family life of their own. It is a question, here, of the coöperative ability of everybody concerned. Sometimes a man's parents are jealous, want to know everything about their son's life, and make difficulties in the new family. His wife feels that she is not sufficiently appreciated and is angry at the interference of her husband's parents. This is particularly apt to occur where a man marries against the wish of his parents. His parents may have been wrong or right. Before their son marries they can oppose his choice, if they are dissatisfied; but after he has married they have only one course open to them — they must do everything they can to secure the success of the marriage. If family differences cannot be avoided, the husband should understand the difficulties and not worry about them. He should look on his parents' opposition as a mistake of theirs and do his best to prove that it was the son

who was right. There is no need for the husband and
wife to submit to the wishes of their parents; but it is
obviously easier if there is coöperation and if the wife
can feel that her husband's parents are thinking of her
welfare and advantage, not of their own.

The function that every one expects most definitely of
a father is a solution of the problem of occupation. He
must be trained for an occupation and he must be able to
support himself and the family. In this he may be helped
by his wife and later on, perhaps, by his children; but in
our present cultural conditions the economic responsibility
falls mainly on the man. A solution for this problem
means that he must work and be courageous, that he must
understand his profession and know its advantages and
disadvantages, that he must be able to coöperate with
others in his profession and be well thought of by them.
It means still more. By his own attitude he is helping to
prepare the way in which his children will face the problem of occupation. He should therefore see what is necessary for the successful solution of this problem — to find
work which is useful to the whole of mankind and contributes to its welfare. It does not so much matter, however, that he should consider his work useful; what is important is that it should *be useful*. We do not need to
listen to his words. If he thinks himself an egoist, it is
a pity; but if at the same time the work he is doing
contributes to our common welfare, no great damage is
done.

It is with the solution of the problem of love that we
are now dealing — with marriage and the building up of
a happy and useful family life. The chief demand upon
the husband is that he should be interested in his partner;

and it is very easy to see whether one person is interested in another or not. If he is interested, he interests himself in the same things as the other and makes the welfare of the other his own spontaneous aim. It is not affection only that proves interest; there are too many kinds of affection for us to regard it as a sufficient witness that everything is well. He must also be a comrade to his wife; he must be striving to make life easier and richer for her; and he must take pleasure in pleasing her. It is only when both partners place their common welfare higher than their individual welfare that a true coöperation can occur. Each partner must be more interested in the other than in himself.

A husband should not show his affection for his wife too strikingly before the children. It is true that the love of a husband and wife is not to be compared with their love for their children. They are quite different things and neither can diminish the other. But sometimes children feel, if the parents are too expressive in their affection for each other, that their own place is narrowed. They grow jealous and wish to make dissensions. The sexual partnership should not be taken with so little seriousness. So, too, in giving explanations of sexual matters, the father with the boys and the mother with the girls, they should be careful not to volunteer information, but to explain only as much as the child wishes to know and can understand at his stage of development. I believe that in our own time there is a tendency to explain to children far more than they can grasp properly and to rouse interests and feelings for which they are not prepared. In this way sexual matters are minimized and treated as if they were a mere bagatelle. This fashion is not much better than the old fashion of being dishonest with children and concealing all sexual information from them. It is best to understand what the child wishes to know and answer the problem which he himself is considering; not to force on him what, from our own standards, we think should be known by everybody. We must preserve his trust and his feeling that we are coöperating with him and interested in helping him to find solutions for his problems; and if we do this we cannot go far wrong. Incidentally, the fear of some parents that their children will hear injurious sex explanations from their fellow children has little justification. A child whose training in coöperation and independence has been good will never suffer from the talk of his friends; and very often children are more delicate in these matters than their elders. A "street explanation" never harmed a child who was not already prepared to take a mistaken view.

In our present society men are offered fuller opportunities for experience in social life; for knowledge of the systems of society, with their advantages and disadvantages, and of the moral relations in their own countries and in the world at large. Their sphere of activity is unfortunately still broader than the sphere of activity of women. It thus falls to the father's part to be the adviser of his wife and children in these problems. He should never boast of his greater experience and make capital out of it. He is not the family tutor. He should advise them, rather, as one friend advises another, avoiding every resistance and happy if the others can agree with him. If there is resistance on the side of his wife, who is perhaps not very well trained for coöperation, he should not insist on his point of view or try to use authority, but look around for ways to diminish this resistance. He will not succeed by fighting.

Money should not be overemphasized or made the subject of quarreling. Women who are not earning money themselves are much more sensitive than their husbands generally believe and feel deeply hurt if they are accused of extravagance. Financial affairs should be settled in a coöperative way, within the financial capacity of the family. There is no excuse for the wife or children if they use their influence to make the father pay more than he can afford; and there should be an agreement on expenses made from the beginning so that no one feels dependent or badly treated. A father should not think that he can assure the future of his children by money alone. I read once an interesting pamphlet written by an American, in which he described how a rich man who had been born in a very poor family wished to secure his descendants for many generations from poverty and restriction. He went to a lawyer and asked him how it could be done. The lawyer asked him how many generations would satisfy him; and he replied that he thought he could manage it till the tenth generation. " Yes, you can do it," said the lawyer. " But do you realize that each member of this tenth generation will have more than five hundred ancestors with as much part in him as you have? Five hundred other families will be able to lay claim to him. Is he your descendant any longer? " We can see here another example of the fact that whatever we do for our own descendants we are doing for the whole community. We cannot escape this tie to our fellow men.

If there is no authority in the family there must be a real coöperation. Father and mother must work together and agree together in everything concerned with the education of their children. It is of the utmost importance that neither the father nor the mother should show any favoritism among their children. The dangers of favoritism can hardly be too dramatically put. Almost every discouragement in childhood springs from the feeling that some one else is preferred. Sometimes the feeling is not at all justified; but where there is real equality there should not be an occasion for it to develop. Where boys are preferred to girls, inferiority complexes amongst the girls are almost inevitable. Children are very sensitive and even a very good child can take an entirely wrong direction in life through the suspicion that others are preferred. Sometimes one of the children develops quicker, or in a more likeable way than the others, and it is difficult not to show more liking for this child. Parents should be experienced enough and skillful enough to avoid showing any such preferences. Otherwise the child which develops better will overshadow and discourage all the other children; they will become envious and doubtful of their own abilities, and their ability to coöperate will be frustrated. It is not enough to say that there is no such preference. Parents must observe whether there is even a suspicion of such a preference in the mind of any of their children.

Now we come to an equally important part of the family coöperation, the coöperation of the children among themselves. Unless the children feel equal, mankind will never be well prepared in social interest. Unless girls and boys feel equal, the relations of the two sexes will continue to offer the greatest difficulties. Many people ask, "How does it happen that children in the same family often differ so widely? " Some scientists have attempted to explain it as the result of differing heredity; but we have seen that this is a superstition. Let us compare the growth of children with the growth of young trees. If a group of trees are growing up together, each one of them is really in a quite different situation. If one grows faster because it is more favored by the sun and the soil, its development influences the growth of all the others. It overshadows them; its roots stretch out and take away their nourishment. The others are dwarfed and stunted. The same is true of a family in which one member is too prominent. We have seen that neither a father nor a mother should assume a dominating position in the family. Often, if the father is very successful or very talented, the children feel that they can never equal his achievements. They grow discouraged: their interest in life is blocked. It is for this reason that the children of famous men and women are sometimes a disappointment to their parents and to the rest of society. The children have seen no way open to excel their father or mother. If a father is very successful in his profession, he should never stress his success in the family or his children's development will be hindered.

The same remark holds good among the children themselves. If one child develops especially well, it is quite likely that he will receive most attention and favor. It is a pleasant situation for him; but the other children feel the difference and resent it. It is not possible for a human being to bear, without disgust and irritation, the position of being put on a lower level than some one else. Such a prominent child can damage all the others; and it is not too much to say that the others will all grow up suffering from mental starvation. They will not cease to strive for superiority, for this striving can never cease. Their striving, however, will turn to other directions which may well not be realistic or socially useful.

Individual Psychology has opened up a very wide field for research work by inquiring into the advantages and disadvantages for children according to the order of their birth. To simplify a consideration of this, we shall suppose that the parents are coöperating well and doing their best in the training of the children. The position of each child in the family still makes a great difference and each child will still grow up in quite a new situation. We must insist again that the situation is never the same for two children in a family; and each child will show in his style of life the results of his attempts to adapt himself to his own peculiar circumstances.

Every oldest child has experienced for some time the situation of an only child and has been compelled suddenly to adapt himself to a new situation at the birth of the next oldest. The first-born child is generally given a good deal of attention and spoiling. He has been accustomed to be the center of the family. Too often it is quite suddenly and sharply, without any preparation, that he finds himself ousted from his position. Another child is born and he is no longer unique. Now he must share the attention of his mother and father with a rival. The change always makes a great impression and we can often find in problem children, neurotics, criminals, drunkards and perverts that their difficulties began in such circumstances. They were oldest children who felt very deeply the arrival of another child; and their sense of deprivation had moulded their whole style of life.

Other children may lose position in the same way; but they will probably not feel it so strongly. They had already had experience of coöperation with another child; they had never been the sole object of consideration and care. To the oldest child it is a complete change. If he is in fact neglected on the arrival of the new baby, we cannot expect him to accept the situation with ease. If he bears a grudge, we cannot hold him guilty. Of course, if his parents have allowed him to feel sure of their affection, if he knows that his position is secure, and, above all, if he is prepared for the arrival of a younger child and has been trained to coöperate in its care, the crisis will pass without ill effects. Generally he is not prepared. The new baby really takes away from him attention, love and appreciation. He begins trying to pull his mother back to him and thinking how he can regain attention. Sometimes we can see a mother pulled this way and that by her two children, each struggling to occupy her more than the other. The oldest child is better able to use force and to think of new tricks. We can reckon up what he will do in these circumstances. He will do just what we should do if we were in his circumstances and were pursuing his aim. We should try to worry the mother, and fight her, and develop such characteristics that she could not possibly overlook us. He will do the same. In the end he exhausts his mother's patience. He fights by every possible means, in the wildest way. His mother is tired of the trouble he causes her; and now he really begins to experience what it is like to be no longer loved. He was fighting for his mother's love and the result is that he loses it. He felt pushed into the background and the effect of his actions is that he really is pushed into the background. He feels himself justified. " I knew it," he feels. The others are wrong and he is right. It is as if he were in a trap: the more he struggles, the worse his position becomes. All the time his views of the position are being confirmed. How can he give up the fight when everything tells him he is justified?

In every case of such a fight, we must inquire into the individual circumstances. If mother fights back at him, the child will become high-tempered, wild, critical and disobedient. When he turns against his mother, it often happens that his father gives him a chance to renew the old favorable position. He becomes interested in his father and tries to win his attention and affection. Oldest children frequently prefer their fathers and lean towards their side. We can be sure, wherever a child prefers his father, that this is a secondary phase: at first he was attached to his mother, but now she has lost his affection and he has transferred it to his father as a reproach against her. If a child prefers his father, we know that he has previously suffered a tragedy; he has felt slighted and left out of account; he cannot forget it and his whole style of life is built around this feeling.

Such a fight lasts a long time and sometimes it lasts through a whole life. The child has trained to fight and resist and he goes on fighting in all situations. Perhaps there is no one whose interest he can engage. He then becomes hopeless and imagines that he can never win affection. We find then such characteristics as peevishness, reserve and inability to join in with others. The child trains himself for isolation. All the movements and expressions of such a child are directed towards the past, the bygone time when he was the center of attention. For this reason oldest children generally show, in one way or another, an interest in the past. They like to look back and to speak of the past. They are admirers of the past and pessimistic over the future. Sometimes a child who has lost his power, the small kingdom he ruled, understands better than others the importance of power and authority. When he grows up, he likes to take part in the exercise of authority and he exaggerates the importance of rules and laws. Everything should be done by rule and no rule should ever be changed. Power should always be preserved in the hands of those who are entitled to it. We can understand that influences like these in childhood give a strong tendency towards conservatism. If such an individual establishes a good position for himself, he is always suspicious that other people are coming up behind him with the intention of taking his place from him and dethroning him.

The position of the oldest child offers a special problem, but it is one which can be well met and turned into an advantage. If he has already been trained for coöperation when the younger child is born, he suffers no injury. Among such oldest children we find individuals who develop a striving to protect others and help them. They train to imitate their fathers or mothers; often they play the part of a father or a mother with the younger children, look after them, teach them and feel themselves responsible for their welfare. Sometimes they develop a great talent for organization. These are the favorable cases, though even a striving to protect others may be exaggerated into a desire to keep those others dependent and to rule over them. In my own experience in Europe and America I have found that the greatest proportion of problem children are oldest children; and close behind them come the youngest children. It is interesting that these extreme positions provide the extreme problems. Our educational methods have not yet successfully solved the difficulties of the oldest child.

The second child is in a quite different position, a situation that cannot be compared with that of the other children. From the time he is born, he shares attention with another child; and he is therefore a little nearer to cooperation than an oldest child. He has a greater circle of human beings in his environment; and if the oldest is not fighting against him and pushing him back, he is very well situated. The most significant fact of his position is something different. Throughout his childhood he has a pacemaker. There is always a child ahead of him in age and development and he is stimulated to exert himself and catch up. A typical second child is very easy to recognize. He behaves as if he were in a race, as if some one were a step or two in front and he had to hurry to get ahead of him. He is under full steam all the time. He trains continually to surpass his older brother and conquer him. The Bible gives us many marvelous psychological hints and the typical second child is beautifully portrayed in the story of Jacob. He wished to be the first, to take away Esau's position, to beat Esau and excel him. A second child is irritated by the feeling that he is behind and struggles hard to overtake the others. Often he succeeds. The second child is often more talented and successful than the first. Here we cannot suggest that heredity has any part in this development. If he goes ahead faster, it is because he trained more. Even when he is grown up and outside the family circle, he often makes use of a pacemaker; compares himself with some one whom he thinks more advantageously placed and tries to go beyond him.

It is not only in the waking life that we see these characteristics. They leave their marks on all expressions of the personality and they are easily found in dreams. Oldest children, for example, often have dreams of falling. They are on top, but they are not sure that they can keep their superiority. Second children, on the other hand, often picture themselves in races. They run after trains and ride in bicycle races. Sometimes this hurry in his dreams is sufficient by itself to allow us to guess that the individual is a second child.

We must say, however, that there are no fixed rules in this way. It is not only an actual oldest child that can behave like an oldest. The situation counts, not the mere order of birth. In a large family a later child is sometimes in the situation of an oldest. Perhaps there were two children born close together; for example, a long time intervened before a third was born, and then two other children followed. The third child may show all the features of an oldest. So, too, with a second child; a typical second child may appear after four or five children have been born. Always where two children grow up close together and separated from the others they will show the characteristics of an oldest and a second child.

Sometimes the oldest is beaten in the race; you will then find that the oldest child offers a problem. Sometimes he can keep his position and push back the younger; it is then the second child that gives trouble. It is a very difficult position for the oldest child when he is a boy and the second is a girl. He runs the risk of being beaten by a girl, which, in our present conditions, he will probably feel as being a serious disgrace. The tension between a boy and a girl is higher than the tension between two boys or two girls. In this struggle the girl is favored by nature; till her sixteenth year she develops more quickly, bodily and mentally, than a boy. Such an older boy gives up the fight, grows lazy and discouraged. He looks around for tricks and underhand means of conquering; he boasts or lies, for example. We can almost guarantee that in such a case the girl will win. We shall see the boy taking to all kinds of mistaken paths, while the girl solves her problems with ease and progresses astonishingly. Such difficulties can be avoided; but the danger must be known beforehand and steps taken before damage has been done. Bad consequences can be avoided only in a family which is a unity of equal and coöperative members, where there is no sense in rivalry and no ground for a child to think he has enemies and spend his time fighting.

All other children have followers; all other children can be dethroned; but the youngest can never be dethroned. He has no followers but he has many pacemakers. He is always the baby of the family and probably he is the most pampered. He faces the difficulties of a pampered child; but, because he is so much stimulated, because he has many chances for competition, it often happens that the youngest child develops in an extraordinary way, runs faster than the other children and overcomes them all. The position of the youngest has not changed in human history. In the oldest stories of mankind we have accounts of how the youngest child excelled its brothers and sisters. In the Bible it is always the youngest who conquers. Joseph was brought up as a youngest. Benjamin came seventeen years after Joseph; but Benjamin played no part in his development. Joseph's style of life is exactly typical of the style of life of a youngest. He is always asserting his superiority, even in his dreams. The others must bow down before him; he outshines them all. His brothers understood his dreams very well. It was not hard for them, since they had Joseph with them and his attitude was clear enough. The feelings which Joseph aroused in his dreams they also had felt. They feared him and wanted to get rid of him. From being the last, however, Joseph became the first. In later days he was the pillar and support of the whole family. The youngest child is often the pillar of the whole family and this cannot be accidental. Men have always known it and told stories of the power of the youngest. He is, in fact, in a very favorable situation; helped by his mother, his father and his brothers; with so much to stimulate his ambition and effort; and with no one to attack him from behind or distract his attention.

And yet, as we saw, the second largest proportion of problem children comes from among the youngest. The reason for this generally lies in the way in which all the family spoils them. A spoiled child can never be independent. He loses courage to succeed by his own effort. Youngest children are always ambitious; but the most ambitious children of all are the lazy children. Laziness is a sign of ambition joined with discouragement; ambition so high that the individual sees no hope of realizing it. Sometimes a youngest child will not admit to any single ambition, but this is because he wishes to excel in everything, he wishes to be unlimited and unique. It will be easily understood, also, from what inferiority feelings a youngest child can suffer. Every one in the environment is older, stronger and more experienced.

The only child has a problem of his own. He has a rival, but his rival is not a brother or sister. His feelings of competition go against his father. An only child is pampered by his mother. She is afraid of losing him and wants to keep him under her attention. He develops what is called a " mother complex "; he is tied to his mother's apron strings and wishes to push his father out of the family picture. This, too, can only be prevented if the father and mother work together and let the child be interested in both of them; but, for the most part, the father is less occupied with the child than the mother. Oldest children are occasionally very much like only children: they want to conquer the father and they like people who are older than themselves. Often an only child is scared to death lest he should have brothers and sisters following him. Friends of the family say, " You ought to have a little brother or sister ", and he dislikes the prospect immensely. He wants to be the center of attention all the time. He really feels that it is a right of his and if his position is challenged he thinks it a great injustice. In later life, where he is no longer the center of attention, he has many difficulties. Another point of danger for his development is that he is born into a timid environment. If, for organic reasons, the parents cannot have more children, we can do nothing but apply ourselves to solving the problems of an only child; but we often find these only children in a family where we could expect more children. The parents are timid and pessimistic. They feel they will not be able to solve the economic problem of having more than one child. The whole atmosphere is full of anxiety and the child suffers badly.

If there is a big space of years between the birth of children, each child will have some of the features of an only child. The situation is not very favorable. I am often asked, " What do you think would be the best spacing of a family? " " Should children follow each other very soon or should there be a longer distance between them? " From my experience I should say that the best distance is about three years. At the age of three a child can coöperate if a younger child is born. He is intelligent enough to understand that there can be more than one child in a family. If he is only one-and-a-half or two, we cannot discuss it with him; he cannot understand our arguments. We shall not be able, therefore, to prepare him rightly for the event.

An only boy brought up in a family of girls has a hard time before him. He is in a wholly feminine environment. Most of the day the father is absent. He sees only his mother, his sisters and the maidservants. Feeling that he is different, he grows up isolated. This is especially true where the women-folk make a joint attack on him. They think they must all educate him or they want to prove that he has no reason to be conceited. There is a good deal of antagonism and rivalry. If he is in the middle, he is probably in the worst place of all — attacked from both sides. If he is the oldest, he is in danger of being followed by a girl who is a very keen competitor. If he is the youngest, he is made into a pet. The type of an only boy among girls is one which no one likes very much. The problem can be solved if there is a social life in which the children share and in which he can meet other children. Otherwise, surrounded by girls, he may behave like a girl. A feminine environment is quite different from a mixed environment. If the apartment is not just standardized but furnished according to the taste of the people in it, you may be sure that an apartment where women live will be neat and orderly, that the colors will be chosen with care, and that attention will have been paid to a thousand details. If there are men and boys about it is not nearly so neat; there is much more roughness and noise and broken furniture. Such a boy among girls is apt to grow up with feminine tastes and a feminine outlook on life.

On the other hand, he may fight strongly against this atmosphere and lay great stress on his masculinity. He will then always be on his guard not to be dominated by women. He will feel that he must assert his difference and his superiority; but there will always be tension. His development will proceed by extremes, he will train to be either very strong or very weak. It is a situation which deserves study and inquiry; it is not met with every day; and before we say much about it we must examine more cases. In a rather similar way, an only girl among boys is apt to develop very feminine or very masculine qualities. Frequently she is pursued through life by feelings of insecurity and helplessness.

Wherever I have studied adults, I have found impressions left on them from their early childhood and lasting forever. The position in the family leaves an indelible stamp upon the style of life. Every difficulty of development is caused by rivalry and lack of coöperation in the family. If we look around at our social life and ask why rivalry and competition is its most obvious aspect — indeed, not only at our social life but at our whole world — then we must recognize that people are everywhere pur-

suing the goal of being conqueror, of overcoming and sur-
passing others. This goal is the result of training in early
childhood, of the rivalries and competitive striving of
children who have not felt themselves an equal part of
their whole family. We can get rid of these disadvantages only by training children better in coöperation.

CHAPTER VII

School Influences

The school is the prolonged arm of the family. If parents were able to undertake the training of their children and fit them adequately for solving the problems of life, there would be no need for school education. Often in other cultures a child was trained almost completely in the family. A craftsman would bring up his sons in his own craft and teach them the skill he had acquired from his own father and from his practical experience. Our present culture, however, makes more complex demands on us, and schools are necessary to lighten the work of parents and carry on what they have begun. Social life needs a higher degree of education from its members than we can give them in the home.

In America schools have not gone through all the phases of development which have taken place in Europe; but sometimes we can still see relics of an authoritarian tradition. At first, in the history of European education, only princes and aristocrats received any schooling. They were the only members of society to whom a value was accorded: others were expected to do their work and aspire no higher. Later on, the limits of society were enlarged. Education was taken over by religious institutions and a few selected individuals could be trained in religion, art, the sciences and professional disciplines.

When industrial technique began to develop, these forms of education were quite insufficient. The struggle for a wider education was long drawn out. The school-masters in the villages and towns were often cobblers and tailors. They taught with a stick in their hands and the results were very poor. Only the religious schools and the universities gave instruction in the arts and sciences and sometimes even emperors did not learn to read or write. Now it became necessary for the workers to read and write, do sums and draw, and the public schools as we know them were founded.

These schools, however, were always established in accordance with the ideals of the government; and the governments of the time aimed at having obedient subjects, trained for the benefit of the upper classes and capable of being turned into soldiers. The curriculum of the schools was adapted to this end. I myself can remember a time in Austria when these conditions, in part, survived; when the training for the least privileged classes was to make them obedient and fit them for tasks appropriate to their status. More and more the insufficiencies of this type of education were seen. Freedom grew; the working classes became stronger and made higher demands. The public schools adapted themselves to these demands; and now it is the prevailing ideal of education that children should be taught to think for themselves, should be given the opportunity to familiarize themselves with literature, the arts and sciences, and should grow up to share in our whole human culture and contribute to it. We no longer wish to train children only to make money or take a position under the industrial system. We want fellow men. We want equal, independent and responsible collaborators in the common work of culture.

Whether they know it or not, all who propose some

school reform are seeking a way to increase the degree of coöperation in social life. This is the purpose, for example, behind the demand for character-education; and, if we understood it in this light, it would clearly be the right demand. On the whole, however, the aims and technique of education are not yet thoroughly understood. We must find teachers who can train children not only to earn money but to work in ways beneficial to mankind. They must feel the importance of this task and they must be trained to fulfill it. Character-education is still on its trial. We must exclude from consideration the courts — so far there has been no serious and organized attempt at character-education there. Even in the schools, however, the results are not very satisfactory. Children come to school who have been failures in family life; and their mistakes are not diminished, in spite of all the lectures and exhortations they get. There is nothing left, therefore, but to train the teachers to understand and help the development of children in the school.

This has been a great part of my own work; and I believe that many of the schools in Vienna are ahead of all others. Elsewhere there are psychiatrists to see the children and give advice about them; but, unless the teacher agrees and understands how to carry out the advice, where is the advantage? The psychiatrist sees the child once or twice a week — perhaps even once a day — but he does not really know the influences from the environment, from the family, from outside the family, from the school itself. He writes a note that the child should be better nourished or should have thyroid treatment. Perhaps he gives the teacher hints for the personal treatment of the child. The teacher, however, does not know the purpose of the prescription and is not experienced in avoiding mistakes. He can do nothing unless he himself understands the character of the child. We need the most intimate coöperation between the psychiatrist and the teacher. The teacher must know everything the psychiatrist knows, so that after discussing the child's problem he can proceed on his own, without further help. If any unexpected problem turns up, he should understand what to do, just as the psychiatrist would if he were present. The most practical method seems to be the Advisory Council, such as we have established in Vienna. This method I shall describe towards the end of the chapter.

When the child first goes to school, he is facing a new test in social life; and this test will reveal any mistakes in his development. Now he must coöperate in a wider field than before, and, if he has been pampered at home, he will perhaps be unwilling to leave his sheltered life and join in with the other children. In this way we can see in his very first day at school the limits of social feeling in a pampered child. He will perhaps cry and wish to be taken home. He will not be interested in school tasks and in his teacher. He will not listen to what is said, because he is thinking of himself all the time. It is easy to see that if he continues self-interested he will remain backward at school. Often parents tell us of a problem child that he gives no trouble at home; that problems only arise when he is at school. We can suspect that the child feels himself in an especially favorable situation in the family. No tests are set him there, the mistakes in his development are not manifest. At school, however, he is no longer pampered and he feels the situation as a defeat.

One child, from his first day at school, did nothing but laugh at every remark of the teacher. He showed no interest in any of the school work and it was thought that he must be feeble-minded. When I saw him, I said to him, "Everybody wonders why you are always laughing at school." He replied, "School is a joke made up by the parents. They send children to school to fool them." He had been very much teased at home and he was convinced that every new situation was a new joke against him. I was able to show him that he overemphasized the necessity for preserving his dignity; that not everybody was engaged in making a fool of him. In consequence, he could interest himself in his school work and make good progress.

It is the task of schoolteachers to notice the difficulties of the children and to correct the mistakes of the parents. They find some of the children prepared for this wider social life; they have already been trained in their families to interest themselves in other people. Some are not prepared; and wherever an individual is not prepared for a problem, he hesitates or withdraws. Every child who is backward but not definitely feeble-minded is hesitating before the problem of adjustment to social life; and the teacher is in the best position to help him to meet what is a new situation for him.

But how is he to help him? He must do exactly what a mother should do — connect the child with himself and interest him. It is on the interest of the child that his whole future adjustment depends. He can never be interested by severity or punishment. If a child comes to school and finds it difficult to make a bridge with his teachers and fellow children, the worst thing to do is to criticize him and scold him. This method would show only too clearly that he was right to dislike school. I must confess that if I myself were a child who was always scolded and reproached at school, I should distract my interest as far as possible from my teachers. I should look about for ways of getting into a new situation and avoiding school altogether. It is mainly the children to whom school is thus made an artificially unpleasant environment who play truant, are bad pupils and give the appearance of being stupid and difficult to handle. They are not really stupid; often they display great ingenuity in making up excuses for not attending school or in forging letters from their parents. Outside the school, however, they find other children who have played truant before them. From these companions they gain far more appreciation than they get at school. The circle in which they feel themselves interested and where they have the testimony of being worth while is not the school class but the gang. We can see, in this situation, how children who are not taken into the class as part of the whole are provoked to train themselves towards a criminal career.

If a teacher is to attract the interest of a child, he will understand what the child's interests have been previously and convince him that he can make a success in this interest and in others. When a child feels confident on one point it is easier to stimulate him in other points also. From the first, therefore, we should find out how the child looks at the world and which sense organ has occupied most of his attention and been trained to the highest degree. Some children are most interested in seeing, some in listening, some in moving. Children of a visual type will be easier to interest in subjects in which they have to use their eyes, in geography or drawing. If the teacher gives lectures, they will not listen; they are not so much accustomed to auditory attention. If such children have no opportunity to learn through the eyes, they will be backward. It will perhaps be taken for granted that they have no abilities or talents; and the blame will be put on heredity. If any one is to blame, it is rather the teachers and parents who have not found the right method of interesting the children. I am not proposing that the education of children should be specialized; but an interest which is highly developed should be used to encourage the children in other interests also. In our own time there are some schools where subjects are taught to the children in a way which can appeal to all the senses. Exercises in modeling or drawing, for example, are combined with the lessons. This is a tendency to be encouraged and developed further. The best way to teach subjects is in coherence with the rest of life, so that the children can see the purpose of the instruction and the practical value of what they are learning. A question is often raised whether it is better to teach children subjects or teach them to think for themselves. It seems to me that too severe an antithesis is made in this question. Both methods can be combined. It is a great advantage, for example, to teach a child mathematics in connection with the building of houses, and let him find out how much wood is needed, how many people will live there, and so forth. Some subjects can easily be taught together, and we often find experts in linking one part of life to another. A teacher, for example, can take a walk with the children and find out what they are most interested in. He can teach them at the same time to understand plants and plant structure, the evolution and use of the plant, the influences of climate, the physical features of the country, the history of mankind and indeed almost every aspect of life. We must presuppose, of course, that such a teacher is really interested in the children he teaches; but there is no hope for educating children where we cannot make this presupposition.

Under our present system we generally find that when children first come to school they are more prepared for competition than for coöperation; and the training in competition continues throughout their schooldays. This is a disaster for the child; and it is hardly less of a disaster if he goes ahead and strains to beat the other children than if he falls behind and gives up the struggle. In both cases he will be interested primarily in himself. It will not be his aim to contribute and help, but to secure what he can for himself. As the family should be a unit, with each member an equal part of the whole, so, too, should the class. When they are trained in this way, children are really interested in one another, and enjoy coöperation. I have seen many " difficult " children whose attitude was entirely changed through the interest and coöperation of their fellow children. One child in especial I may mention. He came from a home where he felt that every one was hostile to him and he expected that every one would be hostile to him at school. His work at school had been bad, and when his parents heard of it, they punished him at home. This situation is only too often met with: a child gets a bad report at school and is scolded for it there; he takes it home and is punished again. One such experience is discouraging enough; to double the punishment is terrible. It is no wonder that the child remained backward and a disturbing influence in the class. At last he found a teacher who understood the circumstances and explained to the other children how this boy believed that every one was his enemy. He enlisted their help in convincing him that they were his friends; and the whole conduct and progress of the boy improved beyond belief.

Sometimes people doubt whether children can really be trained to understand one another and help in this way; but it is my experience that children often understand better than their elders. A mother once brought her two children, a girl of two years and a boy of three, into my room. The little girl climbed up on a table and her mother was scared to death. She was so anxious that she could not make a movement, but she cried out, " Come down! Come down! " The little girl paid no attention to her. The boy of three years said, " Stay there! " and the girl immediately climbed down. He understood her better than her mother and knew what to do.

One frequent suggestion for increasing the unity and coöperation of a class is to make the children self-governing; but in such attempts I think that we must go carefully, under the guidance of a teacher, and assuring ourselves that the children are rightly prepared. Otherwise we shall find that the children are not very serious about their self-government: they look on it as a kind of game. In consequence they are much stricter and severer than a teacher would be; or they use their meetings to gain a personal advantage, to air quarrels, to score off one another, or to achieve a position of superiority. In the beginning, therefore, it is necessary that the teacher should watch and advise.

We cannot avoid tests of one kind or another if we are to find out a child's present standard of mental development, character and social behavior. Sometimes, indeed, a test such as the Intelligence Tests can be the salvation of a child. A boy has bad school reports, for example, and the teacher wishes to put him in a lower class. He is given an Intelligence Test and it is discovered that he could really be promoted. It ought to be realized, however, that we can never predict the limits of a child's future growth. The Intelligence Quotient should be used only to acquaint us with a child's difficulties, so that we may find a method to overcome them. In so far as my own experience goes, an Intelligence Quotient, when it does not reveal actual feeble-mindedness, can always be changed if we discover the right method. I have found that where children are allowed to play with Intelligence Tests, become familiar with them, find out the trick and increase their experience of these test examinations, their Intelligence Quotient improves. The Intelligence Quotient should not be regarded as fixing a limit, set by fate or by heredity, to the child's future achievements.

Nor should the child himself or the child's parents be acquainted with his Intelligence Quotient. They do not know the purpose of the tests and they think that they represent a final judgment. The greatest difficulty in education is provided, not by the limitations of the child, but by what he thinks are his limitations. If a child knows that his Intelligence Quotient is low, he may become hopeless and believe that success is beyond him. In education we should be occupied in increasing the courage and interest of a child and in removing the limits which, through his interpretation of life, he has set to his own powers.

Much the same is true of school reports. If a teacher gives a child a bad report, he believes that he is stimulating him to struggle harder. If the child has had a severe upbringing at home, however, he will be afraid to take his report back with him. He may stay away from home or alter the report. Sometimes children have even committed suicide in such circumstances. Teachers should consider, therefore, what may happen later on. They are not responsible for the home life of the child and its effects on him; but they must take it into consideration. If the parents are ambitious, there are probably scenes and reproaches when he comes home with a bad report. If the teacher had been a little milder and more benevolent, the child might have been encouraged to go ahead and succeed. When a child always has a bad school report and every one else thinks he is the worst pupil in the class, he comes to believe it himself and to believe that it is unalterable. Even the worst pupil can improve, however; and there are sufficient examples, among the most famous men, to show that a child who is backward at school may recover his courage and interest and go forward to great achievements.

It is very interesting to see that children themselves, without any help from reports, have generally a quite good judgment of one another's present abilities. They know who is best in arithmetic, spelling, drawing and athletics, and could classify themselves very well. The mistake they most often make is to conceive that they could never do better. They see others ahead of them and believe that they could never catch up. If a child is very firmly fixed in this opinion he will transfer it to the circumstances of his later life. Even in adult life he will calculate his position relative to others and think that he must always remain behind at this point. The great majority of children at school occupy more or less the same position in all the classes through which they go. They are always among the first, in the middle or at the bottom. We should not look on this fact as if it showed that they were more or less gifted by birth. It shows the limits which they have set for themselves, the degree of their optimism and the field of their activity. It is by no means unknown that a child who has been at the bottom of his class should change and begin to make surprising progress. Children should understand the mistake involved in this self-limitation; and both teachers and children should get rid of the superstition that the progress of a child of normal intelligence can be related to his heredity.

Of all mistakes made in education, the belief in hereditary limits to development is the worst. It gives teachers and parents an opportunity to explain away their errors and diminish their efforts. They can be freed from the responsibility of their influence over the children. Every attempt to avoid responsibility should be opposed. If an educator really attributed the whole development of character and intelligence to heredity, I do not see how he could possibly hope to accomplish anything in his profession. If, on the other hand, he sees that his own attitude and exertions influence the children, he cannot find an escape from responsibility in views of inheritance.

I am not referring here to physical heredity. The inheritance of organ deficiencies is beyond all question. The importance of such inherited deficiencies on the development of the mind is understood, I believe, only in Individual Psychology. The child experiences in his mind the degree of functioning of his organs; and he limits his development in accordance with his judgment of his disability. It is not the deficiency itself which affects the mind, but the child's attitude to his deficiency, and his consequent training. If a child suffers, therefore, from any organic disability, it is especially necessary that he should be given no reason to conclude that he is limited in intelligence or character. We have seen in a previous chapter that the same organic deficiency may be taken as a stimulus for greater effort and success or as an obstacle which is bound to hinder development.

At first, when I advanced this conclusion, many people accused me of being unscientific and of putting forward private beliefs of my own that were in conflict with the facts. It was from my experiences, however, that I had formulated my conclusion, and the evidence in its favor has been steadily accumulating. Now many other psychiatrists and psychologists have come round to the same point of view, and the belief in inherited components of character may be called a superstition. It is a superstition which has existed for many thousands of years. Wherever men have wished to avoid responsibility and have taken a fatalistic view of human conduct, the theory that character traits were inherited was almost bound to show itself. In its simplest form it is the belief that a child at birth is already good or bad. In this form it can easily be shown to be nonsense; and only a very strong desire to escape responsibility could allow it to persist. " Good " and " bad ", like other expressions of character, have meaning only in a social context; they are the result of training in a social environment, among our fellow men, and they imply a judgment, "conducive to the welfare of others", or "opposed to the welfare of others." Before a child is born, he has no social environment in this sense. At birth he has potentialities to develop in either direction. The path he chooses to follow will depend on the impressions and sensations he receives from his environment and from his own body, and on the interpretation he makes of these impressions and sensations. Especially it will depend on his education.

It is the same with the inheritance of mental faculties, though perhaps the evidence is not so clear. The greatest factor in the development of mental faculties is *interest;* and we have seen how interest is blocked, not through heredity, but through discouragement and the fear of defeat. It is doubtless true that brain structure is in some degree inherited; but the brain is the instrument not the origin of the mind; and, if the deficiency is not too severe for us to repair in the present state of our knowledge, the brain can be trained to compensate for the deficiency. Behind every exceptional degree of ability we shall find, not an exceptional heredity, but a long interest and training.

Even where we find families which have contributed many gifted members to society in more than one generation, we need not suppose any hereditary influence at work. We may suppose, rather, that the success of one member of the family acted as a stimulus to the others, and that the family traditions enabled the children to follow their interests and train them through exercise and practice. So, for example, when we learn that the great chemist, Liebig, was the son of a drugstore proprietor, we have no need to imagine that his ability in chemistry was in-

herited. It is sufficient if we know that his environment
allowed him to pursue his interest; and that at an age
when most children understand nothing at all of chemistry
he had already familiarized himself with a great deal of
his subject. Mozart's parents were interested in music;
but Mozart's talent was not inherited. His parents wished
him to be interested in music and provided him with
every encouragement. His whole environment from the
earliest age was musical. We generally find among outstanding men this fact of an " early start ": they played
the piano at the age of four, or they wrote stories for
the other members of the family when they were still
very small. Their interest was long and continuous.
Their training was spontaneous and widespread. They
kept their courage and did not hesitate or remain backward.

No teacher can succeed in removing the limits a child
has set to his own development if he himself believes
that there are fixed limits to development. It may ease his
position if he can say to a child, " You have no gift for
mathematics "; but it can do nothing but discourage the
child. I myself have had some experience in this way.
I was for a few years the mathematical dunce of my
school class, quite convinced that I lacked all talent for
mathematics. Fortunately I found myself one day, to my
own astonishment, able to complete a problem which had
stumped my schoolmaster. The success changed my whole
attitude towards mathematics. Where previously I had
withdrawn my interest from the whole subject, now I
began to enjoy it and use every opportunity for increasing my ability. In consequence I became one of the best
mathematicians in my school. The experience helped me,

I think, to see the fallacy of theories of special talents or inborn capacities.

Even in a crowded class we can observe the differences between the children and we can handle them better if we understand their characters than if they remain an undistinguished mass. Crowded classes, however, are certainly a disadvantage. The problems of some of the children are concealed and it is difficult to treat them rightly. A teacher should know all of his pupils intimately or he will not be able to establish interest and coöperation. I think that it is a great help if the children have the same teacher for several years. In some schools the teacher changes every six months or so. No teacher is given much opportunity to live with the children, to see their problems and follow their development. If a teacher stayed with the same children for three or four years, he could more easily find out and remedy mistakes in a child's style of life; and it would be easier, also, to create from the class a coöperative social unit.

It is not often an advantage for a child to skip a class; he is generally burdened with expectations which he does not fulfill. Perhaps promoting a child to a higher class should be considered if he is too old for his classmates or if he develops quicker than the other children in his class. If the class is a unit, however, as we have suggested that it should be, the successes of one member are an advantage to the others. Where there are brilliant children in a class, the progress of the whole class can be accelerated and heightened; and it is unfair to the other members to deprive them of such a stimulus. I should rather recommend that an unusually quick pupil should be given other activities and interests — painting, for example — in addition to the ordinary tasks of the class. His successes in these activities would also widen the interests of the other children and encourage them to go forward.

It is still more unfortunate if children repeat their classes. Every schoolteacher will agree that children who repeat classes are generally a problem in school and at home. It is not always so; a small minority can repeat a class without giving us any problem at all. The great majority of children who repeat classes, however, always remain backward and problematic. They are not well thought of by their fellow children and they have a pessimistic view of their own capacities. This is a difficult question and in our present school routine we cannot easily escape from letting children repeat classes. Some teachers have managed to make it unnecessary for backward children to repeat classes by making use of the vacation to train the children to recognize the mistakes in their style of life. When the mistakes have been recognized, the children could proceed through the next class with every success. Indeed, this is the only way in which we can really help the backward child; by letting him see the mistakes he has made in his estimate of his own capacities, we can set him free to progress by his own efforts.

Wherever I have seen the children divided into grades of quicker and slower pupils and put into different classes, I have noticed one outstanding fact. My experience has been mainly in Europe and I cannot tell whether the same observation would hold good for America. In the slower grades I have found together feeble-minded children and children who came from poor homes. In the quicker grades I have found mainly the children of richer parents. This fact seems intelligible enough. In the poorer homes the preparation of the children is not so good. The parents are confronted with too many difficulties; they cannot spare so much time to prepare their children and perhaps they are not well enough educated themselves to help them. I do not think, however, that children who are not well prepared for school should be placed in slower classes. A well-trained teacher will know how to correct their lack of preparation and they will gain from association with children who are better prepared. If they are placed in slower grades, they are generally quite aware of the fact; and the children in the quicker grades know it too, and look down on the others. This is fertile ground for discouragement and strivings for personal superiority.

In principle, coeducation deserves every support. It is an excellent means for boys and girls to know each other better and to learn to coöperate with the other sex. Those who believe that coeducation meets all problems, however, are making a great error. Coeducation provides a special problem of its own; and unless the special problem is recognized and dealt with as a problem, the distance between the sexes is greater with coeducation than without it. One of the difficulties, for example, is that girls develop quicker than boys until their sixteenth year. If the boys do not understand this, it is difficult for them to preserve their self-esteem. They see themselves excelled by the girls and grow disheartened. In later life they are afraid of competition with the other sex, because they remember their defeat. A teacher who is in favor of coeducation and understands its problems can accomplish a great deal through it, but if he does not wholly approve of it and is not interested in it, he will fail. Another difficulty is that if the children are not properly trained and supervised sexual problems are sure to arise. The question of sexual education in school is very complicated. The classroom is not the right place for sexual education; if a teacher speaks to the whole class he has no means of knowing that each child understands him in the right way. He may thus arouse interests without knowing whether the children are prepared for them or how they will adapt them to their own style of life. Of course, if a child wishes to know more and asks him questions in private, the teacher should give him true and straightforward answers. He has the opportunity, then, of judging what the child really wants to know and setting him on the way to a correct solution. It is a disadvantage, however, if there are always discussions about sex in a class. Some of the children are sure to misunderstand; and it is not useful to treat sex as a matter of no great importance.

For any one who is trained in the understanding of children, it is easy to distinguish different types and styles of life. The child's degree of coöperation can be seen in his posture, in the way he looks and listens, in the distance he keeps from other children, in the ease with which he makes friends, in his capacity for attention and concentration. If he forgets his tasks or loses his schoolbooks, we can gather that he is not interested in his work. We must find the reason why school is distasteful to him. If he does not join in the games of the other children, we can recognize his feeling of isolation and his interest in himself. If he always wishes to be helped in his work, we can see his lack of independence and his desire to be supported by others.

Some children work only if they are praised and appreciated. Many pampered children succeed very well in their school work so long as they can gain the attention of their teachers. If they lose this position of special consideration, trouble begins. They cannot proceed unless they have an audience; if there is no one to watch them their interest stops. Often for such children mathematics offers a great challenge and difficulty. While they are only asked to memorize a few rules or sentences, they acquit themselves admirably; but as soon as they must solve a problem by themselves they are quite at a loss. This may seem a small fault; but it is the child who is always claiming the support and the attention of others who represents the greatest danger to our common life. If the attitude remains unchanged, he will continue in adult life always to need and demand the support of others. Whenever a problem confronts him, he will respond by an action designed to force others to solve it for him. He will go through life making no contribution to the welfare of others but being, as far as he can, a permanent liability to his fellows.

Another type of child who desires to be the center of attention, if the position is not accorded him, will try to gain it by mischief-making, by disturbing the whole class, by corrupting the other children, and by being a general nuisance to everybody. Reproaches and punishments will not alter him; he revels in them. He would rather be thrashed than overlooked; and the pains that ensue on his conduct are no more than the price that he pays for his pleasure. Many children are only challenged to continue in their style of life by punishment. They regard it as a contest or game to see who can hold out longest; and they can always win, because the issue is in their own hands. So children who are fighting with their parents or teachers will sometimes train themselves to laugh when they are punished, instead of crying.

A lazy child, unless his laziness is a direct attack on his parents and teachers, is almost always an ambitious child who is afraid of defeat. Success is a word differently understood by everybody; and it is sometimes astonishing to find out what a child regards as a defeat. There are many people who think themselves defeated if they are not ahead of all others. Even if they are successful, they consider it a defeat if some one has done still better. A lazy child never experiences the real feeling of defeat because he never faces a test. He excludes the problem before him and postpones the decision whether he could compete with others. Everybody else is more or less sure that if he were less lazy he could meet his difficulties. He takes refuge in that blissful country, " If only I tried, I could accomplish anything." Whenever he fails, he can diminish the importance of his failure and keep his self-esteem. He can say to himself, " It is only laziness, not lack of capacity."

Sometimes teachers will say to a lazy pupil, " If you would work harder, you could be the most brilliant pupil in the class." If he can gain such a reputation by doing nothing, why should he risk losing it by working? Perhaps if he stopped being lazy, his reputation for hidden brilliance would come to an end. He would be judged on his accomplishments, not on what he might have achieved. Another personal advantage for the lazy child is that if he does the least bit of work, he is praised for it. Every one sees a hint of reformation in his activity and is eager to stimulate him further. The same piece of work from an industrious child would never even have been noticed.

In this way a lazy child lives on the expectations of other people. He, too, is a pampered child who has trained himself from babyhood to expect everything to come from the efforts of others.

Another type of child, always present and easy to recognize, is the child who takes the lead amongst his fellow children. Mankind has real need of leaders, but only of men who lead in the interests of all others; and such leadership we do not often find. Most children who take the lead are interested only in situations where they can rule and dominate others and will join in with their fellows only on these conditions. Such a type, therefore, is not a type with favorable auspices. Difficulties are bound to occur in later life; and where it is not tragic, it is comic to see the meeting, in marriage, in business or in social relations of two such leaders. Each is looking for an opportunity of dominating the other and establishing his own superiority. Sometimes the older members of a family enjoy seeing a pampered child try to boss them and tyrannize over them. They laugh at him and urge him on. Teachers, however, can soon see that it is not a character-development which is advantageous for social life.

There will always be varieties among children, and it is not in the slightest degree our aim to cut them all to pattern or make so many blocks of wood out of them. We wish, however, to prevent the developments which obviously lead towards defeat and difficulty: and these developments are comparatively easy to correct or prevent in childhood. Where they have not been corrected, the social consequences in adult life are severe and damaging. The line between childhood mistakes and adult failures is direct. The child who has not learned to coöperate is the neurotic, the drunkard, the criminal or the suicide of later years. The anxiety-neurotic was terrified of the dark, or of strange people, or of new situations. The melancholiac was a cry-baby. We cannot, in our present society, hope to reach all the parents and help them to avoid mistakes. The parents who most need advice are the parents who never come for it. We can hope, however, to reach all the teachers and through them to reach all the children; to correct the mistakes which have already been made and to train the children for an independent, courageous and coöperative life. In this work, it seems to me, lies the greatest promise for the future welfare of mankind.

It was with this aim in view that I started to develop, some fifteen years ago, the Advisory Councils in Individual Psychology which have proved so valuable in Vienna and in many other cities of Europe. It is well enough to have high ideals and great hopes; but if a method is not found the ideals all prove worthless. After the experiences of these fifteen years, I think I may say that these Advisory Councils have proved a complete success and offer us the best instrument we possess for dealing with the problems of childhood and educating children to be responsible fellow men. Naturally, I am convinced that Advisory Councils will succeed best if they are grounded in Individual Psychology; but I can see no reason why they should not coöperate with psychologists of other schools. Indeed, I have always advocated that Advisory Councils should be established in connection with each different school of psychology, and a comparison made of the results obtained by each school.

In the method of the Advisory Council, a well-trained

psychologist who is experienced in the difficulties of teachers, parents and children joins with the teachers of a school and discusses with them the problems that have arisen in their work. When he visits the school, one or other of the teachers describes the case of a child and the problem he offers. The child is lazy, perhaps, or quarrelsome, plays truant, steals or is backward in his work. The psychologist contributes his own experiences and a discussion follows. The family life and character and development of the child are described. The circumstances in which the problem first occurred are mentioned. The teachers and the psychologist inquire what the reasons for the problem may be and how it should be dealt with. Since they are experienced, they soon come to a common conclusion.

On the day of the visit both mother and child are in attendance. After they have decided how it is best to speak to the mother and how they can influence her and show her the reason for the child's failure, the mother is called in. The mother has more information to contribute; and a discussion begins between the psychologist and the mother, in which he suggests what can be done to help the child. Generally the mother is very glad of the opportunity for consultation and is prepared to coöperate. If she resists, the psychologist or the teachers can discuss similar cases and draw conclusions from them which she can apply to her own child.

The child then enters the room and the psychologist speaks to him, not about his own mistakes, but about the problems before him. He looks for the opinions and judgments which prevented the child from developing well, for his belief that he is slighted and other children preferred, and so on. He does not reproach the child, but carries on a friendly conversation with him which will give him another point of view. If he mentions the actual mistake, he puts it as a hypothetical case and invites the child's opinion. To any one who is not experienced in this work, it is surprising to see how well the child understands and how quickly his whole attitude can change.

All the teachers whom I have trained in this work are happy in it and would not give it up on any consideration. It makes their whole contact with their school work more interesting and increases the success of all their efforts. None of them feels it as an added burden; for often, in half an hour or less, they can get rid of a difficulty which would have pursued them and worried them for years. The spirit of coöperation in the whole school is heightened and, after a short time, there are no more grave problems and only small mistakes need to be handled. The teachers themselves are really psychologists. They learn to understand the unity of personality and the coherence of all its expressions. And if any problem comes up in the course of the day, they can settle it themselves. Indeed, it would be our hope, if all the teachers could be trained, that psychologists would become unnecessary.

So, for example, if the teacher has a lazy child in the class, he will propose to the children that they have a discussion of laziness. He leads the discussion by asking, " What does laziness come from? " " What is its purpose? " " Why doesn't a lazy child change? " " What is it that should be changed? " The children will speak and reach a conclusion. The lazy child himself does not know that he is the origin of the discussion, but the problem is his own, he is interested in it, and he learns a great deal from the discussion. If he is attacked, he will learn nothing; but if he can overhear, he will consider and perhaps change his opinion.

No one can know the minds of children so well as a teacher who lives with them and works with them. He sees so many types of children and, if he is skillful, establishes a connection with each one of them. It rests with him whether the mistakes a child has made in family life shall continue or be corrected. Like the mother, he is the guardian of the future of mankind, and the service he can render is incalculable.

CHAPTER VIII

Adolescence

There are whole libraries of books on adolescence; and almost all of them deal with the subject as if it were a dangerous crisis at which the whole character of an individual could change. There are many dangers in adolescence, but it is not true that it can change character. It provides the growing child with new situations and new tests. He feels that he is nearing the front of life. Mistakes in his style of life may reveal themselves that were hitherto unobserved. They were present, however, and a practised eye could always have seen them. Now they develop importance and cannot be overlooked.

For almost every child, adolescence means one thing above all else: he must prove that he is no longer a child. We might, perhaps, persuade him that he can take it for granted; and, if we could do it, a great deal of tension would be drawn from the situation. But if he feels he must prove it, naturally enough he will overstress his point. Very many of the expressions of adolescence are the outcome of the desire to show independence, equality with adults, and manhood or womanhood. The direction of these expressions will depend on the meaning which the child has attributed to being " grown-up." If to be " grown-up " has meant to be free from control, the child will fight against restrictions. Many children at this time begin to smoke, to swear and to stay out late at night. Some of them reveal an unexpected opposition to their parents; and their parents are puzzled to know how such an obedient child could suddenly grow so disobedient. It is not really a change of attitude. The apparently obedient child was always in opposition to his parents; but it is only now, when he has more freedom and strength, that he feels able to declare his enmity. One boy, who had always been bullied by his father and had been to all appearance a quiet and submissive child, was only awaiting an occasion for revenge. As soon as he felt himself strong enough, he challenged his father to a fight, thrashed him and left home.

For the most part a child is given more freedom and independence during his adolescence. The parents no longer feel that they have a right to watch over him and guard him all the time. If the parents try to continue their supervision, however, the child will make still stronger efforts to avoid control. The more his parents try to prove that he is still a child, the more he will fight to prove the opposite. Out of this struggle an antagonistic attitude develops; and we are then provided with the typical picture of " adolescent negativism."

We cannot place strict limits on the period of adolescence. It runs generally from about fourteen years of age to about twenty years; but sometimes children are already adolescent at ten or eleven years of age. All the organs of the body are growing and developing at this time and sometimes the coördination of the functions is not easily accomplished. Children grow taller, their hands and feet grow larger; perhaps they are less active and skillful. They need to train this coördination; but if, in the process, they are laughed at and criticized, they will come to believe that they are clumsy. If a child's movements are laughed at, he will become clumsy. The endocrine glands are also contributing to the child's development. They increase their functions. It is not a complete change; the endocrine glands were active even in the pre-natal period; but now their secretions are greater and the secondary characteristics of sex are more apparent. A boy's beard will begin to grow and his voice to break. A girl's figure swells and is more evidently feminine. These are also facts which an adolescent can misunderstand.

Sometimes a child, badly prepared for adult life, feels himself in a panic at the approach of the problems of occupation, social life and society, love and marriage. He loses all hope of ability to meet them. With regard to society, he is bashful and reserved, he isolates himself and stays at home. With regard to occupation, he can find no work that attracts him and is sure that he would be a failure in everything. With regard to love and marriage, he is embarrassed with the other sex and scared at meeting them. If he is spoken to, he blushes; he cannot find words to reply. Every day he is in deeper and deeper despair. At last he is completely blocked towards all the problems of life and no one can understand him any longer. He does not look at others, speak to them, or listen to them. He does not work or study. He is always engaged in fantasy. Only a shabby remainder of sex activity is left. This is insanity, *dementia præcox;* but the whole insanity is a mistake. If it is possible to encourage such a child, to prove that he is not on the right path and to point out to him a better one, he can be cured. It is not easy, for the whole life and the whole life's training must be corrected. The meaning of past, present and future must be seen in a scientific light, not in the light of private intelligence.

All the dangers of adolescence come from a lack of proper training and equipment before the three problems of life. If the children are afraid of the future, it is natural enough that they should try to meet it by the methods which call for least effort. These easy ways, however, are the useless ways. The more such a child is ordered about, exhorted and criticized, the stronger becomes his impression that he is standing before an abyss. The more we push him, the more he tries to draw back. Unless we can encourage him, every effort to help him will be a mistake and will damage him still further. While he is so pessimistic and so frightened, we cannot expect that he should feel he can afford additional efforts.

A few children at this time wish to remain children; they even speak in baby talk, play with children younger than themselves, and pretend that they can remain infantile forever. By far the great majority make some sort of attempt to behave in an adult fashion. If they are not really courageous, they offer a sort of caricature of the adult: they imitate the gestures of men, like to spend money freely, begin flirtations and have love affairs. In more difficult cases, where a boy does not see his way to meet the problems of life yet keeps a certain degree of activity, he begins to embark on a criminal career. This is especially likely if he has already committed delinquencies without being found out and thinks that he can be clever enough to avoid detection again. Crime is one of the easy escapes before the problems of life, and especially before the problem of economics and livelihood. So it happens that between the ages of fourteen and twenty there is a great increase in the number of delinquents. Here again, we are not facing a new development; but greater pressure has revealed the flaws already present in the childhood pattern.

If the degree of activity is smaller, the easy way of escape is neurosis; and it is between these ages, also, that many children begin to suffer from functional diseases and nervous disorders. Every neurotic symptom is designed to provide a justification for a refusal to solve the problems of life, without lowering the sense of personal superiority. Neurotic symptoms appear when an individual is confronted by social problems which he is not prepared to meet in a social way. The difficulty provides a great tension. During adolescence the physical condition is especially responsive to such tensions, and all the organs can be irritated, the whole nervous system affected. This irritation of the organs can again be used as an excuse for hesitation and failure. An individual in such a case now begins to regard himself, privately and before others, as free from responsibility because of his suffering; and the structure of a neurosis is complete. Every neurotic professes the best of intentions. He is quite convinced of the necessity for social feeling and for meeting the problems of life. Only in his case is there an exception to this universal demand. What excuses him is the neurosis itself. His whole attitude says, " I am anxious to solve all my problems, but unfortunately I am prevented." In this he differs from the criminal, whose professions of bad intentions are often quite open and whose social feeling is concealed and suppressed. It is difficult to decide which offers the greater injury to human welfare, the neurotic whose motives are so good, but whose actions apart from these good motives would seem spiteful, egotistic and designed to hold up the coöperation of his fellows; or the criminal, whose hostility is so much more open and who takes pains to subdue the relics of his social feeling.

A great number of failures in adolescence come from the pampered children; and it is easy to see that the approach of adult responsibilities is an especial strain to the children who have been accustomed to have everything done for them by their parents. They still wish to be pampered, but as they grow older they find that they are no longer the center of attention. They reproach life for having deceived and failed them; they have been brought up in an artificially warm atmosphere and the air outside feels bitterly cold. At this time we find apparent reversals of progress. The children of whom most was expected begin to fail in their studies and their work; and children who had previously seemed less gifted begin to overtake them and to reveal unsuspected abilities. It is no contradiction to the previous history. Perhaps a child who was very promising now begins to feel afraid of disappointing the expectations with which he has been burdened. So long as he was helped and appreciated he could go forward; but when the time comes to make independent efforts his courage fails and he retreats. Others are stimulated by their new freedom. They see the road towards the fulfillment of their ambitions clear before them. They are full of new ideas and new projects. Their creative life is intensified and their interest in all the aspects of our human process becomes more vivid and eager. These are the children who have kept their courage, and to whom independence means, not difficulty and the risk of defeat, but wider opportunity to make achievements and contributions.

The children who have previously felt slighted and neglected now, perhaps, when they are more widely connected with their fellows, conceive the hope that they can find appreciation. Many of them are completely hypnotized by this craving for appreciation. It is dangerous enough for a boy if he is only looking for praise; but girls have often less self-confidence and see in the appreciation of others the only way of proving their worth. Such girls easily fall a prey to men who understand how to flatter them. I have often found girls who felt unappreciated at home beginning to have sex relations, not merely to prove that they are grown-up, but because they hope, by this means, to achieve at last a position in which they are appreciated and the center of attention.

Let me take an instance: a girl fifteen years of age came from a very poor family. She had an older brother who, during her childhood, was always sickly. The mother was forced to devote a good deal of attention to him, and when her daughter was born the mother could not give much care to her. In addition, during her early childhood, her father was ill: and his sickness further curtailed the time that her mother could afford her.

Thus the girl was able to notice and understand what it means to be cared for; it was always her desire to achieve this position, but she could not find it in the family. A younger sister was born; and at this time the father recovered and the mother was free to devote herself to the baby. In consequence, the girl whom we are considering felt that she was the only one who had no love and affection. She continued to struggle; was good at home and the best pupil in her school. Because of her success, it was proposed that she should keep on with her studies; and she was sent to a high school where the teacher did not know her. At first, she could not understand the methods of instruction at the new school. Her work began to fall off, her teacher criticized her and she became steadily discouraged. She was too eager for quick appreciation. When she could not be appreciated either at home or at school, what was left?

She looked around for a man who would appreciate her. After a few experiences, she went away and lived with a man for fourteen days. The family was very much worried on her account and tried to find her; but we could predict what would happen. Soon she would discover that she was still not appreciated for herself alone and begin to repent of the episode. Suicide was her next thought and the girl sent a note home, " Do not worry. I have taken poison. I am quite happy." As a matter of fact, she had not taken poison and we can understand why. Her parents were really kind to her and she felt that she could attract their sympathy. In consequence, she did not commit suicide, but waited until her mother came and found her and took her home. If the girl had known what we know, that all her striving was towards appreciation, these difficulties would not have occurred. If the teacher at the high school had understood, this, too, would have prevented them. Previously, the girl's school reports had always been excellent; and if he had seen that the girl was sensitive on this point and needed a little more careful treatment, her position would not have discouraged her.

In another case, a girl was born into a family where both father and mother were weak in character. The mother had always wanted boys and was disappointed at the arrival of a girl. She undervalued the part of women and her daughter was bound to feel it. More than once she overheard her mother say to her father, " The girl is not at all attractive. No one will like her when she grows up "; or, " Whatever shall we do with her when she is older? " After she had been ten years in this poisonous atmosphere she found a letter from one of her mother's friends, consoling her for having had a daughter and saying that since she was still young she was still able to have a son.

We can imagine how the girl felt. A few months later she went to the country to visit an uncle. While she was there she met a country boy of a low degree of intelligence and became his sweetheart. He left her but she continued in the same direction. When I saw her, she had already amassed a great collection of lovers; but in none of her affairs had she felt properly appreciated. She came to me because she was now suffering from anxiety neurosis and could not go out by herself. Dissatisfied by one way of gaining appreciation, she had tried another. She began to worry the family with her pains and sufferings. No one could do anything unless she gave her permission. She wept, threatened to commit suicide, and tyrannized over the whole house. It was hard work to make the girl see her position and to convince her that in her adolescence she had overemphasized the necessity of finding a way to escape the feeling of not being appreciated.

Both girls and boys often overvalue and exaggerate

sexual relations in their adolescence. They wish to prove that they are grown-up, and they go too far. If a girl, for example, is fighting with her mother and always believes that she is being suppressed, she will frequently, as a protest, have sexual relations with any man she meets. She does not care if the mother knows or not; indeed, she is completely happy if she can worry her. So I have often found that a girl, after a quarrel with her mother, and perhaps with her father too, runs out into the street and has relations with the first man she finds. These were girls that were always supposed to be good girls, well brought up, the last people of whom such conduct would be expected. We can understand that the girls are not really guilty. They are wrongly prepared; they have felt themselves in an inferior situation; and this is the only way by which they could conceive that they could achieve a stronger position.

Many girls who have been pampered find it difficult to adjust themselves to their feminine rôle. There is always the impression in our culture that men are superior to women; and in consequence they dislike the thought of being women. Now they reveal what I have called " the masculine protest." The masculine protest can express itself in many varieties of behavior. Sometimes we see only a dislike and avoidance of men. Sometimes they like men well enough but are embarrassed with them and cannot speak to them, do not want to join in gatherings where men are present, and feel generally ill at ease before the sexual problem. Often they insist that they are eager to marry when they are older, but they make no approach to members of the other sex and form no friendships with them. Sometimes we find a dislike of the feminine rôle expressed more actively in adolescence. Girls will behave more boyishly than before. They will wish to imitate boys and will find it easier to imitate them in their vices, in smoking, drinking, swearing, joining gangs and displaying their sexual freedom.

Often they explain that boys would not be interested in them if they behaved in any other way. Where the dislike of the feminine rôle is still further developed, we find the appearance of homosexuality or other perversions and of prostitution. From their early life all prostitutes have had the firm conviction that nobody likes them. They believe that they were born for a lower rôle and that they could never win the real affection or interest of any man. We can understand in these circumstances how they are inclined to throw themselves away, to depreciate their sexual rôle and to regard it only as a means for making money. This dislike of the feminine rôle does not arise during adolescence. We could always find that the girl, from her first childhood, had disliked being a girl; but in her childhood she had not the same need or opportunities for expressing her dislike.

It is not girls only who suffer from a " masculine protest ", but all children who overvalue the importance of being masculine see masculinity as an ideal and are dubious whether they are strong enough to achieve it. In this way, the stress put upon masculinity in our culture can be as difficult for boys as for girls; especially if they are not entirely convinced of their sexual rôle. Many children grow up to be quite old with the half belief that some time or other their sex can be changed; and it is important that from the age of two that children should know quite definitely whether they are boys or girls. Often a boy

who has a rather girlish appearance has a particularly
difficult time. Strangers will sometimes mistake his sex;
and even friends of the family will say to him, " You
ought really to have been a girl." Such a child is very
likely to take his appearance as a sign of insufficiency and
to regard the problem of love and marriage as a test too
severe for him. Boys who are not sure that they can acquit
themselves well in their sexual rôle often, during adolescence, tend to imitate girls, to become effeminate and to
take on the vices of girls who have been pampered, show
themselves coquettish, pose, and cultivate a temperament.

Even the preparation for the attitude to the other sex
has its roots set in the first four or five years of life. The
sex drive is evident in the first weeks of babyhood; but
nothing should be done which can stimulate it before it
can be given an appropriate expression. If it is not stimulated its appearances will be natural and need cause us no
alarm. We should not be afraid, for example, when we
see in a baby's first year of life some signs of local irritation; but we should use our influence to coöperate with
the child and interest it less in its own person and more in
its environment. It is another case if these attempts at
self-gratification cannot be stopped. Then we can be sure
that the child has intentions of his own: he is not the victim of the sex drive but he is making use of it for his
own purposes. Generally, the aim of little children is to
gain attention. They feel that their parents are afraid and
horrified and they know how to play on their feelings.
If their habits no longer serve their purpose of attract-
ing attention, they will give them up.

I have remarked that children should not be physically
stimulated. Often parents are very affectionate with their

children and their children affectionate with them. To increase the affection of the children they are always hug-
ging them and kissing them. They know that this is not
the right way. They should not be so cruel. They should
not stimulate the affections of the child. Nor should a
child be stimulated mentally. Children have often told
me, and adults in recalling their childhood have told me,
of the feelings roused when they discovered some frivol-
ous picture in their father's library or by some motion
picture they have seen. It is better for them not to find
such books or see such films. If we avoid stimulating children, no difficulties can occur.

Another form of stimulation, to which we have already
referred, is the insistence on giving children quite unnecessary and inappropriate sexual information. Many adults
seem to have a perfect craze for imparting sexual information; and are horribly afraid of the dangers of any
one's growing up in ignorance. If we look into our own
pasts and into the histories of others, we shall not find
such catastrophes as they expect. It is better to wait until
the child himself becomes curious and wants to know
something. If the parents are interested, they will understand the child's curiosity even if he does not speak. If
he feels that they are comrades, he will ask and he should
be answered in a manner in which he can understand and
assimilate the information.

It is good, also, that parents should avoid showing expressions of affection to each other before the children. If
it is possible, the children should not sleep in the same
room with the parents, let alone in the same bed; and it
is also advisable that they should not sleep in the same
room with a sister or brother. Parents must be attentive

to their children's development and should not hoodwink themselves. If they are not acquainted with the characters and striving of their children, they will never know where they are being influenced or in what way.

There is an almost universal superstition that adolescence is a very special and peculiar time. Generally the periods of human development are given a heightened private meaning and taken as if they were complete changes. Such, for example, is the attitude of most people to the climacteric. These phases are not changes, however; they are only a continuation of life and their phenomena have no critical importance. What is important is what the individual expects in such a phase, the meaning he gives it and the way he has trained to face it. People are often startled at the appearance of adolescence and act as if they had seen a ghost. If we understand that condition rightly, we shall see that children are not affected at all by the facts of adolescence, except in so far as the social conditions call for a new adaptation from their style of life. Often, however, they believe that adolescence is the end of everything; all their worth and value is lost. They have no right any longer to coöperate and contribute: nobody wants them any more. It is from such feelings that all the difficulties of adolescence develop.

If the child has been trained to feel himself an equal member of society and to understand his task of contribution, and especially if he has been trained to regard members of the other sex as comrades and equals, adolescence will give him only an opportunity to begin his creative and independent solution of the adult problems of life. If he feels on a lower level than others, if he suffers from a mistaken view of his circumstances, in adolescence it will appear that he is not well prepared for freedom. If some one is always present to compel him to do what is necessary he can accomplish it. If he is left to himself he is timid and he fails. Such a child would be well adapted for slavery, but in freedom he is lost.

CHAPTER IX

Crime and Its Prevention

Through Individual Psychology we begin to understand all the various types of human beings; and, after all, human beings are not so remarkably different from one another. We find the same kind of failure exhibited in criminals as in problem children, neurotics, psychotics, suicides, drunkards and sexual perverts. They all fail in their approach to the problems of life; and, in one very definite and noticeable point, they fail in precisely the same way. Every one of them fails in social interest. They are not concerned with their fellow beings. Even here, however, we cannot distinguish them as if they were in contradiction to other people. No one can be held up as an example of perfect coöperation or perfect social feeling; and the failures of criminals are only a severer degree of common failures.

One other point is necessary for the understanding of criminals; but in this point they are just like the rest of us. We all wish to overcome difficulties. We are all striving to reach a goal in the future by attaining which we shall feel strong, superior, complete. Professor Dewey refers to this tendency, very rightly, as the striving for security. Others call it the striving for self-preservation. But, whatever name we give it, we shall always find in human beings this great line of activity — the struggle to rise from an inferior position to a superior position, from defeat to victory, from *below* to *above*. It begins in our earliest childhood; it continues to the end of our lives. Life means to go on existing on the crust of this planet, to surmount obstacles and overcome difficulties. We should not be surprised, therefore, when we discover exactly the same tendency among criminals. In all the criminal's actions and attitudes, he shows that he is struggling to be superior, to solve problems, to overcome difficulties. What distinguishes him is not the fact that he is striving in this fashion: it is rather the direction his striving takes. And as soon as we see that it takes this direction because he has not understood the demands of social life and is not concerned with his fellow beings, we shall find his actions quite intelligible.

I want to stress this point very strongly, because there are people who think otherwise. They regard criminals as exceptions to the human race, not like ordinary people at all. Some scientists for example, assert that all criminals are feeble-minded. Others put great emphasis on heredity; they believe that a criminal is born wrong and cannot help committing crimes. Still others hold that crime is something unalterably fixed by the environment: once a criminal always a criminal! Now much evidence can be brought against all these opinions; and we should realize, also, that if we accepted them we should be deprived of the hope of handling the problem of crime. In our own days we want to get rid of this human disaster. We know from the whole of history that crime has always been a disaster; but now we are anxious to do something about it and we can never be content to shelve the problem by saying, " It is all heredity, and nothing much can be done."

There is no compulsion either in environment or in

heredity. Children of the same family and the same environment can develop in different ways. Sometimes a criminal springs from a family of irreproachable record. Sometimes in a family of very bad record, with frequent experiences of prisons and reformatories, we find children of good character and behavior. It happens, too, that some criminals improve in later life; and the psychologists of crime have often been puzzled to explain how a burglar, after he has reached the age of thirty, may settle down and become a good citizen. If crime is an inborn defect, or if it is unalterably built in by the environment, this fact is quite beyond understanding. From our own point of view, however, we can understand it very well. The individual is in a more favorable situation, perhaps; there are fewer demands on him, and the mistakes in his style of living are no longer brought to the surface. Or perhaps he has already gained what he wanted. Perhaps, finally, he is growing older and fatter, less suited for a criminal career: his joints are stiff and he can't climb so well: burglary has become too hard for him.

Before I go any further I wish to exclude the idea that criminals are insane. There are psychotics who commit crimes, but their crimes are of quite a different kind. We cannot hold them responsible: their crimes are a result of a complete failure to understand them and a wrong method of treating them. In the same way we must exclude the feeble-minded criminal, who is really no more than a tool. The true criminals are those who plan the crime. They paint glowing pictures of the prospects, they excite the fancy or the ambitions of feeble-minded individuals; then they hide themselves and leave their victims to execute the crime and run the risk of punishment. The same thing holds, of course, when younger people are made use of by old and experienced criminals. It is the experienced criminal who plans the crime; children are deluded into being the executants.

Now let us return to the great line of activity I have mentioned: the line by which every criminal — and every other human being — is striving to gain a victory, to reach a position of finality. There is much difference and variety in these goals; and we find that the goal of a criminal is always to be superior in a private and personal manner. What he is striving for contributes nothing to others. He is not coöperative. Society needs of its members, we all need of each other, a common usefulness, an ability to coöperate. The goal of a criminal does not include this usefulness to society; and this is the really significant aspect of every criminal career. We shall see later how this comes about. At this moment I want to make clear that the main point to find, if we want to understand a criminal, is the degree and nature of his failure in coöperation. Criminals differ in their ability to coöperate; some of them fail less seriously than others. Some, for example, confine themselves to small crimes and do not go beyond these limits. Others prefer major crimes. Some are leaders, others followers. In order to understand the varieties in criminal careers we must examine further the individual style of life.

The style of life typical of an individual is built up very early; we can already find its main features at the age of four or five. We cannot suppose, therefore, that it is an easy matter to change it. It is a man's own personality; it can be changed only by understanding the mistakes he made in building it up. We can begin to see, therefore, how it happens that many criminals, although they have been punished many times, often humiliated and despised and deprived of every good that our social life can offer, still do not reform, but commit the same crime over and over again. It is not economic difficulty that forces them into crime. Truly enough, if times are hard and people are more burdened, crimes increase. Statistics show that sometimes the number of crimes increases in accordance with a rise in the price of wheat. This is no sign, however, that the economic situation causes the crime. It is much more a sign that many people are limited in their behavior. There are limits to their capacity for coöperation, and when these limits are reached they can no longer contribute. They lose the last remnant of coöperation and have recourse to crimes. From other facts, too, we discover that there are plenty of people who in favorable situations are not criminals, but, if a problem arises for which they are not prepared, it turns out that they, also, can commit crimes. It is the style of life, the method of facing problems, which is important.

After all these experiences in Individual Psychology, we can at last make clear a very simple point. A criminal is not interested in others. He can coöperate only to a certain degree. When this degree is exhausted, he turns to crime. The exhaustion occurs when a problem is too difficult for him. It is interesting to consider the problems of life which we all of us have to face, the problems which a criminal cannot succeed in solving. It will appear, in the end, that we have no problems in our lives but social problems; and these problems can only be solved if we are interested in others.

Individual Psychology has taught us to make three

broad divisions in the problems of life. First let us take the problems of relationship to other men, the problems of comradeship. Criminals can sometimes have friends, but only among their own kind. They can form gangs and they can even show loyalty to one another. But we see here immediately how they have decreased their sphere of activity. They cannot make friends with society at large, with ordinary people. They treat themselves as a body of exiles and do not understand how to feel at home with their fellow men.

The second group of problems includes all those which are connected with occupation. A great number of criminals, if they are questioned about these problems, reply, " You don't know the terrible conditions of labor." They find work terrible; they are not inclined, as others are, to struggle with these difficulties. A useful occupation implies an interest in other people and a contribution to their welfare; but this is exactly what we miss in the criminal personality. This lack of the spirit of coöperation appears early, and most criminals, therefore, are ill prepared to meet the problems of occupation. The great majority of criminals are *untrained and unskilled workers*. If you trace back their history you will find that at school and even before school there was a block here, a stoppage of interest. They never learned to coöperate. Now coöperation must be taught and trained, and these criminals were not trained in coöperation. If they fail before the problems of occupation, therefore, we cannot hold them guilty. We must look on it in nearly the same way as if we were testing a person in geography who had never learned geography. He would either give a wrong answer or no answer at all.

The third group includes all the problems of love. A good and fruitful love life calls equally for interest in the other person and for coöperation. It is revealing to observe that half the criminals who are sent to reformatories are suffering from venereal diseases on their entrance. This would tend to show that they wanted an easy way out for the problems of love. They regard the partner in love merely as a piece of property and very often we find them thinking that love can be bought. Sex life is to such people a matter of conquest and acquisition; it is something they ought to possess, not a partnership in life. " What is the use of life," many criminals say, " if I am not given everything I want? "

We can see, now, where we should begin in our treatment of criminals. We must train them to be coöperative. Nothing much is done if we just stick them in reformatories. Leaving them free is a danger to society and under present conditions it cannot be discussed. Society must be saved from criminals — but that is by no means all. We must think also: " They are not prepared for social life; what shall we do with them? " This lack of coöperation in all the problems of life is no small deficiency. We need coöperation at every moment of the day; and the degree of our ability to coöperate shows itself in the way we look and speak and listen. If I am right in my observations, criminals look and speak and listen in a different way from other people. They have a different language and we can understand that the development of their intelligence is handicapped by this difference. When we speak we intend that everybody should understand us. Understanding itself is a social factor; we give words a common interpretation; we understand in the same way that any one else

might understand. With criminals it is different; they have
a private logic, a private intelligence. We can observe this
in the way they explain their crimes. They are not stupid
or feeble-minded. For the most part they conclude quite
rightly, if we grant them their goal of a fictitious personal
superiority. A criminal will say, " I saw a man who had
nice trousers, and I hadn't; so I had to kill him." Now if
we grant him that his desires are all important, and that
there is no call for him to make a living in a useful way,
his conclusion is intelligent enough; but it is not common
sense. There has recently been a court case in Hungary.
A number of women had committed many murders by
poison. When one of them was sent to prison she said,
" My boy was sick and a loafer and I had to poison him."
If she excludes coöperation, what is left for her to do?
She is intelligent, but she has a different way of looking
at things, a different scheme of apperception. We can understand, then, how criminals, if they see attractive things
and want to obtain them in an easy way, conclude that they
must take them from this hostile world, in which they are
not at all interested. They are suffering from a wrong outlook upon the world, a wrong estimate of their own importance and the importance of other people.

But this is not the most noteworthy point in considering their lack of coöperation. All criminals are cowards.
They are evading problems they do not feel strong
enough to solve. We can see their cowardice apart from
their crimes, in the way in which they face life. We can
see their cowardice, also, in the crimes they commit. They
guard themselves by darkness and isolation; they surprise
somebody and draw their weapons before he can defend
himself. Criminals think they are being courageous; but

we should not be fooled in the same way. Crime is a coward's imitation of heroism. They are striving for a fictitious goal of personal superiority and they like to believe that they are heroes; but this is again a mistaken scheme of apperception, a failure of common sense. We know that they are cowards, and if they were sure we knew it, it would be a big shock to them. It swells their vanity and pride to think of themselves as overcoming the police, and often they think, "I can never be found out." Unfortunately, a very careful investigation of the career of every criminal would reveal, I believe, that he had committed crimes without being found out; and this fact is a very great nuisance. When they *are* found out, they think, "This time I wasn't quite clever enough, but next time I shall outwit them." And if they do get away with it, they feel they have obtained their goal; they feel superior, they are admired and appreciated by their comrades.

We must disturb this common estimate of the criminal's courage and cleverness; but when are we to disturb it? We can do it in the family, in the school, and in reformatories. Later on I shall describe the best point of attack; at present I want to go further into the circumstances in which a failure in coöperation may occur. Sometimes we must put the responsibility on the parents. Perhaps the mother was not skillful enough to draw the child to coöperate with herself: she was so infallible that no one could help her, or she was incapable of coöperation herself. It is easy to see that in unhappy or broken marriages the coöperative spirit is not being properly developed. The child's first tie is with his mother, and the mother, perhaps, did not wish to widen the child's social interest to include the father and other children or grown-ups. Or, again, the child may have felt himself to be the boss of the family; when he is three or four years old, another child comes along and the first one feels that he has suffered a reverse, has been ousted from his position; he refuses to coöperate with his mother or with the younger child. These are all factors to be considered; and, if you trace back the life of a criminal, you will almost always find that the trouble began in his early family experiences. It was not the environment itself that counted; but the child misunderstood his position and there was no one there by his side to explain it to him.

It is always a difficulty for the other children if one child in the family is especially prominent or gifted. Such a child gains most attention and the others feel discouraged and thwarted. They do not coöperate, because they wish to compete but have not enough confidence. We can often see the unhappy development of children who have been outshone in this way, and have not been shown how they themselves could use their own capabilities. Amongst them we may find criminals, neurotics or suicides.

When a child who is lacking in coöperation goes to school, we can notice it in his behavior on the very first day. He cannot make friends with the other children. He does not like the teacher, he is inattentive and does not listen to the lessons. If he is not treated with understanding, he can suffer a new setback. He is reproached and scolded, instead of being encouraged and taught coöperation. No wonder he finds the lessons still more distasteful! He cannot be interested in his school life, if he is all the time suffering new attacks on his courage and self-confidence. Often in the career of a criminal you will find that at the age of thirteen he was in the fourth grade and he was blamed for his stupidity. His whole later life is thus endangered. He loses progressively more and more of his interest in others; his goal is put more and more on the useless side.

Poverty, also, offers opportunities for a mistaken interpretation of life. A child who comes from a poor home may meet social prejudice outside the home. His family suffers many deprivations, they have many trials and sorrows. He himself, perhaps, has to earn money very early in life to help out his parents. Later he comes across rich people who lead an easy life and can buy everything they want; and he feels they have no more right to indulgence than he has. It is not hard to understand why the number of criminals is so high in the big cities, where there are very noticeable extremes of poverty and luxury. No useful goal ever came from envy; but a child in these circumstances can easily misunderstand and think that the way to superiority is to get money without working for it.

The feeling of inferiority can also be centered round an organic deficiency. This was one of my own discoveries; and I am a little guilty, on this point, of having paved the way to theories of heredity both in neurology and psychiatry. But even in the beginning, when I first wrote of organ inferiorities and their mental compensations, I recognized this danger. It is not the organism which is to blame, but our methods of education. If we used the right method, children with organic deficiencies would be interested in others as well as themselves. A child burdened with imperfect organs is only interested in himself alone if nobody is at his side to develop his interest in others. There are many people suffering from endocrine deficiencies, but I should like to make clear that we can never say, once and for all, what the normal functioning of an endocrine gland should be. The functioning of our endocrine glands can be very various without damage to the personality. This factor must therefore be excluded; especially if we want to find the right method for making these children also into good fellow men, with a coöperative interest in other people.

Among criminals there is a large proportion of orphans; and it seems to me a disgrace to our culture that we could not establish the spirit of coöperation in these orphans. In a similar way there are many illegitimate children — no one was present who could win their affection and transfer it to their fellow beings. Unwanted children often take to criminal practices, especially if they know and feel that nobody wanted them. Among criminals, also, we often find ugly persons; and this fact has been used as evidence of the importance of heredity. But think what it feels like to be an ugly child! He is at a great disadvantage. Perhaps he is the child of a race mixture which does not give attractive results, or which meets with social prejudice. If such a child is ugly, his whole life is overburdened: he does not possess what we all like so much,— the charm and freshness of childhood. But all these children, if they were treated in the right way, would develop social interest.

It is interesting to observe, moreover, that we sometimes find among criminals boys and men who are unusually handsome. While the first type might be considered as victims of bad hereditary traits, transferred together with physical stigmata — deformed hands, for example, or cleft palate — what are we to say of these handsome criminals? In reality, they, too, have grown up in a situation where it was difficult to develop social interest; they were pampered children. You will find that criminals are divided into two types. There are those who do not know that there is fellow-feeling in the world and have never experienced it. Such a criminal has a hostile attitude to other people; his look is hostile and he regards everybody as an enemy; he has never been able to find appreciation. The other type is the pampered child; and I have frequently noticed, in the complaints of prisoners, that they assert, " The reason for my criminal career was that my mother pampered me too much." On this point we should say much more; but I mention it here just to emphasize that, in various ways, criminals have not been trained and taught into the right degree of coöperation. The parents may have wanted to make their child into a good fellow man, but they did not know how. If they were dictatorial and severe, they had no chance of succeeding. If they pampered him and let him take the center of the stage, he was taught to consider himself important through the mere fact of his existence, without making any creative effort to deserve the good opinion of his fellows. Such children, therefore, lose the ability to struggle; they want always to have notice taken of them and are always expecting something. If they do not find an easy way to satisfaction, they blame the environment for it.

Now let us turn to some cases and see whether we can discover these points, in spite of the fact that the descriptions were not written for this purpose. The first case I shall give is from " 500 Criminal Careers " by Sheldon and Eleanor T. Glueck; the case of " Hard-boiled John." This boy explains the genesis of his criminal career:

I never thought I would let myself go. Up to fifteen or sixteen I was about like other kids. I liked athletics and took part in them. I read books from the library, kept good hours, and all that. My parents took me out of school and put me to work and took all of my wages except fifty cents each week.

Here he is making an accusation. If we questioned him about his relation to his parents, and if we could see his whole family situation, we could find out what he really experienced. At present we must regard it only as an affirmation that his parents were not coöperative.

I worked about a year, then I began going with a girl and she liked a good time.

We find this often in the careers of criminals: they attach themselves to a girl who wants a good time. Recall what we mentioned before — this is a problem and tests the degree of coöperation. He goes with a girl who wants a good time and he has only fifty cents a week. We should not call this a true solution for the problem of love. There are other girls, for example. He is not on the right track. In these circumstances I should say, " If she wants a good time she is not the girl for me." These are different estimates of what is important in life.

You can't give a girl a good time these days, even in N——, on fifty cents a week. The old man wouldn't give me any more. I was sore and had it on my mind: how could I make more money?

Common sense would say, " Perhaps you could look around and earn more "; but he wants it easy, and if he wishes to have a girl it is for his own pleasure and nothing more.

One day along came a fellow I got acquainted with.

When a stranger comes along, it is another test for him. A boy with the right ability for coöperation could not be seduced. This boy is on a path which makes it possible for him to be seduced.

He was a " right guy " [that is, a good thief; an intelligent, capable fellow who knows the business, and will " divvy with you and not do you dirt "]. We put through a lot of jobs in N—— and got away with it, and I have been at it ever since.

We hear that the parents own their own home. The father is foreman in a factory and the family is only just able to make ends meet. This boy is one of three children; and up to the time of his misconduct no member of the family had been known to be delinquent. I should be curious to hear a scientist believing in heredity explain this case. He admits having first had heterosexual experience at the age of fifteen. I am sure some people would say that he is oversexed. But this boy has no interest in other people and only wants pleasure. Anybody can oversex himself. There is no difficulty in it. He is searching for appreciation in this respect — he wants to be a sexual hero. At sixteen he was arrested with a companion for breaking and entering and larceny. Other points of interest follow and confirm what we have said. He wants to be a conqueror in appearances, to attract the attention of girls, to win them by paying for them. He wears a wide-brimmed hat, red bandanna handkerchief, and a belt with a revolver in it. He assumes the name of a Western outlaw. He is a vain boy: he wants to appear a hero and has no other way. He admits having done whatever he was accused of,

" and a lot more." He has no scruples about property rights.

I do not think that life is worth living. For humanity in general I have nothing but the utmost contempt.

All these conscious thoughts are really unconscious. He does not understand them; he does not know what they mean in their coherence. He feels that life is a burden, but he does not understand why he is discouraged.

I have learned not to trust people. They say thieves won't do each other, but they will. I was with a fellow once, treated him white; and he did me dirt.

If I had all the money I wanted, I would be just as honest as anybody. That is, if I had enough so I could do what I wanted to without working. I never liked work. I hate it and never will work.

We can translate this last point as follows: " It is repression which is responsible for my career. I am compelled to repress my wishes and therefore I am a criminal." It is a point deserving much thought.

I have never committed a crime for the sake of doing the crime. Of course there is a certain " kick " in driving up to a place in an automobile, putting through your job, and making your get-away.

He believes it is heroism and does not see it is cowardice.

When I was caught before at one time I had fourteen thousand dollars' worth of jewellery, but I didn't know any better than to go and see my girl, and cashed in only enough to pay my expenses to go to her, and they caught me.

These people pay their girls and so gain an easy victory. But they think of it as a real triumph.

They have schools here in the prison and I am going to get all the education I can get — not to reform myself, but to make myself more dangerous to society.

This is the expression of a very bitter attitude toward mankind. But he does not want mankind. He says:

If I had a son I would wring his neck. Do you think I would ever be guilty of bringing a human being into the world?

Now how are we going to improve such a person? There is no other way than to improve his capacity for coöperation and to show him where his estimate of life is mistaken. We can convince him only when we trace back the misunderstandings of his earliest childhood. I do not know what happened in this case. The description is not occupied with the points which I believe important. Something happened in his childhood that made him such an enemy of mankind. If I had to guess, I would suggest that he was the eldest boy; very much pampered at first, as oldest children generally are. Later on, he felt dethroned because another child was born. If I am right, you will find that things as small as this can block the development of coöperation.

John remarks further that he was treated roughly at an industrial school to which he was committed and he left this school with a feeling of intense hatred toward society. I must say something on this point. From the psychologist's standpoint, all harsh treatment in prison is a challenge. It is a trial of strength. In the same way, when criminals continually hear, " We must put an end to this crime wave ", they take it as a challenge. They want to be heroes, and they are pleased to have the gauge thrown down to them. They take it as a sport: they feel that society is daring them and continue all the more stubbornly. If a man thinks he is fighting the whole world, what could give him a bigger " kick " than to be challenged? In the education of problem children, too, it is one of the worst errors to challenge them: " We'll see who is stronger! We'll see who can hold out longest! " These children, like criminals, are intoxicated with the idea of being strong; and they know they can get away with it if they are clever enough. In reformatories they sometimes challenge the criminals; and this is a very mischievous policy.

Now let me give you the diary of a murderer who was hanged for his crime. He cruelly murdered two people and before he did it he wrote down his intentions. This will afford me an opportunity of describing the kind of planning which goes on in the criminal's mind. No one can commit a crime without planning it; and into the planning there always enters a justification of the deed. In all the literature of such confessions I have never found an instance where the crime was described quite simply and distinctly, and I have never found an instance where the criminal did not try to justify himself. Here we see the importance of social feeling. Even the criminal must try to reconcile himself with social feeling. At the same time he must prepare himself to kill his social feeling, to break through the wall of social interest, before he can commit the crime. So in Dostoievsky's story, Raskolnikov lies in bed two months, considering whether he shall commit a crime. He drives himself on with the thought: "Am I Napoleon, or am I a louse?" Criminals deceive themselves and spur themselves on with such imaginations. In reality, every criminal knows that he is not on the useful side of life and he knows what the useful side is. He rejects it, however, out of cowardice; and he is cowardly because he has not the ability to be useful: the problems are problems demanding coöperation and he has not been trained in coöperation. Later in life criminals want to relieve themselves of their burden; they want, as we have shown, to justify themselves and plead extenuating circumstances. "He was sick and a loafer," and so forth.

Here are the extracts from the diary:

I was disowned by my people, the subject of disgust and contempt [he had an affection of the nose], almost destroyed by the greatness of my misery. There is nothing to keep me back. I feel I cannot bear it any longer. I might resign myself to my abandoned condition; but the stomach, the stomach can not be dictated to.

He produces the extenuating circumstances.

It was prophesied that I should die on the gallows; but the thought came to, "What is the difference whether I die of starvation or on the gallows?"

In one case the mother of a child prophesied: "I am sure that one day you will strangle me." When he was seventeen he strangled his aunt. A prophecy and a challenge act in the same way.

I am not concerned with the consequences. I have to die in any case. I am nothing, no one will have anything to do with me. The girl I want shrinks from me.

He wanted to allure this girl, but he had no grand clothes and no money. He looked on the girl as a piece of property. This was his solution of the problems of love and marriage.

It is all the same. I will procure my salvation or my ruin.

I will say here, though I wish I had more space for an explanation, that all these people like violent contradiction or antitheses. They are like children. It must be everything or nothing. " Starvation or gallows "; " Salvation or ruin."

Everything is planned for Thursday. The victim is chosen. I am awaiting my opportunity. When it comes it will be something that not everybody can do.

He is a hero to himself: " It is dreadful, and not everybody could do it." He took a knife and killed a man by surprise. Not everybody could do it!

As the shepherd drives his sheep, the stomach drives man to the darkest crime. Possibly I shall not see another day, but I do not care. The worst thing is to be tormented by hunger. I am embittered by an incurable illness. The last annoyance will come when they sit in judgment on me. A man must pay for his sins, but it is a better death than by starvation. If I die of hunger, no one will take notice of me. But now how many people will be there! and perhaps some one will be sorry for me. What I have resolved I shall have done. No man has ever been afraid as I have been afraid this night.

So he is not a hero after all, as he believes himself to be! Under cross-examination he said, " Although I did not hit on a vital part I have committed murder. I know

I am destined for the hangman: but the man had such. wonderful clothes and I knew I should never have clothes like them." He no longer says that the stomach is his reason; it is the clothes now that have become a fixed idea. " I did not know what I was doing," he pleaded. This you will always find, in one way or another. Sometimes criminals drink before their crimes, in order to be irresponsible. All this proves how hard they must struggle to break through the wall of social interest. In every description of a criminal career I believe I could show all the points I have brought out.

We are now really faced with the problem, what shall we do? What shall we do if I am right, and we can always find in the criminal career the striving for a fictitious personal superiority in an individual who is lacking in social interest and has not been trained in coöperation? With the criminal, as with the neurotic, we can do absolutely nothing, unless we can succeed in winning him for coöperation. I cannot stress this point too strongly: everything is secured if we can win the interest of the criminal for human welfare, if we can win his interest for other human beings, if we can train him for coöperation, if we can set him on the way towards solving the problems of life by coöperative means. If we fail to do this, we can do nothing. The task is not quite as simple as it looks. We cannot win him by making things easy for him, any more than by making them hard for him. We cannot win him by pointing out that he is wrong and arguing with him. His mind is made up. He has been seeing the world in this way for years. If we are to change him we must find the roots of his pattern. We must discover where his failures first began and the circumstances which provoked them. The main features of his personality had already been decided by the time he was four or five years old: by that time he had already made those mistakes in his estimate of himself and of the world which we see displayed in his criminal career; and it is these primitive mistakes which we must understand and correct. We must look for the first development of his attitude.

Later on, he turns everything which he experiences into a justification for his attitude; and if his experiences do not quite fit into his scheme he broods on them and licks them into shape until they are more amenable. If a man has the attitude, " Other people misuse me and humiliate me," he will find plenty of evidence to confirm him. He will be looking for such evidence and evidence on the other side will not be noticed. The criminal is interested only in himself and his own point of view. He has his own way of looking and listening and we can often see that he pays no attention to things which do not agree with his own interpretation of life. We cannot convince him, therefore, unless we can get behind all his interpretations, all his training in his own point of view, and discover the way in which his attitude first began.

This is one reason why corporal punishment is ineffective. The criminal sees it as a confirmation that society is hostile and impossible to coöperate with. Something of the same sort happened to him, perhaps, at school. He was not trained to coöperate and so he did his work badly, or misbehaved in class. He was reproached and punished. Now is that going to encourage him in coöperation? He feels only that the situation is still more hopeless. He feels that people are against him. Which of us would cultivate a liking for a place where we expected to be reproached and punished? The child loses his remainder of confidence. He is not interested in school tasks, or in his teachers, or in his schoolmates. He begins to play truant and to hide himself away where he cannot be discovered. In these places he finds other boys who have had the same experience and have taken the same road. They understand him; they do not reproach him; on the contrary they flatter him, play on his ambitions, and give him the hope of making his mark on the useless side of life. Of course, since he is not interested in the social demands of life, he takes them for his friends and society in general for his enemies. These people like him and he feels better among them. It is in this way that thousands of children join criminal gangs; and if in later life we treat them in the same fashion, they will find only new testimony that we are their enemies and only criminals are their friends.

There is no cause at all why such a child should be defeated by the tasks of life. We should never allow him to lose hope and we could stop it very easily if we organized our schools so that such children were given confidence and courage. We shall deal more fully with this proposal later: we are using this example at present to show how a criminal will interpret punishment only as a sign that society is against him, *as he always thought*.

Corporal punishment is ineffective for other reasons, also. Many criminals are not very fond of their lives. Some of them at certain moments of their lives are very near suicide. Corporal punishment does not terrify them. They can be so intoxicated by their desire to outdo the police that it does not even hurt them. This is part of their whole response to what they regard as a challenge.

If attendants are harsh, or if they are severely treated, they are put on their mettle to resist. This increases again their feeling of being cleverer than the police. As we have seen, they interpret everything in this fashion. They see their contact with society as a sort of continuous warfare, in which they are trying to gain the victory; and if we take it in the same way ourselves we are only playing into their hands. Even the electric chair can act as a challenge in this sense. The criminal conceives himself as playing against odds; and the higher the penalty, the greater is his desire to show his superior cunning. It is easy to prove that many criminals think of their crimes only in this way. A criminal who is condemned to be electrocuted will often spend his time considering how he might have avoided detection: " If only I had not left my spectacles behind! "

Our only remedy is to find out the block to coöperation which the criminal suffered in childhood. Here Individual Psychology has opened up for us the whole dark territory. We can see much clearer. By the age of five years a child's psyche is a unit: the threads of his personality have been drawn together. Heredity and environment contribute something to his development; but we are not so much concerned with what a child brings into the world, or with the experiences he encounters, as with the way he utilizes them, how he turns them to account and what he effects with them. It is all the more necessary that we should understand this point, since we really do not know anything of inherited abilities or disabilities. All we need consider is the possibilities of his situation, and the degree in which he has made full use of them.

The extenuating circumstance for all criminals is that they have a certain degree of coöperation, but not suffi-

cient for the demands of our social life; and on this point
the first responsibility rests with the mother. She must understand how to enlarge the bonds of this interest; how to
spread the interest in herself until it becomes an interest
in other people. She must behave in such a way that the
child can be interested in the whole of mankind and his
own whole future life. But perhaps the mother does not
want the child to be interested in any one else. Perhaps
she is unhappy in her marriage: the two parents do not
agree: they are considering divorce, or they are jealous
of each other. Perhaps, therefore, the mother wishes to
keep the child all to herself, spoils him and pampers him
and will not let him be independent of her. It is quite
obvious how limited the development of coöperation will
be in such circumstances.

Interest in other children is also very important for the
development of social interest. Sometimes if one child is
the mother's favorite, the other children are not very
much inclined to include him in their friendship and interest. When this circumstance is misunderstood, it can
serve as the starting point of a criminal career. If there is
one boy of outstanding gifts in a family, the boy next to
him is often a problem child. The second son, for example, is more amiable and charming, and his older
brother feels deprived of affection. It is easy for such a
child to deceive himself and intoxicate himself with the
feeling that he is neglected. He looks for evidence to
prove that his reproach is true. His behavior becomes
worse; he is treated with more severity; he finds a confirmation for his belief that he is thwarted and put in a
back seat. Because he feels deprived, he begins to steal;
he is found out and punished and now he has still more

testimony that he is not loved and that other people are his enemies.

When parents complain of bad times and bad circumstances before their children, they can conduce to a block in the development of social interest. The same thing can happen if they are always making accusations about their relatives or neighbors, always criticizing others and showing bad feeling and prejudice. It would be no wonder if the children grew up with a distorted view of what their fellow men were like; nor should we be surprised if in the end they turned against their parents too. Wherever the social interest is blocked, only an egoistic attitude is left. The child feels: " Why should I do anything for other people? "; and, as he cannot solve the problems of life in this frame of mind, he is bound to hesitate and look for an evasion and an easy way out. He finds it too difficult to struggle and he does not feel concerned if he hurts others. It is a warfare; and everything is fair in war!

Let me give you a few examples in which you can trace the development of the criminal pattern. In one family, the second son was a problem child; as far as we could see, he was quite healthy and had no hereditary disabilities. The oldest boy was the favorite, and the younger brother was always trying to catch him up in his achievements, as if he were running a race and trying to beat his pacemaker. His social interest was not developed — he depended very much on his mother and he wanted to get all he could out of her. He had a difficult task in trying to rival his older brother; his brother was at the top of his class in school and he himself was at the bottom. His desire to rule and dominate was very clearly shown. He used to give orders to an old maidservant in the house, march her around the room and drill her like a soldier. The maidservant was fond of him and she let him play at being a general even when he was twenty years of age. He was always worried and over-impressed by the things he had to accomplish; and at the same time he never accomplished anything. He could always get money from his mother when he was in a difficulty, though he was reproached and criticized for his conduct. Suddenly he married and increased all his difficulties. All he cared for, however, was that he had married before his elder brother; and he looked on this as a great triumph. This is witness that his estimate of himself was really very low — he wanted to be a conqueror in such ridiculous things. He was not at all well prepared for marriage and he and his wife always quarreled. When his mother could no longer afford to help him as much as she had done before, he ordered pianos and sold them without paying for them. This was what brought him to prison. In this history we can observe the roots in early childhood of his later career. He grew up overshadowed by an older brother, like a little tree overshadowed by a bigger one. He gathered the impression that he was slighted and neglected in comparison with his good-natured older brother.

Another example I will give is of a girl of twelve, very ambitious and spoiled by both her parents. She had a younger sister of whom she was very jealous and her rivalry showed itself both at home and at school. She was always trying to find instances in which her younger sister was preferred, obtained more candy or more money. One day she stole money from the pockets of her schoolmates, was found out and punished. Fortunately I was able to explain the whole situation to her and free her from the opinion that she could not compete with her younger sister. At the same time, I explained the circumstances to her family and they contrived to stop the rivalry and to avoid giving the impression that the younger sister was preferred. This happened twenty years ago. The girl is now a very honest woman, married, with a child of her own, and she has made no great mistakes in her life since that time.

We have already considered the situations in which the development of children is especially endangered; but I should like to recall them briefly at this point. We must emphasize them, since, if the findings of Individual Psychology are right, it is only by recognizing the effect of such situations on the criminal's outlook that we can really help him to coöperative activity. The three main types of children with special difficulties are: first, children with imperfect organs; secondly, pampered children; and thirdly, neglected children. Children with imperfect organs feel deprived of their birthright by nature, and, unless their interest in others is specially trained, they are apt to be more than usually preoccupied with themselves. They look for opportunities of ruling others, and I have seen a case where such a boy, feeling humiliated because a girl rejected his advances, persuaded a younger and more stupid boy to kill her. Pampered children remain anchored to the parents who spoil them — they cannot spread their interest to the rest of the world. No child is wholly neglected or it could not live through the first months of infancy; but we find children we may call neglected among orphans, illegitimate children, unwanted children, ugly and deformed children. It is easily understood that we find among criminals two main types — the Ugly-neglected and the Handsome-pampered.

I have tried among criminals with whom I have been in contact myself, and in the descriptions of crime I have read in books and newspapers, to find the structure of the criminal personality and I have always found that the key of Individual Psychology can give us an understanding of the circumstances. Let me choose a few further illustrations from an old German book by Anton von Feuerbach. I may remark in passing that it is often in old books that I have found the best descriptions of criminal psychology.

(1) The case of Conrad K., who murdered his father with the help of a servant. The father had neglected the boy, treated him cruelly, and mishandled the whole family. Once the boy struck back at him and his father brought him before the courts. The judge said: " You have a wicked and quarrelsome father and I can see no way out." You notice how the judge himself provided the boy with an excuse. The family tried in vain to find a remedy for their troubles. They were confronted with a difficult problem and in despair. The father took a woman of bad reputation to live with him and drove his son out of the house. The boy made the acquaintance of a day laborer who had a passion for putting out hens' eyes. The laborer counseled him to kill his father. He hesitated because of his mother; but the situation went from bad to worse. After long deliberations, the son agreed, and killed his father with the aid of the laborer. Here we see how the son was not able to spread his social interest even to a father. He was still deeply related to his mother and esteemed her highly. Before he could pierce through the

remainder of his social interest, he needed to have extenuating circumstances suggested. It was only when he gained support from the day laborer, with his passion for cruelty, that he could intoxicate himself into committing the crime.

(2) Margaret Zwanziger, called "the famous poison murderess." She was a charity child, in appearance small and deformed; therefore, as Individual Psychologists would say, stimulated to be vain and anxious to attract attention. She was grovelingly polite. After many adventures, which brought her nearly to despair, she tried three times to poison women in the hope of securing their husbands for herself. She felt deprived and could not think of any other way to " get her own back." She pretended pregnancy and attempted suicide in order to secure these men. In her autobiography (so many criminals delight to compose autobiographies) she writes, giving unconscious testimony to the views of Individual Psychology, but unable to understand her statement: " Whenever I did anything wicked, I thought, ' No one is ever sorry for me: why should I worry if I make others sorry? ' "

In these words we can see how she works up to the crime, drives herself on, and provides extenuating circumstances. It is a remark I often hear when I propose coöperation and interest in others:—" But others don't show any interest in me! " My answer is always: " Somebody has to begin. If the others are not coöperative it is not your affair. My advice is that you should begin and not care whether the others are coöperative."

(3) N. L., oldest son, badly brought up, lame in one foot, takes the place of father to his younger brother. We can recognize this tie, too, as a goal of superiority, till now

probably on the useful side. Perhaps, however, it was pride and a desire to show off. Later on, he drove his mother out of the house to beg, saying, " Be off with you, you beast." We can be sorry for this boy: he is not interested even in his mother. If we had known him as a child we could have seen how he was developing towards a criminal career. For a long time he was out of work. He had no money. He contracted a sexual disease. One day, on his way home from a futile search for work, he killed his younger brother in order to gain control of his small income. Here we see the limits of his coöperation — no work, no money, a sexual disease. There are always these limits, beyond which the individual feels incapable of proceeding.

(4) A child who was early orphaned was given over to a foster mother who spoiled him beyond belief. In this way he is a pampered child. He develops badly in later years, is very clever at business, constantly tries to impress everybody, always wants to be in front. His foster mother encourages him and falls in love with him. He turns into a liar and a swindler and gets money wherever he can. His foster parents belong to the lesser nobility: he puts on aristocratic airs, squanders all their money and drives them out of their house. Bad training and pampering have spoiled him for honest work. He sees his task in life as if he must overcome by lying and cheating. This makes every one an enemy to be outwitted. His foster mother preferred him to her own children and to her husband. This treatment gave him the feeling that he had a right to everything, but his low estimate of himself is shown in the fact that he does not feel able to succeed by normal means.

We have pointed out already that there is no reason why any child should suffer from this discouragement, this deep inferiority feeling that it is useless to coöperate. No man need be defeated before the problems of life. The criminal has chosen the wrong means; we must show him where he has chosen them and why, and we must train him in the courage to be interested in others and to coöperate. If it were fully recognized everywhere that crime is cowardice and not courage, I believe that the greatest self-justification would be taken away from criminals and no child would choose to train himself for crime in the future. In all criminal cases, whether they are correctly described or not, we can see the influence of a mistaken childhood style of life, a style showing a lack of the ability to coöperate. I should like to say that this ability to coöperate must be trained. There is no question of its being hereditary. There is a potentiality for coöperation, and this potentiality must be regarded as inborn; but it is common to every human being, and to be developed it must be trained and exercised. All other points of view about crime seen to me unnecessary, unless we can produce persons who were trained in coöperation and yet became criminals. I have never met such a person, and I have never heard of anybody who *had* met one. The right protection against crime would be the right degree of coöperation. So long as this is not recognized, we cannot hope to avoid the disaster of crime. Coöperation can be taught in the same way that geography can be taught; for it is a truth and we can always teach the truth. If a child, or an adult, is tested in geography and he is not prepared, then he fails. If a child, or an adult, is tested in situations which need a knowledge of coöperation and he is not prepared, then he fails. All our problems need a knowledge of coöperation.

We have come to the end of our scientific investigations of the problem of crime; and now we must be courageous enough to face the truth. After thousands and thousands of years, mankind has still not found the right method of coping with this problem. The means that have been applied seem all to have been useless and this disaster is still with us. Our investigation has told us why: the right steps have never been taken to change the criminal style of life and to prevent the development of mistaken styles of life. Short of this, no measures can be really effective.

Let us recall our results. We have found that the criminal is not an exception to the human race; he is much like other people and his behavior is a comprehensible variety of human behavior. This is a very important conclusion: if we understand that crime is not an isolated thing in itself but the symptom of an attitude to life, and if we can see how this attitude arises, then, instead of having an insoluble problem before us, we can set to work with the confidence that we can accomplish a change. The criminal, we discovered, has trained himself for a long time in non-coöperative thoughts and actions; and the roots of this lack of coöperation go back to his early childhood, the first four or five years of his life. During those years a block occurred in the development of his interest in others. We have described how this block is connected with his relation to his mother, his father, and his fellow children, with the social prejudices around him, with the difficulties of his environment and with other such factors. We have found that the greatest common denominator among all the greatest varieties of criminals and among all failures of every kind is this lack of coöperation, lack of interest in other people and in the welfare of mankind; and, if we are to do anything at all, this ability to coöperate must be trained and taught. There is no other way of accomplishing a result. Everything depends from this single factor, the ability to coöperate.

The criminal differs from other failures in one point. Through his old and continuous training against coöperation he has lost, as the others have also lost, the hope of achieving success in the normal tasks of life; he retains, however, a certain activity, and he throws this remainder of activity on the useless side of life. He behaves actively enough on the useless side, and to a certain extent he can coöperate there with those whom he sees as like himself, with his own type, with other criminals. Here he differs from the neurotic, the suicide or the drunkard. He is very much limited, however, in his sphere of activity; sometimes nothing is left but the possibility of crime; and not even the whole territory of crime, but just one kind of crime, which he commits over and over again. This is the size of his world of action; he is kept and trapped in this narrow stable. We can see in this circumstance how much he is lacking in courage; and he is bound to lack courage, for courage is only a part of the ability to coöperate.

All the time the criminal is preparing his thoughts and emotions for his criminal career: he plans during the day and he dreams during the night in an attempt to break down the last remnant of his social interest. He always looks for excuses and justifications, for extenuating circumstances and for reasons that " force " him to be a criminal. It is not easy to pierce through the wall of social feeling; it offers a great resistance; but if he is to commit a crime he must find a way — perhaps through brooding over his wrongs, perhaps through intoxication — to get rid of this hindrance. This helps us to understand how continuously he is making an interpretation of his circumstances which will confirm him in his attitude; helps us to understand, also, why we can achieve nothing by arguing with him. He sees the world with his own eyes, and he is prepared with a lifetime of argument. Unless we can discover how his attitude developed we cannot hope to change it. There is one advantage we possess, however, in which he cannot compete: it is our *interest in others*, which will allow us to seek out the real way in which we can help him.

The criminal begins to plot and prepare a crime when he is in a difficulty, has not the courage to face it in a coöperative way, and looks for an easy solution. It is especially likely to occur, for example, when he is confronted with the need to make money. Like every human being he is looking for a goal of security and superiority. He is wishing to solve difficulties and overcome obstacles. His striving, however, is outside of the framework of society: his goal is a goal of imaginary personal superiority, and he will try to achieve it by feeling himself the conqueror of the police, of our laws, of the organization of society. It is a kind of game he is playing with himself — to break the laws and escape detection, to be so cunning that no one finds him out. He will believe, for example, that it is a great personal victory to use a bottle of poison; and he will fool and intoxicate himself all the time. He has generally some success before he is convicted for the first time; and his only thought when he is discovered is, " If I had been cleverer, I should have escaped."

In all this we can see his inferiority complex. He is running away from the conditions of labor and from the tasks of life in association. He feels himself incapable of normal success. His training away from coöperation has genuinely added to his difficulties — the majority of criminals are unskilled laborers. He hides his feeling of inadequacy by developing a cheap superiority complex. He thinks how brave and how exceptional he is; but can we call a man a hero when he is a deserter from the front of life? The criminal is really carrying out his life in a dream: he does not know reality; he must fight against knowing reality or he would be forced to give up his career. We find him thinking, therefore, " I am the strongest man in the world, because I can shoot everybody "; or, " I am cleverer than everybody else, because I can commit crimes without being found out."

We have identified, also, the roots of the criminal pattern: how criminals come from among those children who were overburdened in their first years of life, or from among the children who were spoiled and pampered. Children who suffer from imperfect organs need especial care to direct their interest towards others: otherwise they will become interested only in their own persons and will be unable to develop in the right way. Neglected children, unwanted, unappreciated, or hated children, are in a similar situation: they have never experienced the coöperation of others; they have not learned that it is possible to be liked, to win affection, to solve problems by coöperation. Pampered children have not been taught to gain things by their own effort; they think that it is sufficient that they should want something and that the world should hasten to fulfill their demands; and if they are not given everything they want, they feel unfairly treated and refuse to coöperate. Behind every criminal we shall be able to trace a history of this kind. They are not trained in coöperation; they are not yet capable of it; and wherever they meet problems they do not know how to approach them. We know, therefore, exactly what we must do. We must train them in coöperation.

We have the knowledge, and by now we have enough experience. I am convinced that Individual Psychology shows us how we could change every single criminal. But consider what a work it would be to take every single criminal and treat him so that we changed his style of life. Unfortunately, in our culture, the majority of men would exhaust their ability to coöperate if their difficulties went beyond a certain point, and we find that in hard times the number of criminals always increases. I believe that if we were to be sure of abolishing crime in this way we would have to treat a great part of the human race, and I am not sure that it would be practicable to have an immediate aim of making every criminal or potential criminal a fellow man.

There is plenty that we can do, however. If we cannot alter every criminal, we can do something to relieve the burdens of those people who are not strong enough to cope with them. With regard to unemployment, for example, and the lack of occupational training and skill, we should make it possible that every one who wants to work can secure a job. This would be the only way to lower the demands of our social life so that a great part of mankind should not lose the last remnant of their ability to coöperate. It is unquestionable that if this were done there would be a decrease in the number of criminals. Whether our time is ripe for this relief to our economic conditions I do not know; but we should certainly work for this change. We should also train children better for their future occupation, so that they can face life better and with a greater sphere of activity. Such training can be given also in our prisons. To some extent steps have already been taken in this direction and perhaps all we need do here is to increase our efforts. While I do not believe it would be possible to give every criminal an individual treatment, we could contribute much by a mass treatment. I should propose, for instance, that we should have discussions with a great number of criminals on social problems, exactly as we have been considering them here. We should question them and let them answer; we should enlighten their minds and waken them from their lifelong dream; we should free them from the intoxication of a private interpretation of the world and so low an opinion of their own possibilities; we should teach them not to limit themselves and diminish their fear of the situations and the social problems which they must meet. I am very sure that we could achieve great results from such mass treatment.

We should also avoid in our social life everything which can act as a challenge to the criminal or to poor and destitute people. If there are great extremes of poverty and luxury, those who are badly off become irritated and are challenged too much. We should therefore diminish ostentation: it is not necessary always to expand on how many millions an individual possesses. We have learned in the treatment of backward and problem children that it is entirely useless to challenge them to a trial of strength. It is because they think that they are engaged in a warfare with their environment that they persist in their attitude. The same thing holds with criminals. Throughout the world we can observe that police officers, judges, and even the laws we make challenge criminals and put them on their mettle. There should never be menaces, and it would be much better if we were more silent, did not mention the names of criminals or give them so much publicity. This attitude needs changing. We should not believe that either severity or mildness can change a criminal. He can be changed only if he understands his own situation better. Of course we should be humane; we should not imagine that criminals can be terrified by the thought of capital punishment: as we have seen, capital punishment sometimes only adds to the excitement of the game, and even when criminals are electrocuted they will think only of the mistake they made through which they were caught.

It would be very helpful if we increased our efforts to discover those who were responsible for crimes. As far as I can see, at least forty per cent. of criminals, and perhaps far more, escape detection; and this fact is always at the back of the mistaken view of a criminal. Almost every criminal has experienced occasions when he committed crimes and was not found out. On some of these points we have already improved and we are going in the right direction. It is also important that criminals should not be humiliated or challenged either in the prison itself or after they leave prison. An increase in the number of probation officers would be useful, if the right type of man is chosen; and probation officers themselves should be enlightened on the problems of society and the importance of coöperation.

By these means we could accomplish very much. We should still not be able, however, to decrease the number of crimes as much as we could wish. Fortunately we have another means and it is a method which is very practicable and very successful. If we could train our children to the right degree of ability to coöperate, if we could develop them in social interest, the number of criminals would diminish very considerably, and the effects would be shown in the near future. These children could not then be incited or allured: whatever troubles or difficulties they met in their life, their interest in others would not be wholly destroyed: their ability to coöperate and to solve satisfactorily the problems of life would be much higher than we find it in our own generation. The majority of criminals begin their careers very early. It is generally in adolescence that they start, and perhaps in the years between fifteen and twenty-eight crimes are most frequent. Our success, therefore, would be seen very soon. Not only so; I am sure if children were taught rightly they would influence their whole home life. Independent, forward-looking, optimistic and well-developed children are a help and consolation for their parents. The spirit of coöperation would be immediately spread over the whole world; and the whole social atmosphere of mankind would be raised to a much higher level. At the same time as we influence the children we should be influencing parents and teachers.

The only question that remains is how we can choose the best point of attack, what method we are to find to develop children so that they can stand the tasks and problems of later life. Perhaps we could train all the parents? But no; this proposal does not give us much hope. Parents are hard to get hold of, and the parents who need training the most are the very people whom we never see. We could not reach them and so we must look for another way. Perhaps we could catch all the children, lock them up, put them under probation and keep careful guard over them the whole time? This does not seem a much better proposal. One way there is, however, a way which is practicable and promises a real solution. We can make teachers the instruments of our social progress: we can train our teachers to correct mistakes made in the family, to develop and spread the social interest of the children towards others. This is an entirely natural development of the school. Because the family is not able to bring up the children for all the tasks of later life, mankind has established schools as the prolonged arm of the family. Why should we not use the school to make mankind more sociable, more coöperative, and more interested in human welfare?

You will see that our activity must be based upon the following ideas. I will put them very briefly. All the advantages which we enjoy in our present culture have been made possible by the efforts of people who have *contributed*. If individuals have not been coöperative, have not been interested in others, have made no contribution to the whole, their whole life has been futile, they have disappeared and left no trace behind them. Only the work of those men who have contributed survived. Their spirit continues and their spirit is eternal. If we make this the basis for our teaching of children, they will grow in a natural liking for coöperative work. If they are confronted with difficulties they will not weaken; but they will be strong enough to face even the most difficult problems and solve them to the common benefit.

CHAPTER X

Occupation

The three ties in which human beings are bound set the three problems of life; but none of these problems can be solved separately; each of them demands a successful approach to the other two. The first tie sets the problem of occupation. We are living on the surface of this planet, with only the resources of this planet, with the fertility of its soil, with its mineral wealth and with its climate and atmosphere. It has always been the task of mankind to find the right answer to the problem these conditions set us; and even to-day we cannot think that we have found a sufficient answer. In every age mankind had arrived at a certain level of solution, but it was always necessary to strive for improvement and further accomplishments.

The best means of solving this problem which we possess comes from the solution of the second problem. The second tie in which men are bound is that they belong to the human race and are living in association with others of their kind. The attitude and behavior of a human being would be altogether different if he were the only one of his kind alive on earth. We have always to reckon with others, to adapt ourselves to others and to interest ourselves in them. This problem is best solved by friendship, social feeling and coöperation. With the solution of this problem we have an incalculable advance towards the solution of the first.

It was only because men learned to coöperate that we could make the great discovery of the division of labor; a discovery which is the chief security for the welfare of mankind. To preserve human life would not be possible if each individual attempted to wrest a living from the earth by himself with no coöperation and no results of coöperation in the past. Through the division of labor we can use the results of many different kinds of training and organize many different abilities so that all of them contribute to the common welfare and guarantee relief from insecurity and increased opportunity for all the members of society. It is true that we cannot boast of having achieved everything that could be done; and we cannot pretend that the division of labor has reached its most fruitful development. But every attempt to solve the problem of occupation must take place within this framework of the human division of labor and the coöperative effort to contribute by our work to the advantage of others also.

Some people attempt to evade this problem of occupation; to do no work or to occupy themselves outside of common human interests. We shall always find, however, that if they dodge this problem, they will in fact be claiming support from their fellows. In one way or another they will be living on the labor of others without making a contribution of their own. This is the style of life of the pampered child: to demand whenever a problem faces him that it should be solved for him by the efforts of his fellows; and it is chiefly the pampered child who holds back the coöperation of mankind and throws unfair burdens on those who are actively engaged in solving the problems of life.

The third tie of a human being is that he is a member of one of the two sexes and not of the other. On his approach to the other sex and the fulfillment of his sexual rôle depends his part in the continuance of mankind. This relationship between the two sexes also sets a problem; and it, too, is a problem which cannot be solved apart from the other two problems. For a successful solution of the problem of love and marriage, an occupation contributing to the division of labor is necessary, as well as a good and friendly contact with other human beings. As we have already seen, in our own day, the highest solution for this problem, the solution most coherent with the demands of society and of the division of labor, is monogamy. In the way in which an individual answers this problem the degree of his coöperation can always be seen. These three problems are never found apart; they all throw crosslights on one another; a solution of one helps towards the solution of the others; and indeed we can say that they are all aspects of the same situation and the same problem — the necessity for a human being to preserve life, and to further life, in the environment in which he finds himself.

Here we might repeat that a woman who contributes to the life of mankind by the occupation of motherhood is taking as high a place in the division of human labor as any one else could take. If she is interested in the lives of her children and is paving the way for them to become fellow men, if she is spreading their interests and training them to coöperate, her work is so valuable that it can never be rightly rewarded. In our own culture the work of a mother is undervalued and often regarded as a not very attractive or estimable occupation. It is paid only indirectly and a woman who makes it her main occupation is generally placed in a position of economic dependence. The success of the family, however, rests equally upon the work of the mother and the work of the father. Whether the mother keeps house or works independently, her work as a mother does not play a lower rôle than the work of her husband.

A mother is the first influence in the development of her children's occupational interests. The efforts and training of the first four or five years of life are decisive for the child's main sphere of action in adult life. If ever I am called on for vocational guidance, I always ask how the individual began and what he was interested in during his first years. His memories of this period show conclusively what he has trained himself for most continuously: they reveal his prototype and his underlying scheme of apperception. To the importance of first memories I shall return later on.

The next step for training is made by the schools; and I believe that our schools now are giving more attention to the future occupation of the child, to training his hands, ears and eyes, his faculties and functions. Such training is as important as the teaching of special subjects. We should not forget, however, that the teaching of subjects is also important for the child's occupational development. In later life we often hear people say that they have forgotten the Latin or French which they learned at school; but, perhaps, all the same, it was not a mistake to teach these subjects. In the study of all these subjects, we have found, through the combined experience of the past, an excellent occasion to train all the functions of the mind. There are modern schools which pay much attention to craftsmanship and handiwork; and in this way, too, we can increase the experience of a child and raise his self-confidence.

A child's development is much simpler if he knows from his childhood onwards the occupation which he would like to take up in later life. If we ask children what they would like to be, most of them will give an answer. Their answers are not clearly considered; and when they say that they want to be æroplane pilots or engine drivers they do not know why they are choosing this occupation. It is our task to recognize the underlying motives, to see the way they are striving, what is pushing them forward, where they are placed, their goal of superiority and how they feel they can make it concrete. The answer they give shows us only one kind of occupation which seems to them to represent superiority; but from this occupation we can see also other opportunities for helping them to reach their goal.

A child of twelve or fourteen should already know much more of the occupation which he will follow; and I am always sorry to hear at this age that a child does not know what he wishes to be in later life. His apparent lack of ambition does not mean that he has no interest at all. He is probably extremely ambitious and not courageous enough to mention what his ambitions are. In such a case we must take pains to find out his chief interest and training. Some children, when they finish high school at the age of sixteen, are still unsettled over their future occupation. Often they are brilliant pupils but have no idea of how their life will continue. These children we can recognize to be very ambitious but not really coöperative. They have not felt their way in the division of labor and they cannot find in time a concrete method of fulfilling their ambitions. It is thus an advantage to ask children early what their occupation is going to be; and I often put this question in schools so that the children are led to consider the point and cannot forget the problem or wish to hide their answer. I ask them also why they have selected this occupation and I am often told very revealing details. In a child's choice of an occupation we can observe his whole style of life. He is showing us the main direction of his striving and what he values most in life. We must let him value as he chooses; since we ourselves have no means of saying which occupation is higher and which is lower. If he really does his work and occupies himself in a contribution to others, he is on the same level of usefulness as any one else. His only task is to train himself, try to support himself, and set his interest in the framework of the division of labor.

There are some people who could choose any occupation and never be satisfied. What they wish is not an occupation but an easy guarantee of superiority. They do not wish to meet the problems of life, since they feel that it is unfair of life to offer them problems at all. These, again, are the pampered children who wish to be supported by others. Perhaps a great majority of men and women are really interested in the direction in which they have trained themselves in the first four or five years and cannot forget these interests; but they have felt compelled by economic considerations or by the pressure of their parents to take a different direction and engage in an occupation which does not interest them. This is another sign of the importance of childhood training. If in a child's first memories we see an interest in visual things, we can conclude that he will be more apt for an occupation in which he can use his eyes. In vocational guidance, first memories should be considered very important. A child mentions impressions of some one talking to him, of the sound of the wind or of a bell ringing. We know that he is an acoustic type and we can guess that he might be suited for some profession connected with music. In other recollections we can see impressions of movement. These are individuals who demand more activity; perhaps they would be interested in occupations which demanded outside labor or travel.

One of the most frequent strivings is the attempt to excel other members of the family; and especially to go farther than the father or mother. This can be a very valuable striving; we are glad to see an advancement on the position of older generations and, to a certain degree, if a child wishes to surpass the achievements of his father in his own occupation, his father's experience can provide him with an excellent start. Often a child born into a family where the father was a policeman has the ambition of being a lawyer or a judge. If his father is employed in the office of a doctor, the child wants to be a doctor himself. If the father is a teacher, the child wants to be a professor at a university.

By watching children we can often see them training for an occupation in adult life. Sometimes, for example, a child wishes to be a teacher; and we can notice how he brings younger children together and plays school with them. The games of children can give us a hint of their interests. A girl who looks forward to being a mother will play with dolls and train herself to a greater interest in babies. This interest in training to take the rôle of a mother should be encouraged and we need not be afraid of giving little girls dolls to play with. Some people feel that if we give them dolls we are distracting them from reality; but in fact they are training themselves in identification and in fulfilling the tasks of a mother. It is valuable that they should begin so early in life; since if they came to train when it was too late, their interests would already have crystallized. Many children show great mechanical and technical interest; and this, too, is a promise of a fruitful occupation in later life if they can accomplish what they wish.

There are still other children who never wish to be placed in a leading position. Their chief interest is to find a leader to look up to, another child or adult to whom they can subordinate themselves. This is not a very favorable development and I should be pleased if we could decrease such submissive tendencies. If we cannot stop them, such children will be unable to take a leading position in later life and of their own accord will chose positions where they have the tasks of a minor official, where their work is routine work and where everything which they should do is prescribed for them.

Children who meet the problem of sickness or death without preparation always remain with a great interest in these facts. They wish to be doctors, nurses or chemists. Their strivings, I believe, should be encouraged, since I have always found that children with such interests who became doctors began their training very early and had a great liking for their profession. Sometimes an experience of death can be compensated in another way. The child will have the ambition to survive death through artistic or literary creation; or he may become devoutly religious.

The mistaken training of avoiding an occupation, being distracted or lazy, also begins early in life. When we see such a child heading for difficulties in later life, we must find out the reasons for his mistake in a scientific way and try to correct him by scientific means. If we lived on a planet which offered us everything we needed without work, it would perhaps be a virtue to be lazy and a vice to be industrious. As far as we can understand from our relation to our own planet, earth, the logical answer to the problem of occupation, the only answer in accordance with common sense, is that we should work, coöperate and contribute. This has always been felt in the intuitions of mankind: we can see its necessity, now, from the scientific angle.

The training from early childhood has always been evident in geniuses; and I believe that the question of genuis can throw light on the whole subject. Mankind only calls those individuals geniuses who have contributed much to the common welfare. We cannot imagine a genius who has left no advantage to mankind behind him. The arts are the product of the most coöperative of all individuals, and the great geniuses of mankind have raised the whole level of our culture. Homer in his poems makes mention of only three colors; and these three had to serve for all discriminations. Doubtless at the time, people could notice more differences; but it was not necessary to name them, since the differences seemed so slight. Who has taught us to distinguish all the colors which we can now name? We must say that it is the work of artists and painters. Composers have refined our hearing to an extraordinary degree. If we speak now in harmonious tones instead of in the rough tones of primitive mankind, it is the musicians who have taught us; it is they who have enriched our minds and taught us to train our functions. Who increased the depths of our feelings and taught us to speak better and to understand better? These were the poets. It is they who have enriched our language, made it more flexible and adapted it to all the purposes of life. There can be no question but that geniuses have been the most coöperative of all human beings. In some aspects of their behavior and their attitude we could perhaps not see their coöperative ability; but we can see it in the whole picture of their lives. It was not so easy for them to coöperate as for others. They went a difficult way and they had many obstacles to contend with. Often they started with gravely imperfect organs. In almost all outstanding people we find some organ imperfection; and we gather the impression that they were sorely confronted at the beginning of life but struggled and overcame their difficulties. We can notice especially how early they fixed their interests and how hard they trained themselves in their childhood. They sharpened their senses, so that they could make contact with the problems of the world and understand them. From this early training we can conclude that their art and their genius was their own creation, not an undeserved gift of nature or inheritance. They strove and we are blessed.

This early striving is the best foundation for later success. Suppose we have a girl of three or four who has been left alone. She begins to sew a hat for her doll. When we see her at work we tell her what a nice hat it is and suggest how it could be made still better. The little girl is encouraged and stimulated. She increases her strivings and her skill. But suppose we had said, " Put that needle down! You will hurt yourself. There's no need for you to make a hat at all. We'll go out and buy you a far nicer one." She would give up her strivings. If we compared the two girls in later life we should find that the first had developed her artistic taste and was interested in working: the second would not know what to do with herself and she would think that she could always buy better things than she could make.

If the value of money is overstressed in family life, the children will be tempted to look at the problem of occupation only in the light of the money they can make. This is a great mistake; for such a child does not follow an interest in which he contributes to mankind. That every one should earn his living is a truth; and it is true, also, that we find people who neglect this point and make themselves a charge on others. But if a child is only interested in making money he can easily lose the path of coöperation and look only after his own advantages. If " to make money " is his only goal and no social interest is bound up with it, there is no possible reason why he should not make money by robbing and swindling other people. Even if the position is not so extreme but there is only a small degree of social interest combined with the goal, the individual may make plenty of money but his activities will not be of much advantage to his fellows. In our complicated times, it is possible to be successful along these lines and to become rich. Even a mistaken way may sometimes seem to be successful in one point. We need not be astonished; and we cannot hold out a promise that an individual who goes through life with the right attitude will meet immediate success. We can promise, however, that he will keep his courage and will not lose his self-esteem.

An occupation can sometimes be used to evade and be made into an excuse for evading the problems of society and love. Very often in our social life an exaggeration of activity in business can be chosen as a means to get rid of the problem of love and marriage. Sometimes we find it used as an excuse for failure. A man devotes himself furiously to his business, and thinks, " I have no time to spare for my marriage, and so I am not responsible for its unhappiness." It is especially frequent amongst neurotics that these two problems of society and love are the problems that they try to evade. They make no approach to the other sex or they make wrong approaches. They have no friends and they do not interest themselves in other people. But they are occupied day and night with their business. They think of it and dream of it in bed. They throw themselves into a tension; and in their tension the neurotic symptom appears; stomach irritation or some such trouble. They feel now that their stomach trouble excuses them from meeting the problems of society and love. In other cases the man is always changing his occupation. He can always think of an occupation which would suit him better. In the end it appears that he is not occupied at all; he is always vacillating from one thing to another.

Our first point with problem children is to find out their main interest. Through this it is easier to encourage them on the whole. In cases of young people who have not been able to settle on an occupation, or older people who have been occupational failures, their real interest should be found out and used, in the right hands, to give them vocational guidance, combined with an effort to find them employment. This is not always easy. In our own time the great number of unemployed is a matter for alarm. This is not the right expression for a time in which people are trying to improve coöperation. I believe therefore that everybody who has seen the importance of coöperation should strive to see that there are no unemployed individuals, that work is open to everybody who wants it. We may be helped in this way by furthering movements for training schools, technical schools and adult education. Many of the unemployed are untrained and unskilled. Some of them, perhaps, have not been interested in social life. It is a great burden for mankind to have untrained members of society and members who are not interested in the common welfare. These people really feel themselves backward and at a disadvantage; and we can understand it if untrained and unskilled people make up a large proportion of criminals, neurotics and suicides. Because of their lack of training, they lag in the rear of mankind. All parents and teachers and all who are interested in the future development and improvement of mankind should make efforts that all children are better trained and that such a great number of them do not come into adult life with no special place in the division of labor.

CHAPTER XI

Man and Fellow Man

The oldest striving of mankind is for men to join with their fellow men. It is through interest in our fellow men that all the progress of our race has been made. The family is an organization in which interest in other people is essential; and as far back as we can go into our history we find this tendency for human beings to group themselves in families. Primitive tribes held themselves together by common symbols, and the purpose of the symbol was to unite men with their fellows in coöperation. The simplest primitive religion is the worship of a totem. One group would worship a lizard, another a bull or serpent. Those who worshipped the same totem lived together and coöperated, and each member of the group felt himself a brother of the other members. These primitive customs were one of the greatest steps of mankind in fixing and stabilizing coöperation. On the festival of these primitive religions, every man who worshipped the lizard would join his fellows, and they would discuss together questions of the harvest, and of how they could defend themselves against animals and the powers of the air. This was the meaning of the festival.

Marriage was regarded as an affair in which the interests of the whole group were involved. Each brother who worshipped the same totem had to find his partner outside of his group, in accordance with social restrictions. It should still be realized that love and marriage are not private affairs, but common tasks in which the whole of mankind should take part in mind and spirit. There is a certain responsibility in marrying, since it is a task expected by the whole of society, and the whole of society is interested that healthy children should be born and that they should be brought up in the spirit of coöperation. All mankind should, therefore, be willing to coöperate in every marriage. The means of primitive societies, their totems and their elaborate systems to control marriage, may now seem to us ridiculous; but their importance in their time can hardly be overrated; and their real end was to increase human coöperation.

The most important task imposed by religion has always been, " Love thy neighbor." Here again, in another form, we have the same striving to increase interest in our fellow men. It is interesting, too, that now from a scientific standpoint we can confirm the value of this striving. The pampered child asks us, " Why should I love my neighbor? Does my neighbor love me? " and so reveals his lack of training in coöperation and his interest in himself. It is the individual who is not interested in his fellow men who has the greatest difficulties in life and provides the greatest injury to others. It is from among such individuals that all human failures spring. There are many religions and confessions which try in their own way to increase coöperation; and I, for my own part, would agree with every human effort which recognized coöperation as the final goal. There is no need to fight, criticize and undervalue. We are not blessed with the possession of the absolute truth and there are several ways leading towards the final goal of coöperation.

In politics we know that the best means can be abused;

but nobody could accomplish anything by politics if he did not create coöperation. Every politician must have as his final goal the improvement of mankind; and the improvement of mankind means always a higher degree of coöperation. Often we are not very well equipped for judging which politician or which political party can really lead towards improvement. Each individual judges in accordance with his own style of life. But if a political party creates fellow men in its own circle, we have no cause to resent the activity. So, too, with national movements; if it is the aim of those engaged in such movements to bring up the children as real fellow men and to increase social feeling, they may proceed along their own traditions, worship their own nationality, and attempt to influence and change the laws as they think best: we should not disagree with their effort. Class movement, also, is group movement and coöperation, and, if its goal is the improvement of mankind, we should avoid prejudice. So all movements should be judged only in accordance with their ability to further interest in our fellow men and we shall find that there are many ways to help in increasing coöperation. Perhaps there are better and worse ways; but, if the goal of coöperation is granted, it is useless to attack one method because it may not be the best.

What we must disagree with is the view of life in which people are looking only for what is given them, looking only for a personal advantage. This is the greatest conceivable obstacle to individual and common progress. It is only through our interest in our fellows that any of our human capacities develop. To speak, to read and write all presuppose a bridge with other men. Language itself is a common creation of mankind, the result of social interest. Understanding is a common matter, not a private function. To understand is to understand as we expect that everybody should understand. It is to connect ourselves in a common meaning with other people, to be controlled by the common sense of all mankind.

There are some people who are seeking mainly for their own interests and for personal superiority. They give a private meaning to life; life should exist for them alone. This is no understanding, however; it is an opinion which no one else in the whole wide world could share. We find, therefore, that such people are unable to connect themselves with their fellow men. Often when we see a child who has trained towards interest in himself, we find that he has a hangdog or vacant look in his face; and we can see something of the same look in the faces of criminals or of the insane. They are not using their eyes to connect with others. They are not seeing in the same way. Sometimes such children and adults will not even look at their fellow beings; they turn their eyes away and look elsewhere. The same failure of connection is shown in many neurotic symptoms; very noticeably, for example, in compulsive blushing, in stammering, in impotence or premature ejaculation. These all reveal an inability to join with other human beings, rising from a lack of interest in them.

The highest degree of isolation is represented by insanity. Even insanity is not incurable if the interest in others can be aroused; but it represents a greater distance from fellow men than any other expression except, perhaps, suicide. It is an art to cure such cases, and a very difficult art. We must win the patient back to coöperation; and we can do it only by patience and the kindliest and friendliest manner. Once I was called in to do what I could for a girl with *dementia præcox*. She had suffered from this condition for eight years and for the last two years had been in an asylum. She barked like a dog, spat, tore her clothes and tried to eat her handkerchief. We can see how far she had turned away from interest in human beings. She wanted to play the rôle of dog and we can understand this. She felt that her mother had treated her as a dog; and perhaps she was saying, " The more I see of human beings, the more I should like to be a dog." I spoke to her on eight successive days and she did not answer a word. I continued to speak to her and after thirty days she began to talk in a confused and unintelligible way. I was a friend to her and she was encouraged.

If a patient of this type is encouraged he does not know what to do with his courage. His resistance against his fellow men is very strong. We can predict the conduct he will try when his courage comes back to some degree but he still does not wish to be coöperative. He is like a problem child: he will try to be a nuisance: he will break anything he can lay hands on, or he will hit the attendant. When I next spoke to this girl she hit me. I had to consider what I should do. The only answer that would surprise her was to put up no resistance. You can imagine the girl,— she was not a girl of great physical strength. I let her hit me and looked friendly. This she did not expect; it took away every challenge from her. She still did not know what to do with her reawakened courage. She broke my window and cut her hand on the glass. I did not reproach her, but bandaged her hand. The usual way of meeting such violence, to confine her and lock her in her room, was the wrong way. We must act differently if we wish to win this girl. It is the greatest mistake to expect an insane person to act as a normal person. Almost every one is annoyed and irritated because the insane do not respond like ordinary beings. They do not eat, they tear their clothes, and so on. Let them do it. There is no other possibility of helping them.

After this, the girl recovered. A year passed and she had continued perfectly healthy. One day when I had to visit the asylum in which she had been confined, I met her on the way. " What are you doing? " she asked me. " Come with me," I answered. " I am going to the asylum where you lived for two years." We went to the asylum together and I asked for the doctor who had treated her there. I suggested that he should talk with her while I saw another patient. When I came back, the doctor was very much out of temper. " She is perfectly healthy," he said, " but there is one thing about her that displeases me. She does not like me." I still see this girl from time to time and she has remained in good health for ten years. She earns her own living, is reconciled to her fellows, and no one who saw her would believe that she had ever suffered from insanity.

Two conditions which reveal with especial clarity the distance from other human beings are paranoia and melancholia. In paranoia the patient accuses all mankind; he thinks that his fellow men are organized in a conspiracy against him. In melancholia, the patient accuses himself: he says, for example, " I have ruined my whole family ", or " I have lost all my money and my children must starve." If a person accuses himself, however, this is only the outside face he shows; he is really accusing others. A woman of much prominence and influence, for example, had an accident and could no longer continue with her social activities. She had three daughters who had married and she felt very much alone. About the same time she lost her husband. She had been pampered before and she tried to replace what she had lost. She began to travel abroad in Europe. She no longer felt as important as she had been, however, and while she was in Europe she began to suffer from melancholia. Her friends left her. Melancholia is a disorder which is a great trial for those in the environment. She cabled for her daughters to come, but each of them had an excuse and none of them came over to her. When she returned home, her most frequent words were, " My daughters have been so very kind." Her daughters had left her alone, they had let a nurse take care of her, and now that she had come back they visited her only at intervals. We cannot take her words at their surface value. They are an accusation, and every one who knew the circumstances would know that they were an accusation. Melancholia is like a long-continued rage and reproach against others, though for the purpose of gaining care, sympathy and support, the patient seems only to be dejected about his own guilt. A melancholiac's first memory is generally something like this: " I remember I wanted to lie on the couch, but my brother was lying there. I cried so much that he had to leave."

Melancholiacs are often inclined to revenge themselves by committing suicide, and the doctor's first care is to avoid giving them an excuse for suicide. I myself try to relieve the whole tension by proposing to them, as the first rule in treatment, " Never do anything you don't like." This seems to be very modest, but I believe that it goes to the root of the whole trouble. If a melancholiac is able to do anything he wants, whom can he accuse? What has he got to revenge himself for? " If you want to go to the theater," I tell him, " or to go on a holiday, do it. If you find on the way that you don't want to, stop it." It is the best situation any one could be in. It gives a satisfaction to his striving for superiority. He is like God and can do what he pleases. On the other hand, it does not fit very easily into his style of life. He wants to dominate and accuse others and if they agree with him there is no way of dominating them. This rule is a great relief and I have never had a suicide among my patients. It is understood, of course, that it is best to have some one to watch such a patient, and some of my patients have not been watched as closely as I should have liked. So long as there is an observer, there is no danger.

Generally the patient replies, " But there is nothing I like doing." I have prepared for this answer, because I have heard it so often. " Then refrain from doing any- thing you dislike ", I say. Sometimes, however, he will reply, " I should like to stay in bed all day." I know that, if I allow it, he will no longer want to do it. I know that, if I hinder him, he will start a war. I always agree.

This is one rule. Another attacks their style of life still more directly. I tell them, " You can be cured in fourteen days if you follow this prescription. Try to think every day how you can please some one." See what this means to them. They are occupied with the thought, " How can I worry some one." The answers are very interesting. Some say, " This will be very easy for me. I have done it all my life." They have never done it. I ask them to think it over. They do not think it over. I tell them, " You can make use of all the time you spend when you are unable to go to sleep by thinking how you can please some one, and it will be a big step forward in your health." When I see them next day, I ask them, " Did you think over what I suggested? " They answer, " Last night I went to sleep as soon as I got into bed." All this must be done, of course, in a modest, friendly manner, without a hint of superiority.

Others will answer, "I could never do it. I am so worried." I tell them, " Don't stop worrying; but at the same time you can think now and then of others." I want to direct their interest always towards their fellows. Many say, " Why should I please others? Others do not try to please me." " You must think of your health ", I answer. " The others will suffer later on." It is extremely rarely that I have found a patient who said, " I have thought over what you suggested." All my efforts are devoted towards increasing the social interest of the patient. I know that the real reason for his malady is his lack of coöperation and I want him to see it too. As soon as he can connect himself with his fellow men on an equal and coöperative footing, he is cured.

Another clear example of a lack of social interest is the so-called " criminal negligence." A man lets a lighted match fall and starts a forest fire. Or, as in a recent case, a worker leaves a cable stretched across a road when he goes home for the day; an automobile runs into it and the occupants are killed. In neither case did the individual mean any harm. He does not seem to be guilty in a moral sense for the actual disaster. But he has not been trained in thinking of other people; he does not spontaneously take precautions to secure their safety. It is a higher degree of the same lack of coöperation that we see in untidy children and in people who stand on other people's toes, break dishes and plates, or knock ornaments off the mantelshelf.

Interest in our fellow men is trained in the home and the school; and we have seen already what hindrances may be put in the way of a child's development. Social feeling is not, perhaps, an inherited instinct; but the potentiality for social feeling is inherited. This potentiality is developed in accordance with the mother's skill and her interest in the child, and in accordance with the child's own judgment of his environment. If he feels that other people are hostile, if he feels that he is surrounded by enemies and has his back against the wall, we cannot expect him to make friends and to be a good friend himself. If he feels that others should be his slaves, he will wish, not to contribute to others, but to rule them. If he is interested in his own sensations and in his physical irritations and discomforts, he will shut himself off from society.

We have seen how it is best for a child to feel himself an equal part of his family and to take an interest in all the other members. We have seen that the parents should themselves be good friends to each other and should have good and intimate friendships in the outer world. In this way their children come to feel that trustworthy human beings exist outside the family, also. We have seen how, in the school, the child should feel himself a part of the class, a friend to the other children and able to rely on their friendship. Life in the family and life at school are preparations for a larger whole. Their aim is to educate the child to be a fellow man, an equal part of the whole of mankind. Only in these conditions will he preserve his courage and meet the problems of life without tension, finding solutions for them which increase the welfare of others.

If he can be a good friend to all men and contribute to them by useful work and by a happy marriage, he will never feel inferior to others or defeated by them. He will feel that he is at home in the universe, in a friendly place, meeting people he likes and equal to all his difficulties. He will feel, " This world is my world. I must act and organize, not wait and expect." He will be wholly sure that the present time is only one time in the history of mankind, and that he belongs to the whole human process,— past, present and future; but he will feel also that this is the time in which he can fulfill his creative tasks and make his own contribution to human development. It is true that there are evils and difficulties and prejudices and disasters in this world; but it is our own world and its advantages and disadvantages are our own. It is our world to work in and improve and we can hope that if any one takes up his tasks in the right way he can do his part in improving it.

To take up his tasks means to assume responsibility for solving the three problems of life in a coöperative way. All that we demand of a human being, and the highest praise that we can give him, is that he should be a good fellow worker, a friend to all other men, and a true partner in love and marriage. If we are to put it in a word, we may say that he should prove himself a fellow man.

CHAPTER XII

Love and Marriage

In a certain district of Germany there is an old custom
for testing whether an engaged couple are suited for
married life together. Before the wedding ceremony, the
bride and bridegroom are brought to a clearing where a
tree trunk has been cut down. Here they are given a two-
handed saw and set to work to saw the trunk across. By
this test it is found out how far they are willing to coöperate with each other. It is a task for two people. If there
is no trust between them, they will tug against each other
and accomplish nothing. If one of them wishes to take
the lead and do everything by himself, then, even if the
other gives way, the task will take twice as long. They
must both have initiative, but their initiatives must combine together. These German villagers have recognized
that coöperation is the chief pre-requisite for marriage.

If I were asked to say what love and marriage mean, I
should give the following definition, incomplete as it
may be:

"Love, with its fulfillment, marriage, is the most intimate devotion towards a partner of the other sex, expressed in physical attraction, in comradeship, and in the
decision to have children. It can easily be shown that love
and marriage are one side of coöperation — not a coöperation for the welfare of two persons only, but a coöperation also for the welfare of mankind."

This standpoint, that love and marriage are a coöperation for the welfare of mankind, throws light on every aspect of the problem. Even physical attraction, the most important of all human strivings, has been a most necessary development for mankind. As I have explained so often, mankind, suffering from imperfect organs, has been none too well equipped for life on the crust of this poor planet, earth. The chief way to preserve human life was to propagate it; hence our fertility and the continual striving of physical attraction.

In our own days, we find difficulties and dissensions arising over all the problems of love. Married couples are confronted with these difficulties, parents are concerned with them, the whole of society is involved in them. If we are trying, therefore, to come to a right conclusion, our approach must be quite without prejudice. We must forget what we have learned and try to investigate, as far as we can, without letting other considerations interfere with a full and free discussion.

I do not mean that we can judge the problem of love and marriage as if it were an entirely isolated problem. A human being can never be wholly free in this way: he can never reach solutions for his problems purely along the line of his private ideas. Every human being is bound by definite ties; his development takes place within a definite framework and he must conform his decisions to this framework. These three main ties are set by the facts that we are living in one particular place in the universe and must develop with the limits and possibilities which our circumstances set us; that we are living among others of our own kind to whom we must learn to adapt ourselves; and that we are living in two sexes with the future of our race dependent on the relations of these two sexes.

It is easy to understand that if an individual is interested in his fellows and in the welfare of mankind, everything he does will be guided by the interests of his fellows, and he will try to solve the problem of love and marriage as if the welfare of others were involved. He does not need to know that he is trying to solve it in this way. If you ask him, he will perhaps be unable to give a scientific account of his aims. But he will spontaneously seek the welfare and improvement of mankind and this interest will be visible in all his activities.

There are other human beings who are not so much concerned with the welfare of mankind. Instead of taking as their underlying view of life " What can I contribute to my fellows? " " How can I fit in as part of the whole? ", they ask rather, " What is the use of life? What can I get out of it? What does it pay? Are other people considering me enough? Am I properly appreciated? " If this attitude is behind an individual's approach to life, he will try to solve the problem of love and marriage in the same way. He will ask always: " What can I get out of it? "

Love is not a purely natural task, as some psychologists believe. Sex is a drive or instinct; but the question of love and marriage is not quite simply how we are to satisfy this drive. Wherever we look, we find that our drives and instincts are developed, cultivated, refined. We have repressed some of our desires and inclinations. On behalf of our fellow beings, we have learned how not to annoy each other. We have learned how to dress ourselves and how to be clean. Even our hunger does not have a merely natural outlet; we have cultivated tastes and manners in eating. Our drives have all been adapted to our common culture; they all reflect the efforts we have learned to make for the welfare of mankind and for our life in association.

If we apply this understanding to the problem of love and marriage we shall see, here again, that the interest of the whole, the interest in mankind, must always be involved. This interest is primary. There is no advantage in discussing any of the aspects of love and marriage, in proposing reliefs, changes, new regulations or institutions, before we have seen that the problem can be solved only in its whole coherence, only by considering human welfare as a whole. Perhaps we shall improve; perhaps we shall find completer answers to the problem; but if we find better answers they will be better because they take fuller account of the fact that we are living in two sexes, on the crust of this earth, where association is necessary. In so far as our answers already take account of these conditions, the truth in them can stand for ever.

When we use this approach, our first finding in the love problem is that it is a task for two individuals. For many people this is bound to be a new task. To some degree we have been educated to work alone; to some degree we have been educated to work in a team or a crowd. We have generally had little experience of working two by two. These new conditions, therefore, raise a difficulty; but it is a difficulty easier to solve if these two people have been interested in their fellows, for then they can learn more easily to be interested in each other.

We could even say that for a full solution of this coöperation of two, each partner must be more interested in the other than in himself. This is the only basis on which love and marriage can be successful. We shall already be able to see in what way many opinions of marriage and many proposals for its reform are mistaken. If each partner is to be more interested in the other partner than in himself, there must be equality. If there is to be so intimate a devotion, neither partner can feel subdued nor overshadowed. Equality is only possible if both partners have this attitude. It should be the effort of each to ease and enrich the life of the other. In this way each is safe. Each feels that he is worth while: each feels that he is needed. Here we find the fundamental guarantee of marriage, the fundamental meaning of happiness in this relation. It is the feeling that you are worth while, that you cannot be replaced, that your partner needs you, that you are acting well, that you are a fellow man and a true friend.

It is not possible for a partner in a coöperative task to accept a position of subservience. Two people cannot live together fruitfully if one wishes to rule and force the other to obey. In our present conditions many men and, indeed, many women are convinced that it is the man's part to rule and dictate, to play the leading rôle, to be the master. This is the reason why we have so many unhappy marriages. Nobody can bear a position of inferiority without anger and disgust. Comrades must be equal, and when people are equal, they will always find a way to settle their difficulties. They will agree, for example, in questions of having children. They know that a decision for sterility involves their own part in giving a pledge for the future of mankind. They will agree in questions of education; and they will be stimulated to solve their problems as they occur, because they know that the children of unhappy marriages are penalized and cannot develop well.

In our present-day civilization people are not often well prepared for coöperation. Our training has been too much towards individual success, towards considering what we can get out of life rather than what we can give to it. It will be easily understood that where we get two people living together in the intimate way which marriage demands, any failure in coöperation, in the ability to be interested in somebody else, will have the gravest results. Most people are experiencing this close relationship for the first time. They are unaccustomed to consulting another human being's interests and aims, desires, hopes and ambitions. They are not prepared for the problems of a *common task*. We need not be surprised at the many mistakes which we see around us; but we can examine the facts and learn how to avoid mistakes in the future.

No crisis of adult life is met without previous training: we always respond in conformity with our style of living. The preparation for marriage is not overnight. In a child's characteristic behavior, in his attitudes, thoughts and actions, we can see how he is training himself for adult situations. In its main features his approach to love is already established by the fifth or sixth year.

Early in the development of a child we can see that he is already forming his outlook on love and marriage. We should not imagine that he is showing sexual promptings in our adult sense of the term. He is making up his mind about one aspect of the general social life of which he feels himself a part. Love and marriage are factors of his environment: they enter into his conception of his own future. He must have some comprehension of them, take up some stand about these problems. When children give such early evidence of their interest in the other sex and choose for themselves the partners whom they like, we should never interpret it as a mistake, or a nuisance, or a precocious sex influence. Still less should we deride it or make a joke of it. We should take it as a step forward in their preparation for love and marriage. Instead of making a trifle out of it, we should rather agree with the child that love is a marvelous task, a task for which he should be prepared, a task on behalf of the whole of mankind. Thus we can implant an ideal in the child's mind, and later in life children will be able to meet each other as very well-prepared comrades and as friends in an intimate devotion. It is revealing to observe that children are spontaneous and whole-hearted adherents of monogamy; and this often in spite of the fact that the marriages of their parents are not always harmonious and happy.

I should never encourage parents to explain the physical relations of sex too early in life or to explain more than their children wish to learn. You can understand that the way in which a child looks on the problems of marriage is of the greatest importance. If he is taught in a mistaken way, he can see them as a danger or as something altogether beyond him. In my own experience children who were introduced to the facts of adult relations in early life, at four, five or six years of age, and children who had precocious experiences, are always more scared of love in later life. Bodily attraction suggests to them also the idea of danger. If a child is more grown-up when he has his first explanations and experiences, he is not nearly so frightened: there is so much less opportunity for him to make mistakes in understanding the right relations. The key to helpfulness is never to lie to a child, never to evade his questions, to understand what is behind his questions, to explain only as much as he wishes to learn and only as much as we are sure he can understand. Officious and intrusive information can cause great harm. In this problem of life, as in all others, it is better for a child to be independent and learn what he wants to know by his own efforts. If there is trust between himself and his parents he can suffer no injury. He will always ask what he needs to know. There is a common superstition that children can be misled by the explanations of their comrades. I have never seen a child, otherwise healthy, who suffered harm in this way. Children do not swallow everything that their schoolmates tell them: for the most part they are very critical, and, if they are not certain that what they have been told is true, they will ask their parents or their brothers and sisters. I must confess, too, that I have often found children more delicate and tactful in these affairs than their elders.

Even the physical attraction of adult life is already being trained in childhood. The impressions the child gains with regard to sympathy and attraction, the impressions given by the members of the other sex in his immediate surroundings — these are the beginnings of physical attraction. When a boy gains these impressions from his mother, his sisters, or the girls around him, his selection of physically attractive types in later life will be influenced by their similarity to these members of his earlier environment. Sometimes he is influenced, also, by the creations of art: everybody is drawn in this way by an ideal of personal beauty. Thus in later life the individual has no longer a *free choice* in the broadest sense but a choice only along the lines of his training. This search for beauty is not a meaningless search. Our æsthetic emotions are always based on a feeling for health and for the improvement of mankind. All our functions, all our abilities, are formed in this direction. We cannot escape it. We know as beautiful those things which look towards eternity, those things which are for the benefit of mankind and for the future of mankind; the symbols of the way in which we wish our children to develop. This is the beauty which is always drawing us.

Sometimes if a boy experiences difficulties with his mother, and a girl with her father (as happens often if the coöperation in marriage is not firm), they look for an antithetic type. If, for example, the boy's mother has nagged him and bullied him, if he is weak and afraid of being dominated, he may find sexually attractive only those women who appear not to be dominating. It is easy for him to make mistakes: he can look for a partner whom he can subdue, and a happy marriage is never possible without equality. Sometimes, if he wants to prove himself powerful and strong, he looks for a partner who also seems to be strong, either because he prefers strength or because he finds in her more of a challenge to prove his own strength. If his disagreement with his mother is very great, his preparation for love and marriage may be hindered and even physical attraction to the other sex may be blocked. There are many degrees of this obstruction; where it is complete he will exclude the other sex entirely and become perverted.

We are always better prepared if the marriage of our

parents has been harmonious. Children gain their earliest impression of what marriage is like from the life of their parents; and it is not astonishing that the greatest number of failures in life are among the children of broken marriages and unhappy family life. If the parents are not able themselves to coöperate, it will be impossible for them to teach coöperation to their children. We can often best consider the fitness of an individual for marriage by learning whether he was trained in the right kind of family life and by observing his attitude towards his parents, sisters and brothers. The important factor is where he gained his preparation for love and marriage. We must be careful on this point, however. We know that a man is not determined by his environment but by the estimate he makes of his environment. His estimate can be useful. It is possible that he had very unhappy experiences of family life in his parents' home but this may only stimulate him to do better in his own family life. He may be striving to prepare himself well for marriage. We must never judge or exclude a human being because he has an unfortunate family life behind him.

The worst preparation is when an individual is always looking for his own interest. If he has been trained in this way, he will be thinking all the while what pleasure or excitement he can get out of life. He will always be demanding freedom and reliefs, never considering how he can ease and enrich the life of his partner. This is a disastrous approach. I should compare him to a man who tries to put a horse's collar on from the tail end. It is not a sin, but it is a mistaken method. In preparing our attitude to love, therefore, we should not always be looking for mitigations and ways of avoiding responsibility. The comradeship of love could not be firm if there were hesitation and doubt. Coöperation demands a decision for eternity; and we only regard those unions as real examples of love and real marriages in which a fixed and unalterable decision has been taken. In this decision we include the decision to have children, to educate them and train them in coöperation, and to make them, as far as we can, real fellow men, real equal and responsible members of the human race. A good marriage is the best means we have for bringing up the future generation of mankind; and marriage should always have this in view. Marriage is really a task; it has its own rules and laws; we cannot select one part and evade the others without infringing the eternal law of this earth crust, coöperation.

It is impossible to have the real intimate devotion of love if we limit our responsibility to five years or regard the marriage as a trial period. If men or women contemplate such an escape, they do not collect all their powers for the task. In none of the serious and important tasks of life do we arrange such a " get-away." We cannot love and be limited. All those very well-meaning and good-hearted people who are trying to find a relief for marriage are on the wrong path. The reliefs they propose would damage and restrict the efforts of couples who were entering marriage; they would make it easier for them to find a way out and to omit the work they should do in the task on which they have decided. I know that there are many difficulties in our social life and that they hinder many people from solving the problem of love and marriage in the right way, even though they would like to solve it. It is not love and marriage, however, that I want to sacrifice; I want to sacrifice the difficulties of our social life. We know what characteristics are necessary for a love partnership — to be faithful and true and trustworthy, not to be reserved, not to be self-seeking. . . . You can understand that if a person believes that unfaithfulness is all in the day's work, he is not properly prepared for marriage. It is not even possible to carry through a true comradeship if both partners have agreed to preserve their freedom. This is not comradeship. In comradeship we are not free in every direction. We have bound ourselves to our coöperation.

Let me give an example of how such a private agreement, not adapted to the success of the marriage or the welfare of mankind, can harm both the partners.

I remember a case where a divorced man and a divorced woman married. They were cultivated and intelligent people and hoped very much that their new venture in marriage would be better than the last. They did not know, however, how their first marriages had come to ruin; they were looking for a right way without having seen their lack of social interest. They professed themselves free-thinkers, and they wished to have an easy marriage in which they would never run the risk of being bored by each other. They proposed, therefore, that each of them should be perfectly free in every direction; they should do whatever they wanted to do, but they should trust each other enough to tell everything that happened. On this point the husband seemed to be more courageous. Whenever he came home he had many gay experiences to tell his wife and she seemed to enjoy them vastly and to be very proud of her husband's successes. She was always intending to begin a flirtation or a love-relation herself; but before she had taken the first step she began to suffer from agoraphobia. She could no longer go out alone; her neurosis kept her to her room; if she took a step beyond the door she was so scared that she was compelled to return. This agoraphobia was a protection against the decision she had made; but there was more to it than this. At last, since she was unable to go out alone, her husband was compelled to stay by her side. You see how the logic of marriage broke through their decision. The husband could no longer be a free-thinker because he must remain with his wife. She herself could make no use of her freedom because she was afraid to go out alone. If this woman were cured, she would be forced to reach a better understanding of marriage, and the husband, too, would have to regard it as a coöperative task.

Other mistakes are made at the very beginning of the marriage. A child who has been pampered at home often feels neglected in marriage. He has not been trained to adapt himself to social life. A pampered child may develop into a great tyrant in marriage; the other partner feels victimized, feels himself in a cage, and begins to resist. It is interesting to observe what happens when two pampered children marry each other. Each of them is claiming interest and attention and neither can be satisfied. The next step is to look for an escape; one partner begins a flirtation with some one else in the hope of gaining more attention. Some people are incapable of falling in love with one person; they must fall in love with two at the same time. They thus feel free; they can escape from one to the other, and never undertake the full responsibilities of love. Both means neither.

There are other people who invent a romantic, ideal or unattainable love; they can thus luxuriate in their feelings without the necessity of approaching a partner in reality. A high ideal of love can also be used to exclude all possibilities, because no one will be found who can live up to it. Many men, and especially many women, through mistakes in their development, have trained themselves to dislike and reject their sexual rôle. They have hindered their natural functions and are physically not capable, without treatment, of accomplishing a successful marriage. This is what I have called the Masculine Protest and it is very much provoked by the overvaluation of men in our present culture. If children are left in doubt of their sexual rôle, they are very apt to feel insecure. So long as the masculine rôle is taken to be the dominant rôle, it is natural that they should feel, whether they are boys or girls, that the masculine rôle is enviable. They will doubt their own ability to fulfill this rôle, will overstress the importance of being manly, and will try to avoid being put to the test. This dissatisfaction with the sexual rôle is very frequent in our culture. We can suspect it in all cases of frigidity in women and psychic impotence in men. In these cases there is a resistance to love and marriage and a resistance in the right place. It is impossible to avoid these failures unless we truly have the feeling that men and women are equal; and so long as one half of the human race has reason to be dissatisfied with the position accorded to it, we shall have a very great obstacle to the success of marriage. The remedy here is training for equality; and we should never permit children to remain ambiguous about their own future rôle.

I believe that the intimate devotion of love and marriage is best secured if there have not been sexual relations before the marriage. I have found that secretly most men do not really like it if their sweetheart is able to give herself before marriage. Sometimes they regard it as a sign of easy virtue and are shocked by it. Moreover, in this state of our culture, if there are intimate relations before marriage the burden is heavier for the girl. It is also a great mistake if a marriage is contracted out of fear and not out of courage. We can understand that courage is one side of coöperation and if men and women choose their partners out of fear it is a sign that they do not wish for a real coöperation. This also holds good when they choose partners who are drunkards or very far below them in social status or in education. They are afraid of love and marriage and wish to establish a situation in which their partner will look up to them.

One of the ways in which social interest can be trained is through friendship. We learn in friendship to look with the eyes of another person, to listen with his ears and to feel with his heart. If a child is frustrated, if he is always watched and guarded, if he grows up isolated, without comrades and friends, he does not develop this ability to identify himself with another person. He always thinks himself the most important being in the world and is always anxious to secure his own welfare. Training in friendship is a preparation for marriage. Games might be useful if they were regarded as a training in coöperation; but in children's games we find too often competition and the desire to excel. It is very useful to establish situations in which two children work together, study together and learn together. I believe that we should not undervalue dancing. Dancing is a type of activity in which two people have to accomplish a common task, and I think it is good for children to be trained in dancing. I do not exactly mean the dancing we have to-day, where we have more of a show than of a common task. If, however, we had simple and easy dances for children, it would be a great help for their development.

Another problem which also helps to show us the preparation for marriage is the problem of occupation. To-day the solution of this problem is put before the solution of love and marriage. One partner, or both, must be occupied so that they can earn their living and support a family and we can understand that the right preparation for marriage includes also the right preparation for work.

We can always find the degree of courage and the degree of capacity to coöperate in the approach to the other sex. Every individual has his characteristic approach, his characteristic gait and temperament in wooing; and this is always congruous with his style of life. In this amative temperament we can see whether he says " Yes " to the future of mankind, is confident and coöperative; or is interested only in his own person, suffers from stage fright, and tortures himself with the question, " What sort of a show am I making? What do they think of me? " A man may be slow and cautious in wooing, or rash and precipitate; in any case, his amative temperament fits in with his goal and his style of life, and is only one expression of it. We cannot judge a man's fitness for marriage entirely by his courtship; for there he has a direct goal before him and in other ways he may be indecisive. Nevertheless we can gather from it sure indications of his personality.

In our own cultural conditions (and only in these conditions) it is generally expected that the man should be the first to express attraction, that the man should make the first approach. So long as this cultural demand exists, therefore, it is necessary to train boys in the masculine attitude — to take the initiative, not to hesitate or look for an escape. They can be trained, however, only if they feel themselves to be a part of the whole social life and accept its advantages and disadvantages as their own. Of course, girls and women are also engaged in wooing, they also take the initiative; but in our prevailing cultural conditions, they feel obliged to be more reserved, and their wooing is expressed in their whole gait and person, in the way they dress, the way they look, speak and listen. A man's approach, therefore, may be called simpler and shallower, a woman's deeper and more complicated.

We can now advance a step farther. The sexual attraction towards the other partner is necessary but it should always be molded along the line of a desire for human welfare. If the partners are really interested in each other, there will never be the difficulty of sexual attraction coming to an end. This stop implies always a lack of interest; it tells us that the individual no longer feels equal, friendly and coöperative towards his partner, no longer wishes to enrich the life of his partner. People may think, sometimes, that the interest continues but the attraction has ceased. This is never true. Sometimes the mouth lies or the head does not understand; but the functions of the body always speak the truth. If the functions are deficient, it follows that there is no true agreement between these two people. They have lost interest in each other. One of them, at least, no longer wishes to solve the task of love and marriage but is looking for an evasion and escape.

In one other way the sex drive in human beings is different from the sex drive among other beings. It is continuous. This is another way in which the welfare and continuance of mankind is guaranteed; it is a way by which mankind can increase, become numerous, and secure its welfare and survival by the greatness of its numbers. In other creatures life has taken other means to ensure this survival: in many, for example, we find the females produce a very great number of eggs which never come to maturity. Many of them get lost or destroyed but the great number secures that some of them always survive. With men, also, one method of surviving is to have children. We shall find, therefore, that in this problem of love and marriage those people who are most spontaneously interested in the welfare of mankind are the most likely to have children, and those who are not interested, consciously or unconsciously, in their fellow beings, refuse the burden of procreation. If they are always demanding and expecting, never giving, they do not like children. They are interested in only their own persons and they regard children as a bother, a trouble, a nuisance; something that will prevent them from keeping their interest in themselves. We can say, therefore, that for a full solution of the problem of love and marriage a decision to have children is necessary. A good marriage is the best means we know for bringing up the future generation of mankind, and marriage should always have this in view.

The solution of the problem of love and marriage in our practical and social life is monogamy. Any one who starts the relation which demands such an intimate devotion, such an interest in another person, cannot shake the fundamental basis of this relation and search for an escape. We know that there is the possibility that there will be a break in the relation. Unfortunately we cannot always avoid it: but it is easiest to avoid if we are regarding marriage and love as a social task which confronts us, a task which we are expected to solve. We shall then try every means to solve the problem. These breaks generally happen because the partners are not collecting all their powers: they are not creating the marriage: they are only waiting to receive something. If they face the problem in this way, of course they will fail before it. It is a mistake to regard love and marriage as if they were a paradise; and it is a mistake, too, to regard marriage as if it were the end of a story. It is when two people are married that the possibilities of their relationship begin; it is during marriage that they are faced with the real tasks of life and the real opportunity to create for the sake of society. The other point of view, the point of view of marriage as an end, as a final goal, is very much too prominent in our culture. We can see it, for example, in thousands of novels, in which we are left with a man and a woman, just married, and really at the beginning of their life together. Yet the situation is often treated as if marriage itself had solved everything satisfactorily: as if they were at the end of their task. Another point important to realize is that love by itself does not settle everything. There are all kinds of love, and it is better to rely upon work, interest, and coöperation to solve the problems of marriage.

There is nothing at all miraculous in this whole relationship. The attitude of every individual towards marriage is one of the expressions of his style of life: we can understand it if we understand the whole individual, not unless. It is coherent with all his efforts and aims. We shall be able to find out, therefore, why so many people are always looking for a relief or escape. I can tell exactly how many people have this attitude: all the people who remain pampered children. This is a dangerous type in our social life — these grown-up pampered children whose style of life has been fixed in the first four or five years of life and who always have the scheme of apperception: " Can I get all I want? " If they can't get everything that they want, they think life is purposeless. " What is the use of living," they ask, " if I cannot have what I want? " They become pessimistic: they conceive a " death wish." They make themselves sick and neurotic and out of their mistaken style of life they construct a philosophy. They feel that their mistaken ideas are of unique and tremendous importance: they feel that it is a piece of spite on the part of the universe if they have to repress their drives and emotions. They are trained in this way. Once they experienced a favorable time in which they obtained everything they wanted. Some of them, perhaps, still feel that if they cry long enough, if they protest enough, if they refuse coöperation, they will obtain their own desires. They do not look to the coherence of life but to their own personal interests. The result is they do not want to contribute, they always wish to have things easy, they want to be refused nothing; and, therefore, marriage itself they wish to have on trial or return, they want companionate marriages, trial marriages, easier divorces: at the very beginning of marriage they demand freedom and a right to unfaithfulness. Now if one human being is really interested in another, he must have all the characteristics belonging to that interest; he must be true, a good friend; he must feel responsible, he must make himself faithful and trustworthy. I believe that at the least a human being who has not succeeded in accomplishing such a love life or such a marriage should understand that on this point his life has been a mistake.

It is necessary, too, to be interested in the welfare of the children; and if a marriage is based upon different outlooks from the one I have supported, there are great difficulties for the bringing up of children. If the parents quarrel and look on their marriage as a trifle, if they do not see it as if its problems could be solved and the relationship could be continued successfully, it is not a very favorable situation for helping the children to be sociable.

Probably there are reasons why people should not live together; probably there are cases where it would be better that they should be apart. Who should decide the case? Are we going to put it in the hands of people who themselves are not rightly taught, who themselves do not understand that marriage is a task, who themselves are interested only in their own persons? They would look at divorce in the same way as they look at marriage: " What can be got out of it? " These are obviously not the people to decide. You will see very often that people divorce and remarry again and again and always make the same mistake. Then who ought to decide? Perhaps we might imagine that if something is wrong with a marriage, a psychiatrist should decide whether or not it should be broken. There is difficulty there. I do not know whether it holds true of America, but in Europe I have found that psychiatrists for the most part think that personal welfare is the most important point. Generally, therefore, if they are consulted in such a case, they recommend a sweetheart or a lover and think that this might be the way to solve the problem. I am sure that in time they will change their mind and cease to give such advice. They can only propose such a solution if they have not been rightly trained in the whole coherence of the problem, the way it hangs together with the other tasks of our life on this earth; and it is this coherence that I have been wishing to offer for your consideration.

A similar mistake is made when people look upon marriage as a solution for a personal problem. Here again I cannot speak of America, but I know that in Europe, if a boy or girl becomes neurotic, psychiatrists often advise them to have sweethearts and to begin sex relations. They advise adults, also, in the same way. This is really making love and marriage into a mere patent medicine, and these individuals are bound to lose very greatly. The right solution of the problem of love and marriage belongs to the highest fulfillment of the whole personality. There is no problem more closely involved with happiness and a true and useful expression in life. We cannot treat it as a trifle. We cannot look on love and marriage as a remedy for a criminal career, for drunkenness or neurosis. A neurotic needs to have the right treatment before he is fitted for love and marriage; and if he enters them before he is capable of approaching them rightly, he is bound to run into new dangers and misfortunes. Marriage is too high an ideal and the solution of the task demands too much of our effort and creative activity for us to load it with such additional burdens.

In other ways, also, marriage is entered into with inappropriate aims. Some people marry for the sake of economic security; they marry because they pity some one; or they marry to secure a servant. There is no place for such jokes in marriage. I have even known cases where people have married to increase their difficulties. A young man, perhaps, is in difficulties about his examinations or his future career. He feels that he may very easily fail, and if he fails he wishes to be able to excuse himself. He takes on the additional task of marriage, therefore, in order to have an alibi.

I am sure we should not try to depreciate or diminish this problem but to set it on a higher level. In all the reliefs I have heard proposed, it is always the women really who bear the disadvantage. There is no question but that men in our culture already have an easier time. This is a mistake in our common approach. It cannot be overcome by a personal revolt. Especially in marriage itself a personal revolt would disturb the social relationship and the interest of the partner. It can only be overcome by recognising and changing the whole attitude of our culture. A pupil of mine, Professor Rasey of Detroit, made an examination and found that forty-two per cent. of the girls she questioned would like to have been boys; this means that they were disappointed with their own sex. Can it be easy to solve the problems of love and marriage while half of mankind is disappointed and discouraged, does not agree with its position and objects to the greater freedom of the other half? Can it be easy to solve them if women are always expecting to be slighted and believe themselves to be only sexual objects for men, or believe it is natural for men to be polygamous and unfaithful?

From all we have said we can draw a simple, obvious and helpful conclusion. Human beings are neither polygamous nor monogamous. The fact that we live on this planet, in association with human beings equal to ourselves, and divided into two sexes, and the fact that we must solve the three problems of life which our circumstances set us in a sufficient way, will help us to see that the fullest and highest development of the individual in love and marriage can best be secured by monogamy.

INDEX

ADOLESCENCE, character not changed by, 182; what it means to the child, 182; expressions of, 182; child given more freedom and independence during, 183; no strict limits to time of, 183; child sometimes put into panic by problems of, 184; dangers of, 185-187; conduct of children at, 185; failures in, 187; craving for appreciation at, 188-190; sexual relations often exaggerated at, 191; the "masculine protest" at, 191-193; superstition regarding, 195, 196

Adolescent negativism, 183

Advisory Councils, 159, 178-181

Agoraphobia, 31, 275; an expression of inferiority complex, 52

American Indians, their view of dreams, 94

Anger, 30, 42; may be expression of inferiority complex, 52

Antithetic attitude, 95

Anxiety, 30; and sex, 41; as device for occupying attention, 129

Anxiety dreams, 129

Anxiety neurosis, 85, 178, 190

Apperception, 12, 13, 204, 205, 242, 282

Appreciation, craving for, at adolescence, 188-190

Association, a condition of life, 6. See also Ties

Associations, 19

Atheist, the, 61

Austria, schools in, 157. See also Vienna

BEAUTY, the search for, 271

Birth, order of, 144-154

Blushing, compulsive, 255

Body, and mind, interactions of, 25-48; Kretschmer's types of, 44-46

Brain, and mind, 43, 44; improvement of, 44; structure of, in some degree inherited, 169

CHARACTER, no reasons for development of, 124; imperfect organs not sufficient to explain bad traits of, 130; the belief in inherited components of, 168; influence of environment and education on, 168, 169; not changed by adolescence, 182

Character-education, 158

Childhood, interpretation of situations of, 13; situations of, leading to mistaken meanings, 14-19; memories of early, 19-22, 74-92; the meaning of life fixed at end of fifth year of, 34, 47; mistakes of, and adult failures, the connection between, 177, 178; physical attraction of adult life trained in, 270. *See also* Children; Failures

Children, problem, 8; with imperfect organs, 14-16, 35, 36, 207; suffering from infirmities during infancy, 14-16, 207, 224, 232; with abnormal glandular secretions, 15; pampered, 16, 22, 39, 54, 65, 87-92, 97, 98, 127-130, 151, 152, 159, 175, 177, 187, 191, 209, 224, 232, 240, 244, 275; neglected, 17-19, 222, 232; illegitimate, 18, 208, 224; orphan, 18, 208, 224; suffering from enuresis, 20, 21, 37-39; left-handed, 36; can train successfully to compensate for defects, 36, 37; neurotic, 38; delinquent, 38; "backward," 55, 172; if without coöperation, are driven to inferiority complex, 56; mother's coöperation with, 120, 121; relationship with mother, 124-127; devices of, for occupying attention, 127-130, 175, 193; relationship with father, 132; their first idea of marriage gained from marriage of parents, 133; affection of husband for wife not to be shown too strikingly before, 139, 194; explanation of sexual matters to, 139, 140, 174, 194, 269, 270; favoritism among, to be avoided, 142; education of, 142; inter-coöperation of, 142, 143; as to order of birth of, 144-152; an only child, 152; best space of years between birth of, 153;

only boy in family of girls, 153, 154; only girl among boys, 154; on first going to school, 159, 160; must be interested by teacher, 160-163; should be trained in coöperation rather than in competition, 163, 164; as to making them self-governing, 164; as to tests for, 165; effect of school reports on, 166; self-limitation of, 166, 167, 170; and heredity, 167-170; influence of environment and education on, 168, 169; lazy, 175-177; between ages of fourteen and twenty, 185-187; should not be stimulated physically or mentally, 193, 194; should not sleep in same room as parents or as brothers or sisters, 194; responsibility for their becoming criminals, 205-209, 221-224; unwanted, 208, 224, 232; ugly, 208, 224; should be better trained for future occupation, 234, 251; should be developed in social interest, 236-238; early interest in other sex, 269; their preparation for family life, 271, 272; on the having of, 280; grown-up pampered, 282; necessary for parents to be interested in welfare of, 283. *See also* Adolescence; Childhood; Occupation; Problem children; Pupils

Circumstances, always experienced through interpretation, 3

Class movement, 254

Classes. *See* School-classes

Climacteric, 195

Coeducation, in schools, 173

Common sense, dreams antagonistic to, 100, 102; an aspect of coöperation, 101; always better to follow, 106

Competition, training in, to be discouraged, 163

Complaints, a capable weapon for disturbing coöperation, 53

"Conscious" and "unconscious," 95

Conservatism, 147

Contradictions and variations, 95, 96, 128

Contribution, is the true meaning of life, 8, 10, 11, 237. *See also* Coöperation

Coöperation, 6, 8, 23, 24, 44, 46-48; the meaning of life, 9, 10; not learned by pampered or neglected child, 16-18; safeguard against development of neurotic tendencies, 22; safeguard against inferiority complex, 56; new opportunities, constantly made, 57; concrete goals should have to do with, 68-70; treatment an exercise in, and a test of, 72; common sense an aspect of, 101; between mother and baby, 120; the striving of motherhood related to, 124; can never be won by force, 132; of the family, 139-155; in school, 159, 163, 164; results of lack of, in childhood, 177, 178; the criminals' failure in, 200-209, 228-230; the cure for crime, 236; led to division of labor, 240; in geniuses, 247,

248; fixing and stabilizing of, 252; marriage an affair of, 252, 253, 263, 266, 267; imposed by religion, 253; created by politics, 253, 254; movements should be judged by, 254; human capacities developed through, 254, 255; in solving the three problems of life, 262; testing, 263; preparation for, generally lacking, 268

Craftsmanship, training in, 243

Crime, summary of results of scientific investigation of, 229-233. *See also* Criminals

Criminal negligence, 260

Criminal psychology, illustrations of, 225-227

Criminals, 8, 38, 144, 178, 185; fail in social interest and coöperation, 197, 200-204, 228-230; their goal, 198, 200: not made by heredity or environment, 198, 199; are not insane, 199; feeble-minded, 199: style of life of, 200, 201; problems which they cannot solve, 201-203; are mostly untrained and unskilled workers, 202; are cowards, 204, 205, 228: responsibility for, 205-209, 221-224, 232, 233; ugly and handsome, 208, 209; cases of, 209-217, 225-227; the planning done by, 214, 215; the cure of, 217-220, 228-234; corporal punishment ineffective with, 218-220; two main types of (ugly-neglected and handsome-pampered), 225; summary of results of scientific investigation of, 229-233; have inferiority complex, 232; social problems should be discussed with, 234; should be given less publicity, 235; increased efforts should be made to discover, 235; should not be humiliated or challenged, 235

Cry-babies, 53, 178

Culture, is the changes made in environment, 29; based upon feelings of inferiority, 55

DANCING, 277

"Death wish," 282

Delinquents, increase of, between ages of fourteen and twenty, 185, 186. *See also* Criminals

Dementia præcox, 184, 256

Determinism, the theory of, 14

Dewey, Prof. John, 197

Disinterested affection, 17

Division of labor, 240

Divorce, 282, 283

Dolls, 245, 246

Dostoievsky, Feodor M., 214

Dream books, 94

Dreams, 19, 73; recurrent, 20, 90, 91; used to stir up emotions, 38; two theories of interpretation of, 93; considered as bearing on the future, 94, 95; sacred, 94; induced, among American Indians, 94; in the Old Testament, 94; considered as offering solution to problems, 95, 96; referred to sexual background, 96; considered as expressing unconscious desire to die, 96; life of, relation to day life, 96-99; feelings aroused by, 98; are a disturbance of calm and tranquil sleep, 99; the purpose of, 99, 100; are adversaries of common sense, 101; rare and frequent, explanation of, 101; are a form of self-deception, 101, 102, 105-107; choice of pictures, incidences, and occurrences in, 102; use metaphors and symbols, 102-104; some typical forms of, 107-119, 149; anxiety, 129; of first and second children, 149; of Joseph, 151

Drives, 265

Drunkards, 8, 61, 144, 178, 197

ECONOMIC RESPONSIBILITY, 138

Education, European, 156; taken over by religious institutions, 156; founding of public schools, 157; changes in public schools, 157; influence of, on character, 169. *See also* Schools

Egyptians, their view of dreams, 94

Ejaculation, premature, 55, 255

Emotion, bodily expression of, 40-43

Emotional tone, 31

Endocrine glands, 40, 184, 208

Enuresis, 20, 21, 37-39

Environment, 26; changes in, 29; influence of, 169; and criminals, 198, 199, 220

Eugenic selection, schemes of, 15

Examinations, dreams of, 108

Experience, qualified by human purposes, 3; shock of, 14, 48

Extraverts, 45

FAILURES IN LIFE, 8, 18; mother's part in causing, 123, 124; whence they in great part come, 132, 253, 272; the line between childhood mistakes and, is direct, 177, 178; in adolescence, 187

Falling, dreams of, 108, 149

Family, the mother's part in, 120-132; the father's part in, 132-141; financial affairs of, 141; favoritism among children of, to be avoided, 142; intercoöperation of children of, 142, 143; order of birth among children of, 144-154; experiences in, as source of crime, 205-209, 221-224, 229, 232, 233; as an institution, 252

Family differences, 137

Father, his part in family life, 132-135; his influence on children, 135-136; should be an integral part of the family, 136, 137; his parents, 137, 138; economic responsibility of, 138; must be interested in wife, 138, 139; should advise wife and children on systems of society, 140; his success should not be stressed in family, 143

Favoritism among children, to be avoided, 142

Fear, of pampered children, 128, 129

Feelings, stirred by phantasies and identifications, 29; never in contradiction to the style of life, 30; as related to the attainment of goal, 31; appear and disappear at need, 31; belonging to sex, 31; of guilt, 32, 33; aroused by dreams to support style of life, 98-101, 103, 104, 107; aroused voluntarily, 104, 105. See also Dreams

Feuerbach, Anton von, 225

Flying, dreams about, 107

Foresight, most highly developed in the human mind, 27; by phantasies and identifications, 29

Foster-mothers, 131

French, the study of, 242

Freudian theory, of dreams, 93, 95-97, 102; of the Œdipus Complex, 126

Friendship, problem of, 8; training in, as a preparation for marriage, 277. See also Coöperation

Friendships, 136, 137, 261, 262

GAMES, 277

Gang, the, 161, 202, 219

Genius, defined, 9

Geniuses, 247, 248

Glands, endocrine, 40, 184, 208

Glandular secretions, abnormal, in childhood, 15

Glueck, Sheldon and Eleanor T., "500 Criminal Careers," 209

Goal, of security, 27-29; necessary for overcoming of difficulties, 37; of superiority, 55-61; of godlikeness, 60, 61; and style of life, 61, 62; should be changed rather than symptoms, 62-64; should have to do with coöperation, 68-70; of the criminal, 198, 200. See also Superiority

God. *See* Godlikeness

Godlikeness, the goal of, 60, 61, 124

Grades, quicker and slower, 172, 173

Greeks, their view of dreams, 94

Guilt, feelings of, 32, 33

HANDIWORK, training in, 243

"Hard-boiled John," the case of, 209-214

Headaches, 42

Heredity, influence on character, mistaken belief in, 120, 162, 167-170, 198, 199, 207, 208, 220, 228; physical, 167; mental, 169

Home-making, 122

Homosexuality, 192

Housekeeping, 122

Hungary, recent court case in, 204

Hysterical aphasia, 86

IDEALISTS, 25

Identifications, 29

Immortality, 61

Impotence, 55, 255

Individual Psychology, 7, 12, 15, 123, 197, 201, 220, 224-226, 233; and determinism, 14; on relation of mind and body, 25; on feelings and style of life, 30; possibilities of the educational application of, 44, 47, 48; "inferiority complex" a discovery of, 49; opposed to treatment of symptoms, 62; a difficult psychology to learn and practice, 71, 72; negative and positive transferences never met with in, 72, 73; its method of dream-interpretation, 93, 96; technique of, 110; tries to identify purpose, not causes, of fear, 128; inquiries into advantages and disadvantages of order of birth, 144; importance of inherited organ deficiencies understood in, 167, 168; Advisory Councils in, 178

Inferiority, feelings of, 14; combined with movement toward superiority, 50-54; common to all, 51; the cause of improvements in the position of mankind, 55

Inferiority complex, important discovery of Individual Psychology, 49; use of the term, 49; possessed by every neurotic, 49; definition of, 52; expressed by anger, 52; expressed by agoraphobia, 52, 53; children without coöperation driven to, 56; cases of, 67, 68; caused by favoritism, 142; of the criminal, 232

Insanity, 60, 184, 255-258

Insomniacs, 55

Intelligence Tests, 165

Interest, in others, 9, 10, 12, 18, 261; of the child, to be aroused, 160-163, 170; is the greatest factor in development of mental faculties, 169. *See also* Coöperation; Social interest

Interpretation, of experience, 3, 4, 13; of childhood situations, 13; of memories, 75-92; of dreams, 93, 107

Isolation, symptoms of, 255; the

highest degree of, represented by insanity, 255

KIDNEY TRACT, inferiority of, 37
Kretschmer, his types of mind, 44, 45, 46

LANGUAGE, 254
Latin, 242
Liebig, Justus von, 169
Life, the meaning of, gained through interpretation of experienced circumstances, 3, 4; conditioned by three ties, 5-7; problems of, 5-7, 201-203, 262; failures in, 8; is contribution, interest in others, and coöperation, 9, 10; the highest goal of, 55-61; interest in, comes mainly from lack of certainty, 57; the desire to perpetuate, 61. *See also* Failures in life; Meaning of life; Meanings of life
Love, problem of, 6, 10, 138, 203, 241, 264-266; and social interest, 11; feelings belonging to, 31; of husband and wife and of parents and children, 139; defined, 263; a task for two, 266, 267; preparation for, 271-274; does not of itself settle everything, 281. *See also* Marriage; Wooing
Lying, 68

MARRIAGE, problem of, 6, 10, 241, 264-266; the meaning of, 133, 134; a community affair, 252, 253; a test for fitness for, 263; coöperation the chief prerequisite for, 263; defined, 263; a task for two, 266, 267; selection of partner in, 270, 271; preparation for, 271-274, 277; should have in view the bringing up of future generation, 273, 280; trial, 273, 274, 282; mistakes of, 274, 275, 281-284; case of, with private agreement, 274, 275; of those who had been pampered children, 275; resistance to, 276; without preceding sexual relations, 276, 277; through fear, 277; and occupation, 278; not to be regarded as the end of a story, 281; companionate, 282; not to be considered a personal problem, 284; entered into with inappropriate aims, 284, 285. *See also* Love
"Masculine Protest," 116, 191-193, 276
Masculinity, the stress on, 192
Masturbation, 55
Materialists, 25
Meaning of life, is interest in others and coöperation, 9; fixed at end of fifth year, 12, 34; the correcting of, 13, 34; goal of superiority for the individual depends upon, 57-59. *See also* Meanings of life; Style of life
Meanings of life, gained through interpretation of experienced circumstances, 3, 4; true and mistaken, 4; conditioned by three ties, 5-8; true, the common measure of, 8; mistaken, the common measure of, 8; true, the mark of, 9; and psy-

chology, 12; the correction of, 12, 13; not determined by situations, 14; mistaken, situations of childhood leading to, 14-19; key to personality in, 22; religious ideas as, 61. *See also* Life; Style of life

Melancholia, 53, 178, 257-260

Memories, of early childhood, 19-22, 74-92; one of the most revealing of psychic expressions, 73; used to stabilize a mood, 73; can never run counter to style of life, 74; first, their value in vocational guidance, 74, 242, 245

Mental faculties, the greatest factor in the development of, is interest, 169

Metaphors, 102-104

Migraine, 42, 62

Mind, and body, the interactions of, 25-48; the central principle of (the foreseeing of the direction of movement), 26; the ideal goal of, 27-29; and brain, 43, 44; Kretschmer's types of, 44-46

Money, must not be overstressed in choice of profession, 249

Monogamy, 241, 269, 280, 286

Mood, variations of, 73; structure and balance of, 73

Mother, her coöperation with child, 120, 121; her part in the family life, 122, 123, 134, 135; relationships of, 124; may overstress relationship with child, 124-127; importance of her affection and interest, 131, 132; the first influence in development of child's occupational interests, 242

Mother complex, 152

Motherhood, skill of, 121; preparation for, 121; woman's part in, often under-valued, 121, 122, 241, 242; attitude of women toward, 122; the striving for, 124

Movement, direction of, foreseen by the mind, 26; partial and inclusive, 27; the goal of, 27, 28; mistakes in choosing the direction of, 28; and culture, 29

Movements, should be judged by ability to further interest in fellow men, 254

Mozart, Wolfgang A., 170

"NARROW STABLE," of the neurotic, 53, 54

National movements, 254

Neuralgia, trigeminal, 42

Neurosis, 54, 63, 186

Neurotic patients, 31

Neurotic tendencies, coöperation the safeguard against, 22

Neurotics, 8, 197, 250; have inferiority complex, 49, 53; "narrow stable" of, 53, 54; compulsion, 55; his difficulties, 57; inflexible in regard to concrete expressions of goal, 60; become virtuosos of neurosis, 63, 64; antithetic attitude illustrated among, 95; care of oldest child, 144; case of childhood mistakes, 177, 178; sometimes advised to begin sex relations, 284

Nietzsche, Friedrich Wilhelm, 60
Nightmares, 128

OCCUPATION, mother's influence in determining, 242; training in school for, 242; the choosing of, 243-245; the wish to excel other members of family in, 245; early training for, 245, 246; early training for avoidance of, 247; the question of money in the choice of, 249; is sometimes used to evade problems of society and love, 250; real interest to be found in, 250, 251; children should be trained for, 251; and marriage, 278. *See also* Vocational guidance
Occupational problem, 7, 8, 138, 202, 239, 240. *See also* Occupation
Œdipus Complex, 54, 92, 126, 127
Organs, imperfection of, 14-16, 35, 36, 207; the training of, 34
Orphan asylums, 131
Orphans, 18, 208, 224

PAIN AND PLEASURE, 29
Paranoia, 257
Parents, should not show strong expressions of affection for each other before children, 139, 194; actions of, which block social interest of children, 222. *See also* Father; Mother
Personal advantage, opposed to coöperation, 254, 255
Personality, the key to, 22, 71;

unity of the, 59; the investigation of, 71, 72; importance of memories in investigation of, 73-92; coherence of, 96, 97; in dreams, 102
Perverts, 8, 55, 61, 144, 197
Pessimism, 56
Phantasies, 29
Pleasure and pain, 29
Politics, coöperation created by, 253, 254
Postures, 34, 43
Poverty, 207
Premature ejaculation, 55, 255
Probation officers, 235, 236
Problem children, 8, 123, 127, 129, 130, 144, 148, 149, 151, 159, 172, 197, 214, 221, 222, 235, 250
Problems of life, the three main (occupational, social, sexual), 7, 8, 201-203, 239-241, 262
Prostitutes, 8, 192
Psychiatrist, and teacher, 158, 159
Psychoanalysis. *See* Freudian theory
Psychology, the province of, 12, 28; definition of, 34, 47; the task of, 47, 48. *See also* Individual Psychology
Psychotics, 8, 197, 199
Punishment, ineffectiveness of, 17, 218-220, 235; of children, 135, 136, 175; of criminals, 218-220, 235; corporal, 218-220, 235
Pupils, unusually quick, other activities given to, 171; the repeating of classes by, 172; divided into grades, 172, 173; styles of life of, 174; pam-

pered, 175; desiring to be the center of attention, 175; lazy, 175-177; leadership among, 177. See also Children; School-classes; Schools
Purposive striving, 27
Pyknoids, 44-46

RASEY, PROF., of Detroit, 285
Recollections. See Memories
Reformatories, 203, 205, 214
Relationship, problems of, 202
Religion, concerned with the salvation of man, 11; often misinterpreted, 12; the simplest primitive, 252; a striving to increase interest in fellow men in, 253

SCHIZOIDS, 45, 46
School-classes, crowded, 171; skipping, 171; promoting to higher, 171; repeating, 172; quicker and slower pupils put into different, 172, 173
School reform, 158
School reports, 166
Schools, supplement and carry on the work of the family, 156; in America, 156; religious, 157; the public, 157; in Vienna, 158; coöperation in, 163, 164, 237; as to tests in, 165; classes, 171; coeducation in, 173; sexual education in, 174; should be organized to inspire child with confidence and courage, 219; training for future occupation in, 242. See also Children; Teacher

Science, 12; arises when people feel their ignorance, 55
Security the striving for, 27-29, 197
Self-deception, dreams a form of, 101-107. See also Dreams; Style of life
Self-determination, 14
Self-limitation, 70
Self-preservation, the striving for, 197
Sex, a condition of life, 6, 7; feelings belonging to, 31; and anxiety, 41; and dreams, 96; the explaining of matters of, to children, 139, 140, 174, 194, 269, 270. See also Problems of life
Sex drive, 193, 265, 279, 280
Sexual attraction, 279
Sexual education, in school, 174
Sexual problem, 7, 8. See also Problems of life
Sexual relations, often exaggerated at adolescence, 191; sometimes advised to neurotics, 284
Sickness, as device for occupying attention, 129, 130
Sleep, the dream a disturbance of, 99
Social feeling, 10, 11, 70, 261. See also Social interest
Social interest, 197, 205, 221, 222, 225, 230, 236, 237, 249, 260, 277. See also Coöperation
Social problem, 7, 8. See also Problems of life
Stammering, 54, 255
Stealing, the expression of, 28, 29

Stepmothers, 132

Stimulation, of children, to be avoided, 193, 194

Striving, purposive, 27; early, 245-249; the oldest, 252

Style of life, feelings never in contradiction to, 30, 31, 33; abnormalities induced by mistaken, 32; crystallized by child very early, 43, 44, 47; proper subject-matter of psychology, 48; of one suffering from inferiority complex, 49; the understanding of, 57, 58, 71; and goal of superiority, 61, 62; variations of mood within, 73; memories can never run counter to, 74; of pampered child, 87, 88; supported by dreams against the demands of common sense, 99-102, 107; supported by feelings aroused in waking hours, 100, 104, 105; position in family leaves stamp upon, 154; of children in school, 174; of the criminal, 200, 201; attitude toward marriage an expression of, 281

Suicide, an expression of failure, 8, 197; an expression of retreat before difficulties, 52, 53; the child who has not learned to coöperate, 178; represents isolation, 255

Superiority, pursuit of, 30-35, 55-61, 197; movement toward, by those having feeling of inferiority, 50-54, 67; the goal of, 55-61; the striving for motherhood one aspect of the striving for, 124. See also Goal

Superiority complex, 232. See also Superiority

"Superman," 60

Symbols, 102-104, 252

Teacher, and psychiatrist, 158, 159; should notice difficulties of child and correct mistakes of parents, 160; must interest child, 160-163; should know all his pupils intimately, 171; frequent change of, should be avoided, 171; coöperates with psychologist, 179-181; the guardian of the future of mankind, 181

Teachers, children of, 38

Teaching, the best method of, 162, 163

Tears, a capable weapon for disturbing coöperation, 53

Tension, 42

Tests, 165

Ties, conditioning human life, 5-7, 239-241, 264; problems corrected with, 5-7

Totem, 252, 253

Training, of first four or five years of life, 242; in school, 242, 243; for future occupation, 245, 246; for avoidance of occupation, 247; in geniuses, 247, 248

Transferences, negative and positive, 72, 73

Trauma, 14, 48

"Unconscious" and "conscious," 95

Understanding, 255

Unemployment, 233, 251

Universities, 157

VARIATIONS AND CONTRADICTIONS, 95, 96, 128
Vegetative system, 42
Vienna, schools in, 158; Advisory Council, 159, 178
Vocational guidance, value of early recollections in, 74, 242, 245; real interest of person should be found, 250. *See also* Occupation
Voluntary system, 42

"WATER POWER," 53
Welfare of mankind, 11, 264, 265, 266, 274, 279, 280. *See also* Coöperation; Social interest
Wisdom, universal, the desire for, 61
Woman. *See* Mother; Motherhood
Wooing, one's manner in, 278, 279

ZWANZIGER, MARGARET, "the famous poison murderess," 226

CAPRICORN TITLES

1. *Dewey*, ART AS EXPERIENCE. $1.35 (Hardcover $2.50).
2. *Rilke*, NOTEBOOKS OF MALTE LAURIDS BRIGGE. $1.25.
3. *Adler*, WHAT LIFE SHOULD MEAN TO YOU. $1.25.
4. *Bell*, ART. $1.25.
5. *Whitehead*, MODES OF THOUGHT. $1.15.
6. *Adams*, DEMOCRATIC DOGMA. $1.25.
7. *Olmsted*, SLAVE STATES. $1.25 (Hardcover $2.50).
8. *Jefferson*, AUTO. OF THOS. JEFFERSON. $.95 (Hardcover $2.50).
9. *Matthews*, THE FUGGER NEWSLETTERS. $1.25 (Hardcover $2.50).
10. *Hough*, DARK SUN. $1.25.
11. *Hawkes*, COLERIDGE'S WRITINGS ON SHAKESPEARE. $1.35 (Hardcover $2.50).
12. *Shaw*, ADVENTURES OF THE BLACK GIRL. $.95 (Hardcover $2.50).
13. *Whitehead*, SYMBOLISM. $.95.
14. *Golding*, LORD OF THE FLIES. $1.25.
15. *Chekhov*, ST. PETER'S DAY. $1.25 (Hardcover $2.50).
16. *Nashe*, THE UNFORTUNATE TRAVELLER. $1.15 (Hardcover $2.50).
17. *Weil*, WAITING FOR GOD. $1.25.
18. *Coates*, EATER OF DARKNESS. $1.15.
19a. *Bryce*, THE AMERICAN COMMONWEALTH—Vol. I. $1.35.
19b. *Bryce*, THE AMERICAN COMMONWEALTH—Vol. II. $1.35 (Hardcover 1-vol. ed. $5.00).
20. *Moore*, CONFESSIONS OF A YOUNG MAN. $1.25.
21. *Tolstoy*, LAST DIARIES. $1.35 (Hardcover $2.50).
22. *Wain*, LIVING IN THE PRESENT. $1.25.
23. *diPrima*, VARIOUS FABLES FROM VARIOUS PLACES. $1.15 (Hardcover $2.50).
24. *Lovejoy*, ESSAYS IN THE HISTORY OF IDEAS. $1.45.
25. *Symonds*, THE REVIVAL OF LEARNING. $1.45.
26. *White*, THE BESTIARY. $1.45.
27. *Chesterton*, THE MAN WHO WAS THURSDAY. $1.15.
28. *Dewey*, QUEST FOR CERTAINTY. $1.25.
29. *Wood & Edmunds*, MILITARY HISTORY OF THE CIVIL WAR. $1.35.
30. *Pasternak*, POETRY OF BORIS PASTERNAK. $1.25.
31. *Wish*, ANTE-BELLUM: THREE CLASSIC WRITINGS ON SLAVERY IN THE OLD SOUTH. $1.35 (Hardcover $2.50).
32. *Valency & Levtow*, THE PALACE OF PLEASURE: AN ANTHOLOGY OF THE NOVELLA. $1.45 (Hardcover $2.50).
33. *Adler*, THE PROBLEM CHILD. $1.25 (Hardcover $2.50).

34. *Walter Lord, ed.,* THE FREMANTLE DIARY (THE SOUTH AT WAR). $1.25.

35. *Fowlie,* FOUR MODERN FRENCH COMEDIES. $1.25. (Hardcover $2.50).

36. *Torrey,* LES PHILOSOPHES. $1.65.
    Torrey, LES PHILOSOPHES (Cloth) $3.00.

37. *Ault,* ELIZABETHAN LYRICS. $1.75.

38. *Symonds,* AGE OF THE DESPOTS. $1.65.

39. *White,* MISTRESS MASHAM'S REPOSE. $1.35.

40. *Gilbert,* THE LETTERS OF MACHIAVELLI. $1.65.

41. *Still,* THE WEST. $1.65.
    Still, THE WEST. (Cloth) $2.50.

42. *Myers,* HISTORY OF BIGOTRY IN THE UNITED STATES. $1.65.

43. *Armstrong,* GRAY WOLF. $1.45.

44. *Auerbach,* INTRODUCTION TO ROMANCE LANGUAGES & LITERATURE. $1.65.
    Auerbach, INTRODUCTION TO ROMANCE LANGUAGES & LITERATURE. (Cloth) $2.50.

45. *Viereck,* METAPOLITICS. $1.75.

48. *Symonds,* FINE ARTS. $1.65.

49. *Bemelmans,* SMALL BEER. $.95.

50. *Dangerfield,* STRANGE DEATH. $1.75.

52. *Jaspers,* QUESTION OF GERMAN GUILT. $.95.

53. *Tawney,* EQUALITY. $1.35.

54. *La Guardia,* MAKING OF AN INSURGENT. $1.25.

55. *Cooper,* HOME AS FOUND. $1.35.

56. *Quiller Couch,* ART OF WRITING. $1.35.

57. NEWGATE CALENDAR. $1.45.

58. *Symonds,* LIFE OF MICHELANGELO. $1.75.

59. *Disraeli,* CONINGSBY. $1.75.

CAPRICORN GIANTS

201. *Hauser,* DIET DOES IT. $1.25.

202. *Moscati,* ANCIENT SEMITIC CIVILIZATIONS. $1.65.

203. *Chin P'ing Mei,* HSI MEN AND HIS 6 WIVES. $2.45.

204. *Brockelmann,* ISLAMIC PEOPLE. $1.95.

205. *Salter,* CONDITIONED REFLEX THERAPY. $1.75.

206. *Lissner,* LIVING PAST. $1.95.

207. *Davis,* CORPORATIONS. $2.45.

208. *Rodman,* CONVERSATION WITH ARTISTS. $1.45.

209. *Falls,* GREAT WAR 1914-1918. $1.95.

210. MEMOIRS OF A RENAISSANCE POPE. $1.85.

211. *Schachner,* FOUNDING FATHERS, $2.45.

G. P. PUTNAM'S SONS

210 Madison Avenue ● New York 16, N. Y